Beginning Spring 5

From Novice to Professional

Joseph B. Ottinger
Andrew Lombardi

Apress®

Beginning Spring 5: From Novice to Professional

Joseph B. Ottinger
YOUNGSVILLE, NC, USA

Andrew Lombardi
Laguna Beach, CA, USA

ISBN-13 (pbk): 978-1-4842-4485-2
https://doi.org/10.1007/978-1-4842-4486-9

ISBN-13 (electronic): 978-1-4842-4486-9

Managing Director, Apress Media LLC: Welmoed Spahr
Acquisitions Editor: Steve Anglin
Development Editor: Matthew Moodie
Coordinating Editor: Mark Powers

Cover designed by eStudioCalamar

Cover image designed by Freepik (www.freepik.com)

Distributed to the book trade worldwide by Springer Science+Business Media New York, 233 Spring Street, 6th Floor, New York, NY 10013. Phone 1-800-SPRINGER, fax (201) 348-4505, e-mail orders-ny@springer-sbm.com, or visit www.springeronline.com. Apress Media, LLC is a California LLC and the sole member (owner) is Springer Science + Business Media Finance Inc (SSBM Finance Inc). SSBM Finance Inc is a **Delaware** corporation.

For information on translations, please e-mail editorial@apress.com; for reprint, paperback, or audio rights, please email bookpermissions@springernature.com.

Apress titles may be purchased in bulk for academic, corporate, or promotional use. eBook versions and licenses are also available for most titles. For more information, reference our Print and eBook Bulk Sales web page at http://www.apress.com/bulk-sales.

Any source code or other supplementary material referenced by the author in this book is available to readers on GitHub via the book's product page, located at www.apress.com/9781484244852. For more detailed information, please visit http://www.apress.com/source-code.

To our loved ones and whirled peas.

Table of Contents

About the Authors

Joseph B. Ottinger (@josephbottinger) is a distributed systems architect with experience in many cloud platforms. He was the editor-in-chief of both Java Developer Journal and TheServerSide.com and has also contributed to many, many publications, open source projects, and commercial projects over the years, using many different languages (but primarily Java, Python, and JavaScript). He's also a previously published author online (with too many publications to note individually) and in print, through Apress.

Andrew Lombardi (@kinabalu) is a veteran entrepreneur and systems engineer. He's run the successful boutique consulting firm Mystic Coders for 18 years. With his team they've helped companies as large as Walmart and firms with problems as interesting as helicopter simulation. A few years ago, he authored a book on WebSocket for O'Reilly which focused on the server and client components all written with JavaScript and Node.js. He firmly believes that the best thing he's done so far is being a great dad.

About the Technical Reviewer

Manuel Jordan Elera is an autodidactic developer and researcher who enjoys learning new technologies for his own experiments and creating new integrations. Manuel won the Springy Award – Community Champion and Spring Champion 2013. In his little free time, he reads the Bible and composes music on his guitar. Manuel is known as dr_pompeii. He has tech-reviewed numerous books for Apress, including *Pro Spring, Fourth Edition* (2014); *Practical Spring LDAP* (2013); *Pro JPA 2, Second Edition* (2013); and *Pro Spring Security* (2013). Read his 13 detailed tutorials about many Spring technologies, contact him through his blog at www.manueljordanelera.blogspot.com, and follow him on his Twitter account, @dr_pompeii.

Acknowledgments

Joseph Ottinger would like to think the unthinkable – oh, wait, the itheberg already did that. Instead, he'd like to thank the concept of referring to oneself in the third person, as well as cool flashlights, long run-on sentences, whoever invented the footnote, magnetized toys, Porcupine Tree, idealized drum kits and Rickenbacker basses, and Meltwater, as well as friends like Andrew and Tracy Snell and Darren Thornton, in addition to associates like Josh Long (and everyone else from the Spring project!), Reinier Zwitserloot whose name is still probably not properly spelled, and – most importantly and seriously – his family for putting up with him in the first place, and much more for putting up with him during the book-writing process. I love all of you more than I know how to express.

Andrew would like to thank all the people in his life who put up with the book writing process. Thank you to Joaquín who put up with some blank stares to his questions after I'd searched for written words that would not arrive, and my love Dana who took an immediate interest and helped craft some of our funnier footnotes that hopefully survived.

Thank you to Joe, for being crazy enough to want to write a book with me.

CHAPTER 1

History and Justification

Spring is an application framework providing Dependency Injection features for the Java Virtual Machine – features that enable testability, reliability, and flexibility to application developers. It changed how Java is developed, and here's how and why.

1.1 Setting the Stage for Better Development

Spring, according to Wikipedia, is one of the four temperate seasons, following winter and... no, no, this isn't a book about weather. Let's try again.

A spring is a mechanical device that stores kinetic energy, releasing it when tension stored in the... no, that doesn't sound right either. This is supposed to be a book about programming.

One more try:

Spring, contextually speaking, is an application framework for the JVM. It uses a concept called "Dependency Injection" – described later in this chapter, we promise – as a general model for development, and it has changed how Java programs are written, even if the programs in question avoid the use of Spring itself.

Spring is also an *ecosystem* – a galaxy of extensions and modules with a library called spring-core at its center. The extensions and modules add functionality and features to cover many, many possible use cases. In general, people don't refer to spring-core much; instead they just use "Spring" and expect others to understand that the ecosystem as a whole is being referred to.

The modules are, as mentioned, pretty extensive. Chances are, if you need to work with something in Java, there's a Spring module for it... somewhere.

1

© Joseph B. Ottinger and Andrew Lombardi 2019
J. B. Ottinger and A. Lombardi, *Beginning Spring 5*, https://doi.org/10.1007/978-1-4842-4486-9_1

Spring came from somewhere, first, of course; that "somewhere" was actually "someone," Rod Johnson.

In 2002, Rod wrote a book called *Expert One-on-One J2EE Design and Development*.[1] It was written as a reaction to certain aspects of J2EE, the predominant framework for enterprise application design in Java, and as such represented a bit of a revolution – or a rebirth of joy and ease, if you will – for Java programming. In it, Rod included some example code that Juergen Hoeller and others asked him to make open source, which found its way into a project, called "Spring," which itself later found its way into *another* book, *Expert One-on-One J2EE Development without EJB*.[2] *This* is the book that really got things moving.[3]

To understand the importance of J2EE[4] (and Spring, really), we need to think about how programming was evolving at the time. "Real applications" tended to still be run on minicomputers or mainframes, managed resources were still king, and applications that managed to be relevant running on personal computers were surprising. Everyone knew of Lotus 1-2-3,[5] of course, and dBase was a surprisingly functional database application, and sure, it was fine for students and others of similar low breeding to write documents on personal computers... but to actually run *real applications* meant running on the corporate mainframe.

---

[1]Johnson, Rod (2002), *Expert One-on-One J2EE Design and Development*, Hoboken, NJ: Wiley Press. It's unfortunately out of print, although you might be able to find it on Amazon and other such sites.

[2]Johnson, Rod & Hoeller, Juergen (2004), *Expert One-on-One J2EE Development without EJB*, Hoboken, NJ: Wiley Press. Unlike its predecessor, this one's still in print, although it's out of date as one can expect from a book published well over a decade ago, as of *this* book's publication. I think this footnote is longer than the source paragraph.

[3]For all intents and purposes, *J2EE Development without EJB* was the more significant book, and an autographed copy lives on one of the author's shelves in a place of honor. From here on out, any references to these books will center on this latter book.

[4]"J2EE" is a set of specifications and libraries for "enterprise features" in Java. It's an acronym for "Java 2 Platform, Enterprise Edition," and was renamed in 2006 to "Java EE." In 2018, it was turned over to the Eclipse Foundation and renamed "Jakarta EE."

[5]Lotus 1-2-3 was the first "killer application" for PCs; it was the first truly popular and usable spreadsheet, and revolutionized the PC market all by itself, simply by being respectable and capable. It's still around somewhere, now owned by IBM, but for most people Microsoft Excel killed it off. I'm going to try to minimize footnotes for a while.

Mainframe development would be horribly constraining for developers today; the concept of scheduling jobs to run – even as compilations, or tests – is foreign. We're used to the power of being able to spin up a PostgreSQL[6] instance in Docker,[7] for instance, to which we connect our app for a quick integration test. Today, we think nothing of running an application for two seconds just to see if a function returns the right value... but in the mainframe days, that represented quite a considerable investment of time and money and disk space. You typically had a production database and one test database, both of which were valued more than gold, if only because they were very difficult to replace.

In that kind of environment, the system administrator was king. The sysadmin told you where he or she had located the databases, and how to connect to them, and – more importantly – how much of the system resources were allocated to your program. Exceed those resources, and your program would be terminated, to prevent impacting every other program negatively.

Enter Java, which could be compiled on a wimpy local desktop. Suddenly, the cost of development for applications meant to be run on the mainframe dropped, because no longer was the mainframe as important for anything except running the application. What's more, Java was incredibly strong enough to bring the mainframe ethos ("Real programs run here") into smaller machines like minicomputers and even the personal computer.

J2EE was created as an application framework that provided a set of standards for enterprise development. It had a presentation layer and a computation layer, among others, and incorporated formal standards for communications between those layers. It also used the concept of a "container" into which one deployed J2EE modules – like web modules and other such components – and the container represented a point of control for system administrators. An administrator could control how many connections a given container could make to a specific database, for example.

The most important word in the prior paragraph was "formal." The next most important word was "control," as in "what the container administrator had."

---

[6]PostgreSQL is an open source relational database engine. See www.postgresql.org/ for more details.

[7]Docker is an open source container for virtualized runtimes; basically, it's a program that allows you to deploy "application images" for easy deployment. See https://docker.com/ to learn more. So much for my desire to "minimize footnotes."

Java had a concept that it called the "Java bean," which was meant to be a deployable unit of functionality; you might have a "bean" that followed certain standards and represented some kind of relevant operation; you might have a bean that, for example, served to calculate the points along a curve when provided sample data, or a bean that performed matrix computations.

Likewise, J2EE had the concept of an "Enterprise Java Bean," or "EJB," which was a Java Bean with additional restrictions and capabilities, mostly centering around transactions and the ability to be called remotely. An EJB, when called, represented an interprocess communication, even if it was colocated with its caller.

In practice, this meant that every J2EE programmer was enabled right out of the gate to design working distributed architectures. This is not a small accomplishment at all; distributed architectures are difficult to get right, and J2EE made invoking processes on separate machines trivial.

There's a cost to all of this, of course.

The nature of EJB, especially early in J2EE's lifecycle, meant that when every call could be remote, every call had to be treated as if it were a remote call, with a specific deployment and development cycle (early on, you had a separate packaging compiler for EJB, called ejbc, to build the supporting classes for EJBs to run), and because of the requirement that EJBs be considered to be remote even when they weren't, EJBs were slow.

EJBs were slow to develop, slow to test, slow to deploy, and slow to invoke. And they were everywhere.

J2EE Development without EJB was written as a logical reaction to the entrenched mindset. Rod Johnson and Juergen Hoeller looked at how EJBs were being used (and misused) and their actual cost to developer productivity – which was really quite high, for the value they were providing. To use an EJB, not only did you have to go through a special development and deployment cycle, but then you had to look them up at runtime and handle the exceptions when they weren't available...

Listing 1-1. Looking up an EJB in the olden days

```
// get the JNDI context for the application
Context ctx=new InitialContext();
// Inferencer is the java interface for the EJB

// First, we have to get the "Home" object, which
//     can create the EJB for the caller
```

```
// The deployer should have set up the name to point to /
//      an actual deployed EJB artifact
Object ref=ctx.lookup("java:comp/env/ejb/inferencer");
InferencerHome home=
  (InferencerHome) PortableRemoteObject.narrow(
    ref,
    InferencerHome.class
  );

// now, we use the home object to actually get the EJB
Inferencer engine=home.create();

// presumably, generate an inference using inputs...
engine.generate(input);
```

In Listing 1-1, not only did you have to write the code to grab a component that can create the EJB from somewhere else,[8] but you had to *configure* that reference... and then you had to go through a set of semantics to get something that can actually invoke your EJB. But why go through the development and remote semantics when they were rarely needed and desired? Those semantics were rarely important despite how much they catastrophically affected your code; at a Java Symposium in the early 2000s, attendees were asked how many used EJBs, and most hands went up; the next question was how many of those EJBs were actually invoked remotely. The answer was, anecdotally, about 2%.[9]

That mindset is what drove *J2EE Development without EJB*: a desire to return freedom to the coders, to provide support for programming with necessary complexity. If you needed to call a remote service, well, nothing stops you from doing that, but experience with actual coding showed that it was rarely necessary and, instead, served as a barrier to just getting things done.

Rod's primary insight was that EJBs might be powerful, but they were a little like strapping a V6 engine into a child's bicycle. Most developers didn't need them, or want them; EJB just happened to be the language feature *du jour*, and as a result

---

[8]JNDI, the "Java Naming and Directory Interface," is a standard way for an application administrator to create local names for global references. If it sounds sort of like LDAP, it's because it was derived largely from LDAP. It also meant that in order to look up resources, you had to know how to set up the references, and few bothered. In practice, effectively no one liked doing it as part of development.

[9]TheServerSide Java Symposium, Las Vegas, NV, 2004.

development was slowed down, deployment was more difficult,[10] testing was difficult, and configuration was arcane. Most developers didn't use the "correct techniques" for looking up EJBs because they didn't want to take the time to configure the EJB container. Configuring the container meant that reproducing conditions was more difficult, as well.

It was a mess. It was a productive mess, at times; after all, the technology was created as a response to actual user needs. But even if developers were able to use it to get real things done well, it created a lot of burden on those same developers, and the practices in place weren't making it better. The technology didn't even really *allow* better practices.

1.2 Rod and Juergen Change the (Java) World

In *J2EE Development without EJB*, Rod (and Juergen, but I'll shorten it to Rod and hope Juergen takes no offense!) mapped out a process for J2EE development that focused on six themes:

- Simplicity

- Productivity

- The fundamental importance of object orientation

- The primacy of business requirements

- The importance of empirical process

- The importance of testability[11]

In addition to these themes being obviously fairly important, it's important to recognize that these themes were *secondary* concerns for typical J2EE development.

For example, EJBs were meant to represent *generic* access to remote services, so developing an EJB meant creating something that could be invoked via complex protocols, along with handling fairly complex transactional concerns. If that's what you *actually needed*, then EJB was fine... but most developers *didn't* need to worry about CORBA, and their transactional needs tended to be very simple. EJB represented complexity that the *applications* didn't need.

---

[10]EJB modules were deployed separately from presentation modules, so you had to configure the application to coordinate everything to actually run your code.

[11]Rod Johnson, *J2EE Development without EJB* (Hoboken: Wiley, 2004), 5-6.

If the applications didn't need the complexity, but programmers had to be aware of it, then the complexity represented a direct and unavoidable sunk cost for development.

Further, EJBs tended to be non-Java-like in how they worked. They represented endpoints of functionality, not self-contained objects. Designing an EJB meant stepping outside of the very paradigms that made Java useful in the first place.

Spring was designed to change enterprise development such that it prioritized, well, all six of those themes. It was designed to be simple (and thus productive and by definition focused on actual business requirements), object oriented, and **testable**, a feature whose value is difficult to overvalue.[12]

J2EE Development without EJB then went on a tear, demonstrating a self-contained application context that, despite using XML, was far easier for developers to work with than J2EE's striated developer/deployer model. It returned power to the developers and along the way provided easy ways to create objects that were used solely for testing – a feature EJB provided but only with great difficulty – and ways to change how the application objects acquired resources such that it made sense to most developers.

After all, if you need a `Widget` in your `FooFram`, one doesn't normally think that in ordinary Java the `FooFram` should ask a remote service to provide a `Widget` somehow; normally one has a `setWidget(Widget widget)` method in the `FooFram` object.

Spring went a long way to making Java look like, well, Java again. Objective adoption rates are unclear, but it's safe to say that Java developers were a lot more excited about developing with Spring than with traditional J2EE. However, Spring was not a formal part of the development landscape of J2EE.

Spring had an almost subversive approach; one used J2EE, and Spring was used alongside J2EE to actually get things done. It was a curious, but effective, model. Spring was becoming a standard dependency for many; it was standard idiom without being an actual part of any standards.

Better approaches were possible, with the creation of community processes such that Java application design wasn't decided upon by cloistered architects in San Jose.

---

[12]In other words, *testability* is extremely valuable. Tests allow you to *know* if the code is working as designed; no more cases where a developer says "I think it should work…" followed by delivery to a customer. That still happens, but it's not the failure of the technology: it's a failure of process.

1.3 The Lever: Dependency Injection

The core design pattern that Spring introduced to the wider Java world is called "Dependency Injection."[13] With the "traditional J2EE approach," objects that needed a resource deterministically acquired that resource, with a specific name. (You could, I suppose, *look up* the name you wanted, but then you have to look up the *specific name*, which isn't much better.) Control over which resource was provided was given to the J2EE application server's administrator.

For a developer to use J2EE, he or she had to assume the administrator role and configure the name service somehow. Name services, to borrow a phrase from Barbie, are hard; you have to make sure you have qualifying types (a low barrier, honestly, because most of the things you'd want a name service for would qualify, by design), you have to know how to make sure the objects are constructed properly, you have to know how to set up the names and resources *for your specific application server*, and you then have to know how to set up the application-specific redirected names – again, for each application server, because while most of them were similar, they weren't quite the same, either.

It's a very powerful idea, but it's more than most developers wanted to do – and many of them did only the minimum necessary and didn't bother setting up local names for resources. It also made testing very difficult, because you couldn't just use a `Widget` in a test, you had to **deploy** a `Widget`, set up a name for it, and have your object *look up* the `Widget` in the test. It's doable, certainly – programmers are often inventive and driven – but it's also a pain.

With Dependency Injection, however, the objects that want a `Widget` no longer have to *look up* a `Widget`. Now, when an object that needs a `Widget` is constructed, the Dependency Injection framework (in this book, Spring!) *provides* a `Widget` immediately.[14] The Dependency Injection framework gathers information about `Widget` in a few different ways: the simplest way (and the earliest) was simply to create an XML file that had a reference to a `Widget` and the classes that needed it. In later versions of Java and Spring, the application code can be *searched* for possible instances of injectable resources, making configuration of simple applications very lightweight.

---

[13]It used to be called "Inversion of Control."

[14]There is a distinct lack of nuance here. There are actually lots of ways for this to happen; we'll see many variants and why these variants matter in a later chapter.

When programmers designed code for J2EE, they indebted themselves to the J2EE mindset; everything one did with J2EE involved a lot of, well, J2EE. You couldn't test code that used an EJB without involving yourself in JNDI configuration – a simple test would have to start up a JNDI container (and, possibly, an EJB container), along with populating the JNDI dataset and making sure the EJBs could be resolved. None of that is actually **testing the service** – it's all gruntwork required just to get to the point where you're *able* to test the service. It implies enduring startup time for the containers (which is time wasted even in the best of circumstances) and time spent on testing the configuration.

But if the *goal* is to test something... pragmatism would suggest that configuration of containers and startup times is *all* wasted.

With Dependency Injection, you simply create a Java class that reflects the behavior you want, and supply it to the class you're testing. Your test doesn't even have to depend on Spring or anything else. As an example, let's consider two forms of "Hello, world"[15] – the EJB version (as it would exist around 2005[16]) and a version that represents the class structure that's ready for Dependency Injection.

1.3.1 J2EE Hello World, as of 2005

An EJB back in the first days of Spring needed at least three source files: an interface that described the contract for the EJB, a class that provided the actual executable code for the EJB, and a "home object" that was used to manage the EJB's lifecycle (operations that took place when the EJB was created, or destroyed, among other lifecycle stages). We're not even going to go into the process of developing the actual deployment itself – this is *just* the Java class structure required at *runtime*. Deployment required **at least** one XML descriptor, with each container often requiring yet another container-specific XML file to connect resources inside the container's JNDI tree. It was maddening, even in the *best* case... and the best cases were rather rare.[17]

---

[15]Note that we're going to revisit "Hello, World" in the next chapter, and do it correctly.

[16]Why focus on 2005? Because Spring made J2EE change a lot, something that every Java programmer benefitted from. We're showing *why* Spring was such a benefit to Java.

[17]Sadly, the rarity of the best cases was difficult to measure, because most developers would do things inefficiently just so they could avoid the *normal* deployment model. This is a clear signal that EJB development, while "functional," didn't actually work.

Listing 1-2. The EJB interface

```
interface HelloWorldEJB
  extends EJBObject
{
  String sayHello(String name)
    throws RemoteException;
}
```

In our `HelloWorldEJB`, we're simply saying that we have one method that the EJB provides: `sayHello()`. Since this is an EJB, we have to anticipate the possibility of errors occurring due to the nature of EJBs being remoteable. It's worth pointing out that even the *interface* of our EJB is affected by, well, being an EJB; we have to include the `EJBObject` interface. We can't even develop this much of our EJB without being aware of the fact that it's an EJB. This is *Not Good*; it represents technical debt to J2EE and we haven't even done anything yet.

Listing 1-3. The EJB home object

```
public interface HelloWorldEJBHome
  extends EJBHome
{
  HelloWorldEJB create()
    throws RemoteException,
      CreateException;
}
```

The `HelloWorldEJBHome` interface specifies how a concrete instance of `HelloWorldEJB` can be created. In our case, our interface demonstrates a stateless service (e.g., we don't create it with a default target to greet), so there's nothing special for the creation process... yet we still need to create this interface.

Listing 1-4. The EJB implementation

```
class HelloWorldEJBImplementation
  implements SessionBean
{
  public String sayHello(String name)
  {
    if(name==null)
    {
      name="world";
    }
    return "hello, "+name+".";
  }
}
```

At least, we have meaningful code! It's a simple method; if the argument is `null`, default to saying "Hello, world," but otherwise greet the name provided to the method. It's worth noting here that it doesn't actually implement `HelloWorldEJB` – evidence of an antipattern, indeed.

Listing 1-5. The EJB client code

```
...
try {
  Context ctx=new InitialContext();
  Object ref=ctx.lookup("java:comp/env/ejb/hello");
  HelloWorldEJBHome home= (HelloWorldEJBHome)
    PortableRemoteObject.narrow(
      ref, HelloWorldEJBHome.class);
  HelloWorldEJB greeter=home.create();
  System.out.println(greeter.sayHello("Andrew"));
} catch(Throwable throwable) {
  /*
    bubble up to the next level of the application
    for all exception conditions, since we can
    handle none of them *here* - note that we're
```

```
    handling CreateException, RemoteException,
    and NamingException with one catch block
  */
  throw new RuntimeException(
    throwable.getMessage(), throwable);
}
```

This is what the *caller* of our EJB would have to do as a bare minimum. This doesn't *test* our EJB; it only *calls* it. If we wanted to test our EJB out, we'd have to construct something similar to this, **deploy** our EJB, and add code to pass it known inputs and compare to expected outputs.[18]

I think it's safe to say that this sounds like a burden... but this is what every J2EE developer had to endure.

1.3.2 Spring's Better Vision of Hello World

Now let's take a look at what Rod Johnson encouraged coders to create. We'll have our contract (the interface), an implementation of that interface, and show client code that would use our HelloWorldBean – and then walk a little bit through some of the many reasons this implementation is better.

Listing 1-6. The HelloWorld interface

```
package com.bsg5.hello;

interface HelloWorld
{
  String sayHello(String name);
}
```

Note how clean this interface is: it does nothing more than our EJB's interface does (and in fact HelloWorldEJB could extend this interface, adding only the EJBObject interface as decoration). This class has no technical debt *anywhere* – not to Spring, not to J2EE.

---

[18]Note that the EJB 1.1 source files shown here are *not* part of the book's source code. These files are like time-traveling back to when your choices were death by smallpox or death by the bubonic plague.

Listing 1-7. The HelloWorld implementation

```
package com.bsg5.hello;

public class HelloWorldImplementation
  implements HelloWorld
{
  public String sayHello(String name)
  {
    if(name==null) {
      name="world";
    }
    return "Hello, "+name+".";
  }
}
```

We see the same pattern with HelloWorldImplementation as we do with HelloWorld. It depends on the HelloWorld interface, of course, but that's all. We have nothing in the class that's not focused on actually fulfilling the contract of the HelloWorld interface. The HelloWorldEJBImplementation gets **close** to that idea, but has to implement SessionBean – and *is not supposed to* implement the interface that represents its contract. We've only displayed two example classes and we've got far less technical debt, and our classes conform to idiomatic Java – even the idioms of the day back in 2004 or so, when J2EE was king and dinosaurs roamed the Earth.

Listing 1-8. The HelloWorld client

```
package com3.bsg5.client;

public class Greeter
{
  HelloWorld generator;
  void setGenerator(HelloWorld generator)
  {
    this.generator=generator;
  }
```

```
public void displayHello(String name)
{
  System.out.println(generator.sayHello(name));
}
}
```

Here, you see the generator reference points to a HelloWorld implementation. Greeter doesn't instantiate a HelloWorld (although it could if it wanted); however, the idea here is that something *external* to Greeter provides a HelloWorld, and a Greeter just uses it. It doesn't have to have any acquisition code, has no lookup code, it's just an attribute on a regular Java class.

HelloBean is too simple to actually *need* other implementations... but suppose we needed to wrap some other functionality into an implementation for testing or other diagnosis?[19] We could create the functionality and just use the new implementation for testing; our Greeter class doesn't have to change, and we don't have to do anything special to switch to our new implementation besides using it instead.

This is Dependency Injection; we're injecting the HelloWorld dependency when we need it.

Spring not only recognized the power of this pattern, but the Spring framework provided tools to use it; you would define an XML file that named a helloworld bean (of type com.bsg5.chapter1.HelloWorldImpl), as well as a Greeter instance, and would inject the helloworld reference into the Greeter automatically, with no source-level dependencies on Spring whatsoever.

Spring added some technical debt, if you used certain aspects of the framework: you could have lifecycle hooks in your beans, for example, if you wanted them. (You could still configure lifecycle stages via XML, too, and avoid technical debt in the source files.) But Spring was, and is, largely pragmatic; you, as a developer, had the power to choose how much debt you wanted to incur, as opposed to J2EE's mandated and crushing technical debt.

---

[19]We'll see this sort of thing in Chapter 2.

1.4 Spring Breaks Free and Fixes Java EE

Sun, the original creators and maintainers of Java, created the Java Community Process back in 1998, but opened up membership a few years later. Spring, being an influential aspect *of* the community, participated in the creation of Java EE 6, with J2EE having been renamed to something less confusing.[20] With Spring's participation, Java EE 6 gained a new specification, "Context and Dependency Injection." Standard annotations were added to support CDI and features related to it, and the world rejoiced publicly and privately.

The funny thing is, as Spring became more influential on Java EE, Java EE itself became *less* influential. Spring never stopped innovating; now, you can deploy microcontainers using Spring, leveraging Java EE API specifications, without bothering with Java EE containers as such at all. You can still use a Java EE application server, of course, but the need to do so has lessened.

That represents a loss of control by the "old guard," the system administrators who still think that 2005 represented the "good old days[21]" – but it means that programmers of today have more power and flexibility than they've ever had, and in Java it's fair to say they owe a debt of gratitude to the Spring framework for it.

1.5 Next Steps

In our next chapter, we're going to take a look at "Hello, World" again – and go a lot deeper into the strengths of Dependency Injection, and Spring in particular.

---

[20]"Java 2, Enterprise Edition" made sense, until you realized that it used Java 1.2. Then you had "Java 2, Enterprise Edition, version 1.3," and so on. Sun was a brilliant company with confusing release numbering schemes. It made sense when you dug into the details, but it would have made a lot more sense to just use cohesive and sensible version numbers. We'll talk more about this in Chapter 5 when we discard "J2EE" as a name.

[21]Those old system administrators are probably still on their front porches, shouting "Get off my lawn!"

CHAPTER 2

Hello, World!

It seems appropriate to start learning about Spring by building out our first example as a simple "Hello, World!" application. In this chapter, we're going to take a look at the tools and libraries we're going to rely on – in particular, Gradle and TestNG[1] – and build a simple application to demonstrate how we validate that our application works as designed. Then – at last – we'll leverage Spring in our application. This way, we'll establish the knowledge we'll need to make sense of the rest of the book.

2.1 A Simple Application

Our goal in this chapter will be to take another look at the "Hello, World" application from Chapter 1, except this time we're going to examine tooling and the mindset that drove the design.

First, why "Hello, World?" Traditionally, programming languages (and frameworks) use this application because it's very **simple** – and that means we have room to focus on things like overall syntax, how to design, how to build, and how to run the app. "Hello, World" allows us to do nothing but explore the lifecycle of a "full program."[2]

---

[1]Why TestNG and not JUnit? There's a little more explanation later in this chapter, but just to get it out of the way: TestNG makes certain kinds of tests more convenient. You should be able to use JUnit instead with fairly little difficulty, although you'll need to add a JUnit module to use features like data providers.

[2]We're foisting a "Hello world" on you, but we promise there's no "Pet Store" in this book. If that doesn't give you a palpable sense of relief, well... pretend it does, because it should. Right, Joe? We're not doing the Pet Store, right? We agreed? Yes?

© Joseph B. Ottinger and Andrew Lombardi 2019
J. B. Ottinger and A. Lombardi, *Beginning Spring 5*, https://doi.org/10.1007/978-1-4842-4486-9_2

Spring is going to be incredibly heavy for such a simple application, and we aren't even going to use it for the first iteration, but that allows us to focus on tooling and process, including tests.[3] We'll wire everything together with Spring as we continue – even though it will look a bit silly – because that will demonstrate how we can move configuration around as needed, a feature that's necessary in real-world scenarios.

2.1.1 Suffering-Oriented Programming

Throughout the entire book, we're going to do simple things over and over (and over) again – you'll probably be sick of "Hello, World" as we use it multiple times. This is partly because of the familiarity of "Hello, World" – it has simple, knowable inputs and simple, knowable outputs and therefore allows us to focus on the bits that **surround** the basic process rather than the process of saying "Hello" itself.

A bit of history: "Hello, World" was introduced to the world in Kernighan and Ritchie's *The C Programming Language*.[4] This is an iconic programming book, and it's the most accessible of the classic programming books such as *The Art of Computer Programming* (Knuth) or *Design Patterns* (Gamma, Helm, Johnson, Vlissides). The other books are accessible, too – they're classics for a reason – but *The C Programming Language* stands alone due to its directness, simple and clear presentation of its subject matter, and, well, the time of publication.

"Hello, World" is used as a "sanity check" – a very simple program to make sure the compiler and runtime environment are working, as well as illustrating a general "bare minimum" to get a program running that actually generates output.

---

[3]If you don't write tests, you need to start writing tests. Don't worry, you'll get a ton of exposure in this book. They're easy and fun. After your first 1,203,172 tests, you might get a free toaster.

[4]Kernighan, Brian & Ritchie, Dennis (1978), Englewood Cliffs, NJ; Prentice-Hall.

Many programmers add functionality to it to illustrate additional features; the Free Software Foundation's "Hello, World" (found at `www.gnu.org/software/hello/`) is *184* lines of code, illustrating command line parsing and licensing and other such issues of concern for the FSF – and the downloadable archive is nearly 800K!

Following this time-honored tradition – are there any other kinds of valid traditions? – we'll be following suit in this book, generally using "Hello, World" to make sure our library is doing what it's supposed to, before adding functionality that actually exercises the chapter's subject in question.

We also follow the concept of "suffering-oriented programming," a term coined by Nathan Marz on `http://nathanmarz.com/blog/suffering-oriented-programming.html`. The concept behind this is simple: "First make it possible. Then make it beautiful. Then make it fast."

This mindset says that **working** code is superior to any other kind of code; you should first focus on making your application **run**.

The next most important aspect of your code is to make it **understandable** – or "beautiful," or perhaps "simple." Once you've solved your problem somehow (you've made it work), you are likely to understand your problem more completely than when you first started writing code. Now that you've got working code, you can try to simplify your solution such that it's more clear and maintainable. (Spring helps a lot with this, by the way.) Along the way, if you find your "more beautiful" version doesn't actually work, well... you've still got your baseline code, the code that existed before you started beautifying, so you can refine your attempts to clean up your code until it, too, works.

Lastly, you make your code **fast**. By this point you've presumably got working code written with simple abstractions; now it's time to focus on where the code actually runs inefficiently, such that it uses resources properly. This is where you'd go through the code with a profiler, looking for places where you allocate memory unnecessarily (a small concern with languages like Java, where short-term memory usage is, to use the technical term, "fast as blazes") or where you iterate through data structures more slowly than you could have.

This book focuses heavily on the first two aspects of suffering-oriented programming, because Java's actually fairly spectacular at making simple code run well, but it's worth keeping all three concerns in mind.

2.2 Building

With simplicity in mind, we're going to use an open source build tool called Gradle.[5] Gradle is one of the two major build systems popular in Java, along with Maven, but Gradle has a simpler configuration file – and the goal of this book is to focus on Spring, rather than spend 15 pages explaining how the build system is configured.

Gradle uses a conventional filesystem structure lifted from Maven and a simple domain-specific language for building. Basically, there's a directory for source files called `src` – with typically two directories in it. `src/main` holds the application files – the ones that make up the actual program being built – and `src/test` contains the files that are for testing only. `src/main` and `src/test` themselves have different directories; Java files that are part of the application would go into `src/main/java`, while tests written in Java would be located in `src/test/java`. You might have static resources as part of the build; things meant to be included for delivery would go in `src/main/resources`, where resources meant only for testing would go into `src/test/resources`.

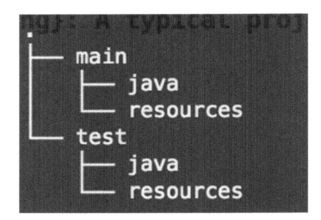

You'll have a lot of opportunities to see these structures over and over again as the book progresses.

First, let's show how to install Gradle for some popular operating systems.[6] After that, we'll walk through `build.gradle`, the file that informs Gradle about how you want your project built.

---

[5]Gradle can be found at `https://gradle.org`. We'll demonstrate how to install Gradle for many operating systems as we go through the chapter.

[6]If your operating system is not addressed, fear not, Brave Reader: `http://gradle.org/` can help.

2.2.1 Installing Gradle

The best method to install Gradle is subjective, but our recommendation is to use a package manager available on your platform.

For Linux, you can use the SDKMAN! package manager[7] and install with:

```
sdk install gradle 5.5.1
```

For MacOS the best option is to use Homebrew[8]:

```
brew install gradle
```

And for those of you unlucky enough to be using Windows, scoop[9] is inspired by Homebrew and looks to be pretty decent:

```
scoop install gradle
```

Most often you will add the Gradle wrapper to your code repository and developers can just use the wrapper for their operating system, either `gradlew` or `gradlew.bat`. To create the Gradle wrapper after installing Gradle from any of the preceding methods, you can do the following:

```
> gradle wrapper
> Task :wrapper

BUILD SUCCESSFUL in 0s
1 actionable task: 1 executed
```

The result will be two files and a directory you can add to your code repository: `gradlew`, `gradlew.bat`, and the directory `gradle/`. (There's also a hidden directory, `.gradle`, that holds a local gradle instance for repeatable builds, but that shouldn't go into a code repository.)

---

[7]SDKMAN! (`https://sdkman.io/`) is a developer-focused environment manager for multiple operating systems, including Linux, Windows, and OSX. It allows you to have localized environments for building and running applications. It's horribly useful, because it disassociates you from the distribution's package-management process.

[8]Homebrew (`https://brew.sh/`) is essential if you run MacOS, so if you don't have it installed already, for the love of all that is good and holy, do it now.

[9]Scoop (`https://scoop.sh/`) is a simple command line installer for Windows.

2.2.2 Building the Project

Gradle uses a plugin-based system to control what simple operations to apply to a given project. For Java, there's a `java` plugin; we'll use that to use the default configurations for building, testing, and bundling Java artifacts.

What's an "artifact?" An artifact is a deliverable element. If you build an application into a file called `myapplication-1.0.jar`, then `myapplication-1.0.jar` is an artifact of your build. A single project might have multiple artifacts; this will show up in a much later chapter. For right now, though, an "artifact" is a deliverable element generated from a project.

What we want to do is define a build that controls a number of **other** builds as subprojects, or "modules." Our top-level file won't actually have anything to compile, but it will instead define variables for use in our chapter modules, as well as setting global preferences. As a result, our chapters' `build.gradle` files will be essentially simple, only containing dependencies and configurations for the chapters that are differentiated from the top-level project.

In practice, this means that the chapters' `build.gradle` files will consist of chapter dependencies themselves, like Spring. Let's take a look at the file in Listing 2-1.

Listing 2-1. Gradle Java plugin definition

```
apply plugin: 'java'
sourceCompatibility = 1.11
targetCompatibility = 1.11

ext {
    springFrameworkVersion = "5.1.5.RELEASE"
    jacksonVersion = "2.9.9"
    testNgVersion = "6.14.3"
}

allprojects {
    apply plugin: 'java'
```

```
    repositories {
        jcenter()
        mavenCentral()
    }

    dependencies {
        testImplementation "org.testng:testng:$testNgVersion"
    }

    test {
        useTestNG()
    }
}
```

Our top-level build file has four sections:

- A `plugin` section that marks this as a Java project. This is meant
  mostly to help with setting the Java version settings, which aren't
  visible in non-Java projects.

- `sourceCompatibility` and `targetCompatibility` settings, which
  target the current (as of publication time) long-term supported
  version of Java, which is Java 11. (At the time of writing, Java 12 had
  been released; however, that version will be deprecated when Java 13
  is released. Java 11 is slated to have support for a few years.)

- An `ext` section that sets variables for use in every other submodule.
  Here, we set our TestNG version and the current Spring release
  version; if a new release of Spring is made, we can update Spring for
  the entire project by changing the value of `springFrameworkVersion`.

- A section marked `allprojects`. This is a set of build directives that
  apply to every project under **this** project. What this means, then, is that
  every chapter will have the `java` plugin applied and will depend on
  TestNG (and use TestNG in tests). They will also look up dependencies
  (like Spring and TestNG) through two common repositories.

However, we've made a reference to subprojects without showing them. Our next
file, `settings.gradle`, is how we can easily tell Gradle that a subdirectory represents a
subproject (Listing 2-2).

Listing 2-2. `/settings.gradle` including submodules

```
rootProject.name = 'bsg5'

// add inclusions as the chapter sources are followed
include 'chapter2'
include 'chapter3'
include 'chapter4'
include 'chapter5'
include 'chapter5common'
include 'chapter5anno'
include 'chapter5xml'
include 'chapter6'
include 'chapter7'
include 'chapter8'
include 'chapter9common'
include 'chapter9test'
include 'chapter9jpa'
include 'chapter9mongodb'
include 'chapter10'
include 'chapter10custom'
include 'chapter10jpa'
```

If you're typing in each chapter's code as you proceed through the book, you'll want to include only the existing directories – if you have only chapter2 as a subdirectory for your project, only use include 'chapter2'.

We have a very flat directory structure. In Maven, one can nest projects deeply; you can do it with Gradle, too, but Gradle uses a slightly different addressing scheme for projects. As a result, it's more efficient for Gradle to have a very flat structure with unique names for each chapter; thus, instead of having a chapter9 directory with common, test, jpa, and mongodb in it, we have chapter9common, chapter9test, and so forth.

We can now define the build.gradle for our submodule in the chapter2 directory. In this chapter, we need three Spring dependencies (spring-core, spring-context, and spring-test) – and every other attribute of the build comes from the build.gradle at the top-level project (i.e., apply the java plugin, use Java 11, include and use TestNG for testing).

Listing 2-3. chapter2/build.gradle

```
dependencies {
    compile "org.springframework:spring-core:$springFrameworkVersion"
    compile "org.springframework:spring-context:$springFrameworkVersion"
    compile "org.springframework:spring-test:$springFrameworkVersion"
}
```

The Gradle default is to run tests under JUnit. As we'll discuss in the next section, we're choosing to use TestNG instead in the examples of the book. TestNG has had support for annotations from the beginning, doesn't require extending a test class, and has other powerful features that we've decided to leverage[10]; you can use JUnit in similar ways but TestNG has earned its way into our hearts.

Now that we've got the basics set up with Gradle, we can run the `gradle` command and see some very mundane but expected output – since we don't have any code yet.

Listing 2-4. Gradle output without any code

```
% gradle
Parallel execution is an incubating feature.

> Task :help

Welcome to Gradle 4.6.

To run a build, run gradle <task> ...

To see a list of available tasks, run gradle tasks

To see a list of command-line options, run gradle --help

To see more detail about a task, run gradle help --task <task>

For troubleshooting, visit https://help.gradle.org

BUILD SUCCESSFUL in 0s
1 actionable task: 1 executed
```

---

[10]TestNG utilized the concept of data providers before JUnit did, and while JUnit supports the feature **now** it's through a library external to JUnit. We've chosen to stick with TestNG, but you can certainly use JUnit instead without hurting our feelings very much; JUnit's nearly caught up with TestNG and in some ways has surpassed it.

In the next section, we'll go into more detail about TestNG and how we'll be using it throughout the many examples in the pages ahead.

2.3 Testing

The best way to ensure that your program is working as intended is not System.out. println all over your codebase. It's to write tests. Tests allow us to write assumptions about what our code does, and have those validated (or not). They help with refactoring and can sometimes be an initial basis for self-documentation of the codebase.

As we saw in Listing 2-1, we've already added TestNG to our configuration for every submodule in our directory structure. So let's assume before we write any implementation that we have a class called HelloWorldGreeter that implements an interface Greeter which defines two methods greet() and setPrintStream().

Listing 2-5 shows our very simple Greeter interface.

Listing 2-5. chapter2/src/main/java/com/bsg5/chapter2/Greeter.java

```
package com.bsg5.chapter2;

import java.io.PrintStream;

public interface Greeter {

    void setPrintStream(PrintStream printStream);

    void greet();
}
```

As mentioned earlier, TestNG makes use of annotations to instrument your test classes. For our test GreeterTest, we will use the method annotation @Test to let TestNG know to run testHelloWorld as a test – if any of the assertions fail, or if an exception is thrown, the test will be considered to have failed.

Listing 2-6. chapter2/src/test/java/com/bsg5/chapter2/GreeterTest.java

```
package com.bsg5.chapter2;

import org.testng.annotations.Test;

import java.io.ByteArrayOutputStream;
```

```java
import java.io.PrintStream;
import java.io.UnsupportedEncodingException;
import java.nio.charset.StandardCharsets;

import static org.testng.Assert.assertEquals;

public class GreeterTest {
    @Test
    public void testHelloWorld() {
        Greeter greeter = new HelloWorldGreeter();
        final ByteArrayOutputStream baos = new ByteArrayOutputStream();
        try (PrintStream ps = new PrintStream(baos, true, "UTF-8")) {
            greeter.setPrintStream(ps);
            greeter.greet();
        } catch (UnsupportedEncodingException e) {
            e.printStackTrace();
        }
        String data = new String(baos.toByteArray(), StandardCharsets.UTF_8);
        assertEquals(data, "Hello, World!");
    }
}
```

You can see in Listing 2-6 that we also have a static import so in our assertions we can type assertEquals(actual, expected) vs. Assert.assertEquals(actual, expected). Using static imports in test code is generally a good idea[11] as this type of code tends to duplicate calls many times in each method and we're not losing any readability since it's fairly constrained. The implementation of a Greeter is that an implementation will output something (the default implementation will send to System.out). A test that can confirm this is a bit difficult, so we inject our own implementation of a PrintStream and use that to assert the test case we expect. Take a look at the snippet of code later and see how we're creating a new HelloWorldGreeter object, a ByteArrayOutputStream, and the PrintStream which our Greeter will use to send data to (which by default is assigned to System.out – we want to override it so we can check the output).

---

[11]Using static imports in your regular code is a code smell, and you don't want your code to smell funky, do you? ... No, you don't.

Now that we have a test we can use to validate expected functionality, let's write the implementation for HelloWorldGreeter so we can get it to compile and run. In Listing 2-7 you'll find a base implementation of the Greeter interface.

Listing 2-7. HelloWorldGreeter without implementation

```java
package com.bsg5.chapter2;

import java.io.PrintStream;

public class HelloWorldGreeter implements Greeter {

    public void setPrintStream(PrintStream printStream) {
    }

    public void greet() {
    }
}
```

With the preceding code in place, we can run gradle test and get the expected failure in Listing 2-8. The failure proves our assumption, that the current implementation of Greeter does in fact not print "Hello, World!" and the test works as expected. (The actual failure record can be seen in chapter2/build/reports/tests/test/index.html, if you're interested, but in this case we know exactly why the test failed: our class doesn't do anything yet.)

Listing 2-8. GreeterTest failure

```
gradle test
Parallel execution is an incubating feature.

> Task :chapter2:test FAILED

Gradle suite > Gradle test > com.bsg5.chapter2.GreeterTest.testHelloWorld
FAILED
    java.lang.AssertionError at GreeterTest.java:26

1 test completed, 1 failed

FAILURE: Build failed with an exception.
```

```
* What went wrong:
Execution failed for task ':chapter2:test'.
> There were failing tests. See the report at:
  file:///./chapter2/build/reports/tests/test/index.html

* Try:
Run with --stacktrace option to get the stack trace. Run with --info or
--debug
  option to get more log output. Run with --scan to get full insights.

* Get more help at https://help.gradle.org

BUILD FAILED in 1s
4 actionable tasks: 2 executed, 2 up-to-date
```

Finally, let's actually write the implementation for HelloWorldGreeter so that we know the test not only works as expected but will pass. We're going to write a non-Spring implementation of HelloWorldGreeter so that in the next section when we add the relevant Spring configuration, you'll have a base of understanding to work from.

Listing 2-9. chapter2/src/main/java/com/bsg5/chapter2/ HelloWorldGreeter.java

```
package com.bsg5.chapter2;

import org.springframework.stereotype.Service;

import java.io.PrintStream;
```

In this section, we wrote a test using TestNG against the Greeter interface and exercised the implementation we wrote called HelloWorldGreeter. Everything has used vanilla Java so far because of the nature of the example and was very simple to achieve. In the next section, we're going to refactor the code in Listing 2-9 to show you how to wire the beans together using the power of Spring's Dependency Injection framework.

2.4 A Simple Application with Spring

What have we done so far? We've built an "application" (in our test) that creates a Greeter and, after supplying it with instances of a PrintStream we can use to test, we exercise it. We are manually building the classes to inject into our Greeter, and we're manually instantiating the actual Greeter implementation as well.

Spring allows us to automate almost everything **but** the test itself – which we don't really want to automate (although I suppose we could, given a scaffolding). We're going to get Spring to do all of the object instantiation and injection for us; the power here is that if we should want to redirect to something different, all we need to do is change the actual objects being injected.

Historically one of the most pervasive arguments for not using Spring was the configuration, which was written in namespaced XML.

While there is definitely a programmatic way of implementing our Spring context,[12] for purposes of this example, we're going to stick with the XML file. Using the conventions from our build system, we can put the config file in src/main/resources and load it from the classpath.

The header of our file in Listing 2-10 pulls in specifics that we'll need from Spring which include the specs for beans.

Note that most IDEs can generate Spring contexts, including most or all of this, for you.

Listing 2-10. applicationContext.xml XML header

```xml
<?xml version="1.0" encoding="UTF-8"?>
<beans xmlns="http://www.springframework.org/schema/beans"
       xmlns:xsi="http://www.w3.org/2001/XMLSchema-instance"
       xsi:schemaLocation="http://www.springframework.org/schema/beans
        http://www.springframework.org/schema/beans/spring-beans-3.0.xsd">
```

---

[12]We'll be showing you programmatic Spring context configuration in Chapter 3.

Let's add our beans to the Spring config. In the section on testing, we checked the output of the HelloWorldGreeter by creating a String from a passed in ByteArrayOutputStream. When we wrote this out without using Spring, we were forced to create the ByteArrayOutputStream, PrintStream, and HelloWorldGreeter implementation like in Listing 2-11.

Listing 2-11. GreeterTest test to validate HelloWorldGreeter

```java
public void testHelloWorld() {
    Greeter greeter = new HelloWorldGreeter();
    final ByteArrayOutputStream baos = new ByteArrayOutputStream();
    try (PrintStream ps = new PrintStream(baos, true, "UTF-8")) {
        greeter.setPrintStream(ps);
        greeter.greet();
    } catch (UnsupportedEncodingException e) {
        e.printStackTrace();
    }
    String data = new String(baos.toByteArray(), StandardCharsets.UTF_8);
    assertEquals(data, "Hello, World!");
}
```

While the preceding code is certainly fine, we can do the entire thing with the Spring context. We will create the ByteArrayOutputStream and PrintStream objects using the Spring context along with our HelloWorldGreeter which will take the PrintStream as a bean reference.

Take a look at Listing 2-12 to see this in action.

Listing 2-12. chapter2/src/main/resources/applicationContext.xml

```xml
<bean id="helloGreeter" class="com.bsg5.chapter2.HelloWorldGreeter">
    <property name="printStream" ref="printStream" />
</bean>
```

```xml
<bean id="printStream" class="java.io.PrintStream">
    <constructor-arg ref="baos"/>
    <constructor-arg value="true"/>
    <constructor-arg value="UTF-8"/>
</bean>

<bean id="baos" class="java.io.ByteArrayOutputStream" />
```

With the preceding code, we can greatly simplify our test because Spring ends up doing all of the work by reading our configuration. We're obviously (hopefully!) great proponents of testing so the way we'll ensure everything is working is to spruce up our test with Spring.

Lastly, we will look at our test class, with a focus on the new `testHelloWorld` method, and see how much it has simplified.

The first thing it does is create an `ApplicationContext` reference, by instantiating a `ClassPathXmlApplicationContext`. This is a concrete instance of an `ApplicationContext` that loads a configuration file from the classpath. As you may (or may not) suspect, this is one of many possible concrete instances of `ApplicationContext`; for most simple uses, this is one that works quite well.

Outside of the creation of the Spring context, the rest of the code is quite simple. With Spring injecting our `HelloWorldGreeter` into the test class, in our method we can simply call `greeter.greet()` and then convert the contents in the injected `ByteArrayOutputStream` into a `String` and assert that it equals what we expect. If all goes well, and it should, we'll get a passing test now.

Listing 2-13. chapter2/src/test/java/com/bsg5/chapter2/
SpringGreeterTest.java

```java
package com.bsg5.chapter2;

import org.springframework.context.ApplicationContext;
import org.springframework.context.support.ClassPathXmlApplicationContext;
import org.testng.annotations.Test;

import java.io.ByteArrayOutputStream;
import java.nio.charset.StandardCharsets;

import static org.testng.Assert.assertEquals;
```

```
public class SpringGreeterTest {
    @Test
    public void testHelloWorld() {
        ApplicationContext context = new ClassPathXmlApplicationContext
        ("/applicationContext.xml");
        Greeter greeter = context.getBean("helloGreeter", Greeter.class);
        ByteArrayOutputStream baos = context.getBean("baos", ByteArray
        OutputStream.class);

        greeter.greet();
        String data = new String(baos.toByteArray(), StandardCharsets.UTF_8);
        assertEquals(data, "Hello, World!");
    }
}
```

When we run this test – by running gradle :chapter2:test, in our top-level directory – we should see something equivalent to the output in Listing 2-14.

Listing 2-14. Output of gradle :chapter2:test in root directory

```
$ gradle chapter2:test
BUILD SUCCESSFUL in 7s
4 actionable tasks: 3 executed, 1 up-to-date
```

There's no output for a successful test – only a successful build. Congratulations, programmer!

One thing: It's **very** important to note the class hierarchy of this test – it **must** extend AbstractTestNGSpringContextTests (or, if you're using JUnit 4, AbstractJUnit4SpringContextTests; JUnit 5 has a different extension mechanism, where you annotate a test class with @ExtendWith(SpringExtension.class) instead of altering the class hierarchy. The new base class of the test is where the context is loaded and any processing occurs, before the tests are run.[13]

---

[13]Worth noting: Not remembering the proper inheritance bit the author for about 30 minutes before he realized that he'd forgotten the required class hierarchy.

If we ignore the extravagant lengths we went to do build a "Hello, World" app and think through the power that can come from loosely coupling our individual classes in a bigger application, the power of Dependency Injection really starts to shine. In this case we simply created and injected an `OutputStream` that gave us the ability to see what had been written into it; we could easily replace this with an `OutputStream` (or `Greeter`) that sent an email, or logged data, or performed a translation into different languages, or any other feature we can think of – and yet our client application doesn't have to change, or even be aware of the differences.

Since the configuration of the structure is **external** to the classes themselves, we can radically change the function of the program – while retaining a fairly high confidence that the program works as designed, because our object model is trivial to test, and our configuration is easily debugged.

2.5 Next Steps

In our next chapter, we're going to shift gears a bit and dive into configuration and bean declaration with Spring.

We're going to expand on our small "Hello, World" example and start exercising more aspects that the Spring framework provides.[14]

---

[14]I promise the next chapter will fly by, configuration talk is super exciting.

CHAPTER 3

Configuration and Declaration of Beans

In this chapter, we're going to explore a decent subset of Spring configuration, and we're going to shift attention away from "Hello, World" into a simple application that will allow us to explore features and configuration. We'll introduce the sample application first, then walk through a few different ways to configure it. There's a lot of code here, much of it redundant on the surface, but we'll use some base classes to help reduce the tendency to repeat ourselves.[1]

3.1 The Container

Spring changed how Java developers thought about class structure and design in their applications,[2] and it's entirely doable to design applications with Dependency Injection in mind – without using Spring – while reaping the benefits of the mindset. However, the central mechanism for using the Dependency Injection mindset, regardless of what framework you use, is the Container.

The Container is responsible for managing instances of what are referred to as "managed objects." Our `HelloWorldGreeter` from Chapter 2, for example, is a manageable object (as most objects would be) but *is* managed when it's created and injected via the `ApplicationContext` – which is a Container. The `ApplicationContext` is the primary interaction point for Spring-managed classes, so when we refer to the "context," this is usually what we're referring to.

---

[1]The redundancies we're going to run into will either be required by Java as boilerplate or deliberate choices to illustrate a point. We'll try to be clear about why such choices are made.

[2]See all of Chapter 1 for how and why – and you thought it'd be okay to skip! ... and you thought there'd be fewer footnotes as the book progressed, too, didn't you?

© Joseph B. Ottinger and Andrew Lombardi 2019
J. B. Ottinger and A. Lombardi, *Beginning Spring 5*, https://doi.org/10.1007/978-1-4842-4486-9_3

Classes that are managed by a Spring container are referred to as "Spring beans."[3]

The Container not only creates instances – the Spring beans – but also provides references to those instances in various ways (through constructors, or mutators and accessors[4]). The process as a whole is referred to as "wiring."

We're going to step through an example application's specification, and then we're going to start showing how to wire the application together with Spring.

3.2 The Sample Application

This next section – the entire heading, actually – has nothing to do with Spring at all. No dependencies on Spring, no Spring references, no rites of Spring, absolutely nothing outside of a reference here and there to remind us that we're in a book about Spring. However, we're introducing an application that gives us enough functionality to explore Spring in some depth; without the application and an understanding of it, we're going to end up saying "Hello, World" in 80 different ways. With the project, we'll have a practical application to keep in mind as we walk through Spring features.

Imagine you're the fan of a band called "Threadbare Loaf."[5] If you were trying to introduce a friend to Threadbare Loaf, they'd probably wonder what song (or songs) they should listen to, to get a sense of what Threadbare Loaf is about as an artist; you might suggest their first hit, "Someone Stole The Flour," or perhaps the single from their second release, "What Happened to Our First Release?"

---

[3]Wouldn't it have been neat for Spring to have been called "Human," so instead of "Spring beans" we had "Human beans?"

[4]A "mutator" is also known as a "setter," and an "accessor" is known colloquially as a "getter." Your Humble Authors find these terms to be rather gross, so we're going to use the correct terms even though they make us sound all hoity-toity and like we're too proud to drink our wine from a box.

[5]There is no artist known as "Threadbare Loaf" at the time this was written. If you still manage to be a fan of the band, that's... interesting.

These two songs might be considered the "hooks" for the artist. Most artists have a song or set of songs that exemplify the band's direction and focus; for the Rolling Stones, it might be "Satisfaction" or "Jumpin' Jack Flash"; for Pink Floyd it might be "Money" or "Comfortably Numb"; for The Beatles it might be "Hey Jude" or "Let It Be"; and so forth and so on.

It's not that the artists' *other* songs aren't great, but that these are songs which a given person might think were perfect to entice someone else to enjoy the band as well.

What we're going to do is create an API for an application to allow users to suggest "hooks" for artists, and for other users to see what users suggested most. It's a simple application, and we're not going to construct a full user experience; we're mostly going to focus on the core API for the application to illustrate Spring concepts.

We're also going to create many, many versions of the API, with each iteration being used to demonstrate different features of Spring. The API will likely improve as we continue, but the goal of the iterations will *usually* be demonstrative and not for the purpose of making the API more "mature" or full-featured.

For the purposes of this book, the application will be called the "band gateway," suggesting that the songs managed by the API are the "gateway songs" to appreciate the artists in question.

We're initially going to have two entities to consider as part of our data model: the Artist and the Song.

An Artist is uniquely referred to by name.[6] We should expect to support only one Artist with a given name, as long as we're working *only* with music.

A Song is scoped to an Artist and does *not* have a unique name – it's perfectly legitimate to have a song called "Come Together" recorded by both The Beatles and Aerosmith, for example, and users might consider these songs the ideal introductions to both bands.[7] We're also aware that artists might have other types of media that serve

---

[6]Strictly speaking, this is not true, but artists usually do try to have unique names. The original names for the example app were intended to be "The Heebie Jeebies" and "The Screaming Meemies," both rejected because there were *actual bands* with these names already. If "Threadbare Loaf" and the other example band names ("Therapy Zeppelin" and "Clancy in Silt") used in this chapter actually exist in the real world, they were created and named rather poorly after the book was written.

[7]Worth noting: The opinions of the ideal introductory songs, or hooks, for every real band mentioned are entirely up to the taste of the individual. You might listen to these songs and be revolted; take every suggestion with a grain of salt, unless it refers to the Canadian band Rush, in which case every suggestion is made *very* seriously.

as "hooks" for the band, such as videos or other artistic works; for the purposes of simplicity, we're assuming that we are *only* managing audio recordings and not, say, videos or paintings that might be associated with a given Artist.

Our application, in its initial form, needs to support a few basic read operations and two write operations.

The operations related to *reading* data are as follows:

- Retrieve songs for an artist, ordered by popularity (the most popular song is the better "hook")

- Retrieve song names for an artist (for use in autocompletion operations)

- Retrieve a list of artist names (for use in autocompletion operations)

Then, we also need to allow people to **contribute** to our database:

- Record that a song exists

- Vote for a song as a hook for a given Artist

3.2.1 The Code for the Band Gateway

We're going to need at least five classes to begin to construct our API: our model consists of two classes (the Artist and Song), and we're going to create an interface (called Normalizer) that represents a method by which we can transform (or "normalize") names for our API, and lastly, an interface for our API (the MusicService) and a base class that contains an in-memory representation of our model (BaseMusicService).

We're also eventually going to build a base class for our tests, for the same reason (it will contain the basic tests we will want to run no matter what the actual implementation of the MusicService is), and our *actual* tests will extend this base class.

Our model will be concrete, but the rest of the interfaces and abstract classes are chosen because we don't want to have eight implementations of the same functionality.[8]

---

[8]We're trying to apply the programming principle known as DRY – "Don't Repeat Yourself." The alternative is all WET – "Write Everything Twice." This concept is given to us courtesy of Andy Hunt and Dave Thomas, in their book *The Pragmatic Programmer*.

The Build

We'll want to create a module for this project. In Chapter 2 we created a top-level project and a chapter2 module under it; in Chapter 3 (this one) we'll follow the same idea and create a chapter3 directory. You'll want to open up your settings.gradle from the top-level directory and make sure it contains a line with include 'chapter3' – which was already shown in Chapter 2, incidentally.

Our chapter3 directory should have a source tree in it, of course, so create src/main/java, src/main/resources, src/test/java, and src/test/resources. If you're using a UNIX-like operating system like OSX or Linux, you can do this trivially with a typical shell like bash or zsh with the following commands, when in the project's top-level directory.

Listing 3-1. Building the chapter3 directory structure

```
mkdir -p chapter3/src/main/java
mkdir -p chapter3/src/test/java
mkdir -p chapter3/src/main/resources
mkdir -p chapter3/src/test/resources
```

Next we need a build.gradle to tell Gradle how to compile and test this chapter's code. It's nearly identical (if not exactly identical! – and it turns out it **is** identical) to Chapter 2's build.gradle.

Listing 3-2. chapter3/src/build.gradle

```
dependencies {
    compile "org.springframework:spring-core:$springFrameworkVersion"
    compile "org.springframework:spring-context:$springFrameworkVersion"
    compile "org.springframework:spring-test:$springFrameworkVersion"
}
```

The Model

First let's take a look at our model classes, Artist and Song. These are simple Java objects, and as such there's a lot of boilerplate with accessors and mutators, equals(), hashCode(), and toString().

Our implementations are also fairly simple – we're choosing mutable classes, with default constructors as well as simple parameterized constructors. We're leaving our classes mutable (thus, an Artist might change names, according to our model). There are reasons to prefer immutable classes (namely, performance, and avoiding having programmers who worship at the Church of Functional Programming say rude things about you), and there are also reasons to expect more complicated constructors that validate arguments and other such things, but we're going to stay simple by choice and acknowledge that there are workable alternatives even though we're not using them here.

Our first class is the Song, which is very simple: it contains the Song name (a String) and a number of votes, basically the number of people who suggest that this Song is a good hook for its artist. It does not have a reference to the Artist (because it will exist only in the context of an Artist, as we'll see in the next code listing – an Artist has a reference to a Set of Song instances).

Most of the code in the listing is, of course, boilerplate; note that we do not consider votes as part of uniqueness, but only the Song name.

Listing 3-3. chapter3/src/main/java/com/bsg5/chapter3/model/Song.java

```java
package com.bsg5.chapter3.model;

import java.util.Objects;
import java.util.StringJoiner;

public class Song implements Comparable<Song> {
    private String name;
    private int votes=0;

    public Song() {
    }

    public Song(String name) {
        setName(name);
    }

    public String getName() {
        return name;
    }
```

```java
public void setName(String name) {
    this.name = name;
}

public int getVotes() {
    return votes;
}

public void setVotes(int votes) {
    this.votes = votes;
}

@Override
public boolean equals(Object o) {
    if (this == o) return true;
    if (!(o instanceof Song)) return false;
    Song song = (Song) o;
    return Objects.equals(getName(), song.getName());
}

@Override
public int hashCode() {
    return Objects.hash(getName());
}

@Override
public String toString() {
    return new StringJoiner(", ", Song.class.getSimpleName() + "[", "]")
            .add("name='" + name + "'")
            .add("votes=" + votes)
            .toString();
}
```

```java
    @Override
    public int compareTo(Song o) {
        int value = Integer.compare(o.getVotes(), getVotes());
        if (value == 0) {
            value = getName().compareTo(o.getName());
        }
        return value;
    }
}
```

Our Artist class consists of a name – again, a simple String – and a Map of Song objects, indexed by name, called songs. Since we're using a Map, the songs are considered to be unique (we can't have two Song instances with the same name, by implication, although we need to make sure that our Song class enforces this).

Listing 3-4. chapter3/src/main/java/com/bsg5/chapter3/model/Artist.java

```java
package com.bsg5.chapter3.model;

import java.util.*;

public class Artist {
    private String name;
    private Map<String, Song> songs=new HashMap<>();

    public Artist() {
    }

    public Artist(String name) {
        setName(name);
    }

    public String getName() {
        return name;
    }

    public void setName(String name) {
        this.name = name;
    }
```

```java
public Map<String, Song> getSongs() {
    return songs;
}

public void setSongs(Map<String, Song> songs) {
    this.songs = songs;
}

@Override
public boolean equals(Object o) {
    if (this == o) return true;
    if (!(o instanceof Artist)) return false;
    Artist artist = (Artist) o;
    return Objects.equals(getName(), artist.getName());
}

@Override
public int hashCode() {
    return Objects.hash(getName());
}

@Override
public String toString() {
    return new StringJoiner(", ", Artist.class.getSimpleName() +
    "[", "]")
            .add("name='" + name + "'")
            .add("songs=" + songs)
            .toString();
}
}
```

The Normalizer Interface

This is a simple single-access method interface, by which we can transform input somehow. The default transformation is to trim whitespace from the edges of the input string, but implementations can obviously change the behavior.

This is only an *interface*. It's not usable without a concrete realization of the interface; we could have made it a base class, but we've chosen to make it an interface so we can use it to illustrate some concepts with Spring later in the chapter.

Listing 3-5. chapter3/src/main/java/com/bsg5/chapter3/Normalizer.java

```
package com.bsg5.chapter3;

public interface Normalizer {
    default String transform(String input) {
        return input.trim();
    }
}
```

The Music Service

The Music Service API itself is represented in a single interface. It really would be better, in a real-world application, to split the API calls related to Artist into an ArtistService, and the other API calls into a SongService, and then have the MusicService delegate to concrete implementations of *those* interfaces, but our initial revision is going to focus on different aspects of the configuration rather than object design.[9]

The interface itself is simple.

Listing 3-6. chapter3/src/main/java/com/bsg5/chapter3/MusicService.java

```
package com.bsg5.chapter3;

import com.bsg5.chapter3.model.Song;

import java.util.List;

public interface MusicService {
    List<Song> getSongsForArtist(String artist);
    List<String> getMatchingSongNamesForArtist(String artist, String prefix);
    List<String> getMatchingArtistNames(String prefix);
```

---

[9]The single class for managing both Artist and Song instances is dictated in *this* chapter by storing all of our data in memory. If we were using an external datastore, like a relational database accessed through JPA or JDBC, split interfaces would be the better approach. In this chapter, and for our purposes, the single interface and implementation is wiser.

```
Song getSong(String artist, String name);
Song voteForSong(String artist, String name);
}
```

We want to have another interface for testing purposes – a Resettable.[10] This allows us to mark a component as being able to be reset – something useful for us during testing.

There are multiple ways to accomplish resetting a class. This just happens to use an interface to expose reset() to other classes, so it meets some object-oriented design requirements while really contributing fairly little value. It's just convenient for testing, especially when we haven't explored the scope of references we get from Spring – which we'll do more in Chapter 4 when we introduce the prototype.

Listing 3-7. chapter3/src/main/java/com/bsg5/chapter3/Resettable.java

```
package com.bsg5.chapter3;

public interface Resettable {
    void reset();
}
```

There's not a lot going on here – we just want implementations to be easily marked as being able to be reset, and we want to know the entry point for actually causing the reset. Since we're not insane, we're going to call the method reset().

We're also going to build a base class that implements each of those methods in both MusicService and Resettable to varying degrees. This class is going to be a little more verbose than it really should be, because it has to anticipate conditions that normal implementations shouldn't have to. Let's take a look at it, and then we'll discuss what it's doing and why.

---

[10]The use of Resettable as an interface name matches the use of Closeable, Serializable, and other such classes in the Java API.

Listing 3-8. chapter3/src/main/java/com/bsg5/chapter3/
AbstractMusicService.java

```java
package com.bsg5.chapter3;

import com.bsg5.chapter3.model.Artist;
import com.bsg5.chapter3.model.Song;

import java.util.*;
import java.util.function.Function;
import java.util.stream.Collectors;

public abstract class AbstractMusicService implements MusicService,
Resettable {
    private Map<String, Artist> bands = new HashMap<>();

    protected String transformArtist(String input) {
        return input;
    }

    protected String transformSong(String input) {
        return input;
    }

    @Override
    public void reset() {
        bands.clear();
    }

    private Artist getArtist(String name) {
        String normalizedName = transformArtist(name);
        return bands.computeIfAbsent(normalizedName,
                s -> new Artist(normalizedName));
    }

    @Override
    public Song getSong(String artistName, String name) {
        Artist artist = getArtist(artistName);
        String normalizedTitle = transformSong(name);
        return artist
```

```
                .getSongs()
                .computeIfAbsent(normalizedTitle, Song::new);
}

@Override
public List<Song> getSongsForArtist(String artist) {
    List<Song> songs = new ArrayList<>(
            getArtist(artist)
                    .getSongs()
                    .values()
    );
    songs.sort(Song::compareTo);
    return songs;
}

@Override
public List<String> getMatchingSongNamesForArtist(String artist,
String prefix) {
    String normalizedPrefix = transformSong(prefix)
            .toLowerCase();
    return getArtist(artist)
            .getSongs()
            .keySet()
            .stream()
            .map(this::transformSong)
            .filter(name -> name
                    .toLowerCase()
                    .startsWith(normalizedPrefix))
            .sorted(Comparator.comparing(Function.identity()))
            .collect(Collectors.toList());
}
@Override
public List<String> getMatchingArtistNames(String prefix) {
    String normalizedPrefix = transformArtist(prefix)
            .toLowerCase();
    return bands
```

```
                .keySet()
                .stream()
                .filter(name -> name
                        .toLowerCase()
                        .startsWith(normalizedPrefix))
                .sorted(Comparator.comparing(Function.identity()))
                .collect(Collectors.toList());
    }

    @Override
    public Song voteForSong(String artistName, String name) {
        Song song = getSong(artistName, name);
        song.setVotes(song.getVotes() + 1);
        return song;
    }
}
```

There's quite a lot going on in this class.

First, we have two methods (transformSong() and transformArtist()) that do nothing but return their input parameters. These are functional stubs, or hooks; classes that extend the AbstractMusicService can (and probably should) override their behavior, possibly by delegating to a Normalizer instance. These methods are meant to be called in order to make sure Song and Artist names are in some sort of consistent form before use.

Next we have our humble reset() method – which, true to its name, simply clears out the in-memory data structure.

After the normalization methods, we have a private method, getArtist(), which maps a String into a valid Artist reference. If the Artist does not exist, we create an instance for future use. We then see the same pattern replicated in getSong(), with the main difference between the methods being that getSong() is exposed as part of the external API. (It fulfills the specification requirement of being able to create a Song without voting for it as a hook for the artist.)

Next we have a series of methods to retrieve a sorted set of Song references for the Artist and return lists of matching names. In nearly every case, we call our transformation methods to make sure the names are in consistent form (even though by default that doesn't change the names at all). Even though some of the chains of methods look quite long (see `getMatchingSongNamesForArtist()` as an example, where *eight* methods are chained together in a row, with a few extra chains embedded), the actual process is expressed rather simply and few of those methods incur any noticeable CPU cost.[11]

One thought that our eagle-eyed readers will probably already have noted: our model classes are mutable (i.e., can be changed) and we're returning the actual instances that represent our model in these methods. In other words, a bad actor (or rookie programmer) could get a song from `voteForSong()`, then call `setVotes(400)` – and the actual "database" would change the votes for that `Song` to 400. This is not wise; you don't want to propagate changes unintentionally. Here, though, we'll allow it because this is a memory-only demonstration[12] and the code's complex enough already without adding a copy step to our methods. Consider it an exercise for the reader.

At long last, it's time for us to start building some concrete implementations and tests, wiring them together with Spring.[13]

3.3 Configuration Through Annotation

Configuration through annotations in Spring is very simple. The main thing to remember is that we want to **tell Spring we're using annotations**. You can do this in a number of ways; we're going to use XML to configure the annotations, since it's simple (and reflects what we've already learned, in Chapter 2).

After that, we have to remember that Spring will work only with *managed* objects: that means we can annotate a class all we like, but if we don't retrieve it from a Spring container (an `ApplicationContext`), the annotations will be irrelevant.

---

[11]In `getMatchingSongNamesForArtist()`, the `sorted()` method for the `Stream` is probably the most expensive method call. Of course, if you really wanted to make sure, you'd crank up your friendly local profiler and check and leave assumptions to authors and other such miscreants.

[12]If our data model was actually being held in secondary storage, i.e, in a file, or in a database, or on punch cards, persistence would have a step that had nothing to do with the references in memory, and therefore the incorrect changes would propagate only to the scope of the instance. This problem is limited to the in-memory form of the data storage.

[13]We really tried to figure out a good way to make the application code we've seen so far related to Spring somehow. That's a terrible idea, honestly; the fact that we've got no technical debt on Spring in our object model is a strength. However, this *is* a book about Spring, so it's time to start accruing some technical debt at last. Thankfully, it'll be beneficial, in the end.

Annotations in Spring generally fall into two categories: component declaration and wiring. Component declaration means that a class is managed by a container, and wiring means that the class has resources that are injected (or "wired") by the container.

3.3.1 Declaring a Spring Bean with @Component

To enable scanning for components, we need to tell Spring to, well, scan for the components. Let's create the first in a series of configuration files, called `config-01.xml`, in `src/test/resources`. This is a baseline Spring configuration for annotations; normally we'd have a *little* more information in this file, but this will serve for our first explorations.

This file has one significant line in it: `<context:component-scan basepackage="com.bsg5.chapter3.mem01" />`. (Well, that's not strictly true: the entire `<beans...>` content is pretty important, too. Most people, including your authors, copy and paste that section, unless there are tools like the Spring Tool Suite that do build the header for you.) What this line does is pretty simple: it scans that package and any others under it for beans marked with the valid annotations for components, like `@Component`, `@Service`, `@Repository`, and others. (The specific meanings will be discussed in later chapters.) Those beans will be registered in the `ApplicationContext` and can be referred to by any other Spring components managed by that `ApplicationContext`, whether scanned in with `<component-scan />` or not.[14]

Now that we've talked about it, let's take a look at our first iteration of the Spring configuration.

Listing 3-9. `chapter3/src/test/resources/config-01.xml`

```
<?xml version="1.0" encoding="UTF-8"?>

<!-- chapter3/src/test/resources/config-01.xml -->

<beans xmlns="http://www.springframework.org/schema/beans"
       xmlns:xsi="http://www.w3.org/2001/XMLSchema-instance"
       xmlns:context="http://www.springframework.org/schema/context"
```

---

[14]Proof that annotated components can be used by anything managed by a given `ApplicationContext` can be seen in our tests. The test classes themselves are managed by the `Context`, and as we've seen (and as we'll see, over and over again), we can wire components into our test classes with wild abandon, and it all works.

```
xsi:schemaLocation="http://www.springframework.org/schema/beans
  http://www.springframework.org/schema/beans/spring-beans.xsd
  http://www.springframework.org/schema/context
  http://www.springframework.org/schema/context/spring-context.xsd">
```

```
<context:component-scan base-package="com.bsg5.chapter3.mem01" />
</beans>
```

We'll need two more classes to make this worthwhile. Our first one will be a concrete realization of the `AbstractMusicService` interface, which will do nothing more than add a `@Component` annotation to the abstract class. (An abstract class in Java can't be instantiated, so telling Spring that an abstract component is a component would be ... unfortunate.)

Listing 3-10. `chapter3/src/main/java/com/bsg5/chapter3/mem01/MusicService1.java`

```java
package com.bsg5.chapter3.mem01;

import com.bsg5.chapter3.AbstractMusicService;
import org.springframework.stereotype.Component;

@Component
public class MusicService1 extends AbstractMusicService {
}
```

We also want to build a test, however. Our first test is going to be very simple and test very little of the `MusicService` interface; we're going to use it to *acquire* a `MusicService`, and we're also going to take a quick look inside the `ApplicationContext` to get a sense of what our simple Spring configuration actually contains.

As we've seen in Chapter 2, Spring-aware tests using TestNG extend `AbstractTestNGSpringContextTests`. We add a class-level annotation, `@ContextConfiguration`, with a reference to our `/config-01.xml` file to specify that this test uses that particular configuration. Let's take a look at the source file for the test, and then we'll discuss what we can learn from it.

Listing 3-11. chapter3/src/test/java/com/bsg5/
chapter3/TestMusicService1.java

```
package com.bsg5.chapter3;

import com.bsg5.chapter3.model.Song;
import org.springframework.beans.factory.annotation.Autowired;
import org.springframework.context.ApplicationContext;
import org.springframework.test.context.ContextConfiguration;
import org.springframework.test.context.testng.
AbstractTestNGSpringContextTests;
import org.testng.annotations.Test;

import java.util.Arrays;
import java.util.HashSet;
import java.util.Set;

import static org.testng.Assert.assertEquals;
import static org.testng.Assert.assertNotNull;
import static org.testng.Assert.assertTrue;

@ContextConfiguration(locations = "/config-01.xml")
public class TestMusicService1 extends AbstractTestNGSpringContextTests {
    @Autowired
    ApplicationContext context;
    @Autowired
    MusicService service;

    @Test
    public void testConfiguration() {
        assertNotNull(context);
        Set<String> definitions = new HashSet<>(
                Arrays.asList(context.getBeanDefinitionNames())
        );
```

```
        /*
        // uncomment if you'd like to see the entire set of defined beans
        for (String d : definitions) {
            System.out.println(d);
        }
        */

        assertTrue(definitions.contains("musicService1"));
    }

    @Test
    public void testMusicService() {
        Song song = service.getSong(
                "Threadbare Loaf", "Someone Stole the Flour"
        );
        assertEquals(song.getVotes(), 0);
    }
}
```

Aside from the @ContextConfiguration annotation on the test class itself, we also have two fields marked with @Autowired. The first one is an ApplicationContext and the second is a MusicService. When Spring sees an @Autowired field, it will look for classes that it manages that fit the description of the field.

The simplest matching is done on the basis of type; if we are wiring a field of type ApplicationContext and Spring is managing only one component that can be assigned to that field, then that component's reference is used in the field.

If the configuration contains more than one component that can be assigned to the reference, then Spring will look for a component whose name matches the reference. Thus, if we had a field named xyzyx, of type Fuzzball, it would look for a *single* component of type Fuzzball, and if it had more than one Fuzzball in the configuration, it would look for the component named xyzyx, and fail to inject that value if such a component wasn't found.

We'll also see the use of @Qualifier for autowired fields in a subsequent test, through which we can tell Spring what specific component name to look for, such that it does not try to derive the component name from the reference. (In other words, we could tell it to look for a component called myxalotl even if the field was xyzyx. We promise: we'll explain more later.)

There are two tests in this file: `testConfiguration()` and `testMusicService()`. The first test, `testConfiguration()`, simply checks our configuration to demonstrate that wiring has occurred properly. It first checks to make sure that the `ApplicationContext` has been provided to the test; if the `context` reference is null, we know something has failed rather dramatically.[15] After it makes sure that the `context` is available, it checks to make sure that a component with a specific name (`musicService1`) is available in the context. This is the name Spring will derive from a component called `MusicService1`, by default. We can override it with `@Component`, and we will do so in a later example; if no name is specified, Spring takes the class name (`MusicService1`) and decapitalizes the first letter (leaving it as `musicService1`).

If you would like to see all of the beans in the context as specified by our current configuration and package structure, you could include the code from the Java comment. For this test, for the record, this code outputs the following.

Listing 3-12. Console output from the commented code in `TestMusicService1`

```
org.springframework.context.event.internalEventListenerProcessor
org.springframework.context.event.internalEventListenerFactory
org.springframework.context.annotation.internalConfigurationAnnotationProcessor
musicService1
org.springframework.context.annotation.internalAutowiredAnnotationProcessor
```

The `org.springframework` classes noted here are components for internal Spring use; they're not really things we care about much, as application designers. What we're looking for in that list is the `musicService1` reference.

The second test simply calls `getSong()` for our mythical band, "Threadbare Loaf," and makes sure that the song should have no votes (as we've not registered any yet).

---

[15]In early versions of this chapter, one of the authors wasted quite a bit of time wondering why the configuration was left unassigned. It turned out that he'd forgotten to extend `AbstractTestNGSpringContextTests`. It's a silly test, but less silly than it could be.

3.3.2 **Wiring Components Together with** `@Autowired`

In our first configuration, we had a single component (a `MusicService`), and our test simply made sure the component scanning was working and that our component was able to be injected into our test.

In our next configuration, we're going to actually have two components and wire them together. We're going to add a good bit of code here, too, to have a repeatable set of tests that we can apply to multiple configurations; when we reach the end of the chapter, we can use this to test nearly all of our implementations in series.[16]

We're going to create another instance of `MusicService`, one that looks almost exactly like our `MusicService1`, except that it's going to override `transformArtist()` and `transformSong()` such that they call an injected `Normalizer` instance. We'll also need to create a concrete type to serve as a `Normalizer` – because we declared it as an interface, so it's non-instantiable in and of itself. We also need another configuration file and two more classes: one will be our base test class (incorporating tests we will want to be able to apply to *every* `MusicService`) and the other will be our actual executable test, which delegates to our base test class.

Our `MusicService2` class is very simple.

Listing 3-13. `chapter3/src/main/java/com/bsg5/chapter3/mem02/`
`MusicService2.java`

```
package com.bsg5.chapter3.mem02;

import com.bsg5.chapter3.AbstractMusicService;
import com.bsg5.chapter3.Normalizer;
import org.springframework.beans.factory.annotation.Autowired;
import org.springframework.stereotype.Component;

@Component
public class MusicService2 extends AbstractMusicService {
    @Autowired
    Normalizer normalizer;
```

---

[16]We're still trying to make sure we're not repeating ourselves very often in code.

```
    @Override
    protected String transformArtist(String input) {
        return normalizer.transform(input);
    }

    @Override
    protected String transformSong(String input) {
        return normalizer.transform(input);
    }
}
```

Our Normalizer is a simple concrete realization of our Normalizer interface; the primary values it conveys are in that it can be marked as a @Component, and it can be instantiated. Since we have a default method body in Normalizer, we don't even have to create the method in our NameNormalizer, unless we want it to do more than simply trim whitespace. (At this point in our application, we're not concerned about the actual functionality; we're demonstrating component wiring.)

Listing 3-14. chapter3/src/main/java/com/bsg5/chapter3/mem02/ SimpleNormalizer.java

```
package com.bsg5.chapter3.mem02;

import com.bsg5.chapter3.Normalizer;
import org.springframework.stereotype.Component;

@Component
public class SimpleNormalizer implements Normalizer {
    /* inherits default transform() method from interface */
}
```

Lastly, our configuration file, config-02.xml.

Listing 3-15. `chapter3/src/test/resources/config-02.xml`

```xml
<?xml version="1.0" encoding="UTF-8"?>

<!-- chapter3/src/test/resources/config-02.xml -->

<beans xmlns="http://www.springframework.org/schema/beans"
       xmlns:xsi="http://www.w3.org/2001/XMLSchema-instance"
       xmlns:context="http://www.springframework.org/schema/context"
       xsi:schemaLocation="http://www.springframework.org/schema/beans
         http://www.springframework.org/schema/beans/spring-beans.xsd
         http://www.springframework.org/schema/context
         http://www.springframework.org/schema/context/spring-context.xsd">

    <context:component-scan base-package="com.bsg5.chapter3.mem02" />
</beans>
```

Now we get to the "fun" part of the code. We're going to build a test class that contains a series of methods usable by a test. They won't be invoked directly by TestNG, but they're designed to be called from test methods that *are* invoked by the test framework.

Why are we doing it this way? Primarily, it's because a test class has a single application context.[17] What we'd like to do is enable ourselves to eventually load a set of configurations on demand and run each test on each individual configuration; this way, we repeat ourselves for the delegation call but little else.

This class is designed to be used through composition – that is, it's designed to be included in an actual class with the tests. This may make you think that it's a good candidate to be a Spring bean – and you're right, it is. We'll show this in practice in a later section of this chapter.

Let's take a look at our `MusicServiceTests` class, and then we'll step through some of the details of what it provides. After we do that, we'll show a test that actually uses this class – and the good news is that the actual test class is far, far shorter than the `MusicServiceTests` class.

---

[17]A test class can load multiple configurations, but it merges them into one context. We have not shown this in operation yet, but the explanation is that a `@ContextConfiguration` annotation can actually accept an *array* of configuration files (and other configuration sources, which we'll learn about later in this chapter), merging them all into one context.

Listing 3-16. chapter3/src/main/test/com/bsg5/chapter3/
MusicServiceTests.java

```java
package com.bsg5.chapter3;

import com.bsg5.chapter3.model.Song;

import java.util.List;
import java.util.function.Consumer;

import static org.testng.Assert.assertEquals;

public class MusicServiceTests {
    private Object[][] model = new Object[][]{
            {"Threadbare Loaf", "Someone Stole the Flour", 4},
            {"Threadbare Loaf", "What Happened To Our First CD?", 17},
            {"Therapy Zeppelin", "Medium", 4},
            {"Clancy in Silt", "Igneous", 5}
    };

    void iterateOverModel(Consumer<Object[]> consumer) {
        for (Object[] data : model) {
            consumer.accept(data);
        }
    }
    void populateService(MusicService service) {
        iterateOverModel(data -> {
            for (int i = 0; i < (Integer) data[2]; i++) {
                service.voteForSong((String) data[0], (String) data[1]);
            }
        });
    }

    void reset(MusicService service) {
        if (service instanceof Resettable) {
            ((Resettable) service).reset();
```

```
    } else {
        throw new RuntimeException(service +
                " does not implement Resettable.");
    }
}

void testSongVoting(MusicService service) {
    reset(service);
    populateService(service);
    iterateOverModel(data ->
            assertEquals(
                    service.getSong((String) data[0],
                            (String) data[1]).getVotes(),
                    ((Integer) data[2]).intValue()
            ));
}

void testSongsForArtist(MusicService service) {
    reset(service);
    populateService(service);
    List<Song> songs = service.getSongsForArtist("Threadbare Loaf");
    assertEquals(songs.size(), 2);
    assertEquals(songs.get(0).getName(), "What Happened To Our First CD?");
    assertEquals(songs.get(0).getVotes(), 17);
    assertEquals(songs.get(1).getName(), "Someone Stole the Flour");
    assertEquals(songs.get(1).getVotes(), 4);
}

void testMatchingArtistNames(MusicService service) {
    reset(service);
    populateService(service);
    List<String> names = service.getMatchingArtistNames("Th");
    assertEquals(names.size(), 2);
    assertEquals(names.get(0), "Therapy Zeppelin");
    assertEquals(names.get(1), "Threadbare Loaf");
}
```

```
    void testMatchingSongNamesForArtist(MusicService service) {
        reset(service);
        populateService(service);
        List<String> names = service.getMatchingSongNamesForArtist(
                "Threadbare Loaf", "W"
        );
        assertEquals(names.size(), 1);
        assertEquals(names.get(0), "What Happened To Our First CD?");
    }
}
```

The first bit worth noticing in this class is the Object[][] model. This may surprise some readers, but this is our starting data model for the tests. Each row represents an artist's song, and the number of times users have indicated that this song is the artist's ideal introductory song. Thus, we have three artists represented, with four songs; two of the artists have "Th" at the beginning of the names, and one of the artists has two songs represented. This allows us to test name matching (for autocompletion) as well as allowing us to test the sorting of songs based on votes.

The first method in the class is iterateOverModel(). This method is designed to allow us to execute a simple method over every row in the model; it accepts a Consumer<Object[]>, which means a lambda that expects an Object[], and calls the lambda for every row; nothing more, nothing less. It can be seen being used in the next method in this class, populateService().

The next method – again, populateService() – creates a lambda that issues a single vote for a song and calls that lambda multiple times for every row in our model. The model has an Integer as the third "column," and populateService() calls voteForSong() for each song as many times as that column indicates. In other words, if we have an artist of "Threadbare Loaf" and a song title of "What Happened To Our First CD?", with a third column of 17 – and this may surprise you, but we do have those things – populateService will call voteForSong() 17 times for that particular song. This method is primarily meant as a utility method, not something to serve as a test itself.

We have another utility method after populateService(), called reset(). This makes sure that the Service is marked as Resettable, and if it's not, it throws an exception; for this chapter, all of our services **are** resettable, and if they're not, we want to know. Assuming they are, then this method simply delegates to the service's reset() method, which **should** empty out the service's data model.

After that, we have four methods that are designed to be delegated to – testSongVoting(), testSongsForArtist(), testMatchingArtistNames(), and testMatchingSongsForArtist(). These all accept a Service reference, and generally exercise the Service, using data that we know about the model. The testSongVoting() method tests the votes for every song in our model.

However, as we've stated, this class isn't actually usable as a test. We want to write a test that delegates to an instance of MusicServiceTests to actually execute the methods that actually represent our tests.

Listing 3-17. chapter3/src/main/test/com/bsg5/chapter3/ TestMusicService2.java

```
package com.bsg5.chapter3;

import org.springframework.beans.factory.annotation.Autowired;
import org.springframework.test.context.ContextConfiguration;
import org.springframework.test.context.testng.
AbstractTestNGSpringContextTests;
import org.testng.annotations.Test;

@ContextConfiguration(locations = "/config-02.xml")
public class TestMusicService2 extends AbstractTestNGSpringContextTests {
    @Autowired
    MusicService service;

    MusicServiceTests tests = new MusicServiceTests();

    @Test
    public void testSongVoting() {
        tests.testSongVoting(service);
    }

    @Test
    public void testGetMatchingArtistNames() {
        tests.testMatchingArtistNames(service);
    }
```

```
    @Test
    public void testGetSongsForArtist() {
        tests.testSongsForArtist(service);
    }

    @Test
    public void testMatchingSongNamesForArtist() {
        tests.testMatchingSongNamesForArtist(service);
    }
}
```

Finally, we have an actual executable test![18] This test has the same scaffolding as `TestMusicService1`, except with a different configuration file. It uses an injected `MusicService` and instantiates a local copy of `MusicServiceTests`; it then has four test methods, each of which delegates to the method of the same name in `MusicServiceTests`. It's very simple. It **also** manages to test *every line of code* in `MusicService2` and its superclass, `AbstractMusicService`, with the sole exceptions being the methods in `AbstractMusicService` that are overridden by `MusicService2`.[19]

3.3.3 Choosing Components with @Qualifier and Bean Names

In the previous section, we injected a normalizer into our `MusicService2` and used it to normalize both the artist names and the song names. This assumes, though, that both sets of names are normalized in the same way. What if they're not?

In that case, we need to use two different kinds of normalizers. Then we're faced with a different kind of problem: how do we tell Spring which normalizer to use, and where?

---

[18]Seriously, run it. Unless something unfortunate's happened to your source code or ours, the build should run without any failures when you use `gradle :chapter3:test` – these tests don't really have visible output, nor should they.

[19]It's a good thing that every line of code is hit, even though all of these are test classes and the code doesn't *really* matter, but don't make the mistake of thinking that 100% code coverage is an "end goal." We have 100% coverage, but we've not tested any edge cases, and no failure conditions. Again, 100% coverage is good, but it's a lousy target; you should aim to fulfil all of the specification's requirements, instead. It just so happens that our "specification" doesn't contain any error conditions to speak of.

It turns out we have a few different options. Since injection is based on types, we could simply create new marker interfaces, like SongNameNormalizer, that simply extend Normalizer. Then we would have a declaration like @Autowired SongNameNormalizer songNameNormalizer and be done; Spring would look at the components it manages, find one component that can be assigned to songNameNormalizer, and be done.

We can also use the component names, as opposed to the components' assignable types. The @Component annotation has an optional value that serves as the component name for Spring. The default component name is the class' name itself, with an initial lowercase letter (thus, MusicService1 is given a component name of musicService1), but if we use @Component("bluePin"), then the component is named, predictably, bluePin instead.

If the autowired reference uses a name that matches a Spring bean – that is, we have MusicService bluePin – then Spring will inject a bean with that name.

That doesn't help us when one of two different circumstances arises in our code, though. If our variable reference doesn't match a component name, *or* we have two of the same types to inject, Spring still won't know how to choose which instance to inject.

We can help Spring decide which component to inject by using the @Qualifier annotation, which requires a value corresponding to the name of the Spring bean you want assigned.

Let's see it in action! We're going to use *two* Normalizer types: one will trim all whitespace from the beginning and the end of the input text (the default behavior, and we're basically replicating the SimpleNormalizer from the last example) and the other will capitalize the start of every word in addition to trimming the whitespace. Then we'll create a MusicService that uses both normalizers, and lastly, we'll have another test.

These listings will all be short, thankfully.

Here's our configuration file. Again, it's *very* similar to our previous configurations, only changing the base-package of the component-scan tag.

Listing 3-18. chapter3/src/test/resources/config-03.xml

```
<?xml version="1.0" encoding="UTF-8"?>

<!-- chapter3/src/test/resources/config-03.xml -->

<beans xmlns="http://www.springframework.org/schema/beans"
       xmlns:xsi="http://www.w3.org/2001/XMLSchema-instance"
       xmlns:context="http://www.springframework.org/schema/context"
       xsi:schemaLocation="http://www.springframework.org/schema/beans
```

```
http://www.springframework.org/schema/beans/spring-beans.xsd
http://www.springframework.org/schema/context
http://www.springframework.org/schema/context/spring-context.xsd">

<context:component-scan base-package="com.bsg5.chapter3.mem03" />
</beans>
```

Our `Normalizer` instances come next. Note that we don't *need* the `@Component` annotations to use names; the two classes would get names of `simpleNormalizer` and `capLeadingNormalizer` by default. Those are boring names, and thus we're changing them to `foo` and `bar`, respectively.[20]

First, the `SimpleNormalizer`, which is basically a copy of what we've seen before, but with a new `package` and a name in the `@Component` annotation.[21]

Listing 3-19. `chapter3/src/main/java/com/bsg5/chapter3/mem03/` `SimpleNormalizer.java`

```
package com.bsg5.chapter3.mem03;

import com.bsg5.chapter3.Normalizer;
import org.springframework.stereotype.Component;

@Component("foo")
public class SimpleNormalizer implements Normalizer {
}
```

Next we have our `CapLeadingNormalizer`. The `transform()` method trims whitespace from the edges of the input and then splits the string into words separated by whitespace and creates a `Stream`. It then filters out tokens that are blank and then (with `map()`) creates a word with a leading capitalized character and the rest of the word lowercased. It then joins the results into a single `String` as output. It looks (and sounds) more complicated than it is.

---

[20]Of course, `foo` and `bar` are just as boring, as is the use of `baz` later in this very chapter. These are known as "metasyntactic variables," a set of meaningless placeholder words used as names when we don't want to communicate specific meaning. In this code, they're actually being used in exactly the wrong sense, since these references *do* have specific meaning, but we're using the meaningless words because they help us illustrate a concept.

[21]Yes, we know, these are the same classes, repeated over and over again! We're painfully aware. We just haven't shown how to build modular configurations yet – and we actually need slightly different codebases because we're changing the configuration that's embedded in the code itself.

Listing 3-20. chapter3/src/main/java/com/bsg5/chapter3/mem03/
CapLeadingNormalizer.java

```java
package com.bsg5.chapter3.mem03;

import com.bsg5.chapter3.Normalizer;
import org.springframework.stereotype.Component;

import java.util.StringJoiner;
import java.util.stream.Stream;

@Component("bar")
public class CapLeadingNormalizer implements Normalizer {
    @Override
    public String transform(String input) {
        StringJoiner joiner = new StringJoiner(" ");
        Stream
                .of(input.trim().split("\\s"))
                .filter(s -> !s.isBlank())
                .map(s ->
                        Character.toUpperCase(s.charAt(0)) +
                                s.substring(1).toLowerCase()
                )
                .forEach(joiner::add);
        return joiner.toString();
    }
}
```

Of course, now we have to wonder: will this code work? The simplest response is
"of course it will," but if you're from Missouri, that isn't likely to fly. We had better cater
to our readers from Missouri and demonstrate that this class does what it's supposed
to do, with a test.[22] Our test can be really simple, simply feeding a set of inputs into our
Normalizer and checking it against expected output.

---

[22]We're programmers. We don't have to be from Missouri, not that there's anything wrong with
that, but we're *supposed* to be a suspicious bunch.

Listing 3-21. `chapter3/src/main/test/com/bsg5/chapter3/`
`TestCapLeadingNormalizer.java`

```java
package com.bsg5.chapter3;

import com.bsg5.chapter3.mem03.CapLeadingNormalizer;
import org.testng.annotations.DataProvider;
import org.testng.annotations.Test;

import static org.testng.Assert.assertEquals;

public class TestCapLeadingNormalizer {
    Normalizer normalizer=new CapLeadingNormalizer();

    @DataProvider
    Object[][] data() {
        return new Object[][] {
                { "this is a test", "This Is A Test"},
                { " This IS a test ", "This Is A Test"},
                { "this    is   a test", "This Is A Test"}
        };
    }

    @Test(dataProvider = "data")
    public void testNormalization(String input, String expected) {
        assertEquals(normalizer.transform(input), expected);
    }
}
```

Now that we have a test that shows that we can trust our `CapLeadingNormalizer`, it's time to show a `MusicService` that uses it. This is a slight variant on `MusicService2`, as you might expect, with the main differences being in the `package` and the use of `Normalizer` references with a `@Qualifier` annotation, matching the names in our `Normalizer` classes. We also add mutators and accessors (again, "setters" and "getters") to expose the `Normalizer` references – we don't really need this yet, but we will.[23]

---

[23]In the writing business, this is called "foreshadowing." It's pretty clumsy foreshadowing, honestly, but when we get to the XML configuration section, we're going to want `MusicService3` to have the mutators and accessors.

Listing 3-22. chapter3/src/main/java/com/bsg5/chapter3/mem03/
MusicService3.java

```java
package com.bsg5.chapter3.mem03;

import com.bsg5.chapter3.AbstractMusicService;
import com.bsg5.chapter3.Normalizer;
import org.springframework.beans.factory.annotation.Autowired;
import org.springframework.beans.factory.annotation.Qualifier;
import org.springframework.context.annotation.Scope;
import org.springframework.stereotype.Component;

@Component
@Scope()
public class MusicService3 extends AbstractMusicService {
    @Autowired
    @Qualifier("bar")
    Normalizer artistNormalizer;
    @Autowired
    @Qualifier("foo")
    Normalizer songNormalizer;

    public Normalizer getArtistNormalizer() {
        return artistNormalizer;
    }

    public void setArtistNormalizer(Normalizer artistNormalizer) {
        this.artistNormalizer = artistNormalizer;
    }

    public Normalizer getSongNormalizer() {
        return songNormalizer;
    }

    public void setSongNormalizer(Normalizer songNormalizer) {
        this.songNormalizer = songNormalizer;
    }
```

```
    @Override
    protected String transformArtist(String input) {
        return artistNormalizer.transform(input);
    }

    @Override
    protected String transformSong(String input) {
        return songNormalizer.transform(input);
    }
}
```

And finally, we want to verify that *this* code works, too, so let's round things out with another (short) test class, which mirrors our previous test classes but changes the configuration file.

Listing 3-23. chapter3/src/test/com/bsg5/chapter3/TestMusicService3. java

```
package com.bsg5.chapter3;

import org.springframework.beans.factory.annotation.Autowired;
import org.springframework.test.context.ContextConfiguration;
import org.springframework.test.context.testng.
AbstractTestNGSpringContextTests;
import org.testng.annotations.Test;

@ContextConfiguration(locations = "/config-03.xml")
public class TestMusicService3 extends AbstractTestNGSpringContextTests {
    @Autowired
    MusicService service;

    MusicServiceTests tests = new MusicServiceTests();

    @Test
    public void testSongVoting() {
        tests.testSongVoting(service);
    }
```

```
@Test
public void testGetMatchingArtistNames() {
    tests.testMatchingArtistNames(service);
}

@Test
public void testGetSongsForArtist() {
    tests.testSongsForArtist(service);
}

@Test
public void testMatchingSongNamesForArtist() {
    tests.testMatchingSongNamesForArtist(service);
}

}
```

Careful readers might note that we're still manually instantiating the `MusicServiceTests` object. In the next section, we'll fix that – and introduce constructor injection. However, we're going to start reusing some of the code from *this* section and introduce some more configuration elements so that you, the reader, don't have to read the same code over and over (and over and over) again.

3.3.4 Constructor Injection with Annotations

There's one more primary mode of bean injection we haven't addressed so far: constructor injection. If you've looked at our example code in an IDE like IDEA (`https://jetbrains.com/idea`) or Eclipse (`https://eclipse.org`), you might have noticed that the IDE was telling you something ominous about the `@Autowired` annotation, like "Field injection is not recommended."

The alternative is to use *constructor injection*, to have a constructor with parameters marked with `@Autowired` and, if necessary, `@Qualifier`. The reason is pretty simple: fields are mutable by implication, and using a constructor argument means that we can mark a field as `final`; *this* means that we can not only *require* a field to be set, but we can also assume that when it's set, it remains at the value that's been set.

In practice, all we need to do to enable constructor injection is, well, to create a valid constructor with the arguments marked for injection. The rules for constructor injection mirror the rules for field injection; we just get more control over it.

One other thing we'd like to do, to save ourselves from endless repetition in later sections (and chapters), is introduce a new configuration tag: `<import>`.[24]

What `<import>` does should be pretty obvious: it imports a separate configuration file into another. It allows us to create modular configurations.

We're going to create two "modules" – meaning configurations with specific purposes. One is going to be a set of `Normalizer` instances, from the `com.bsg5.chapter3.mem03` package; the other is going to be our `MusicServiceTests` class. When we import those two configurations into a *third* configuration, the beans in each configuration will have access to one another.

There's one problem, though: the `mem03` package has a `MusicService` implementation, too! So we're going to introduce an additional attribute for `<context:component-scan />`, called `resource-pattern`.

Let's start building our modules. First, the simplest one, a pure XML configuration for `MusicServiceTests`. We're not going to change that class from the code we've already seen, so there's no annotation; we're going to use a simple XML `<bean />` tag, much as we saw in Chapter 2.

Listing 3-24. `chapter3/src/test/resources/musicservicetest.xml`

```xml
<?xml version="1.0" encoding="UTF-8"?>

<!-- chapter3/src/test/resources/musicservicetest.xml -->

<beans xmlns="http://www.springframework.org/schema/beans"
       xmlns:xsi="http://www.w3.org/2001/XMLSchema-instance"
       xsi:schemaLocation="http://www.springframework.org/schema/beans
         http://www.springframework.org/schema/beans/spring-beans.xsd">

    <bean id="musicServiceTests" class="com.bsg5.chapter3.
    MusicServiceTests" />
</beans>
```

---

[24]If you're wishing we'd have introduced this tag earlier in the chapter… well, us too. However, we're trying to introduce new pieces of information at a deliberately slow pace, to avoid overwhelming readers new to the concepts we're discussing, so this was where we *finally* felt like we had the chance to introduce this one. We've found that people usually learn best when new concepts are introduced piecemeal, so we've chosen to go fairly slowly.

This configuration is quite simple: it declares a bean named `musicServiceTests`, of the type `com.bsg5.chapter3.MusicServiceTests`. Therefore, in any context in which *this* file is referenced, `MusicServiceTests` is a valid candidate for injection, as we'll see.

Listing 3-25. `chapter3/src/test/resources/normalizers.xml`

```
<?xml version="1.0" encoding="UTF-8"?>

<!-- chapter3/src/test/resources/normalizers.xml -->

<beans xmlns="http://www.springframework.org/schema/beans"
       xmlns:xsi="http://www.w3.org/2001/XMLSchema-instance"
       xmlns:context="http://www.springframework.org/schema/context"
       xsi:schemaLocation="http://www.springframework.org/schema/beans
        http://www.springframework.org/schema/beans/spring-beans.xsd
        http://www.springframework.org/schema/context
        http://www.springframework.org/schema/context/spring-context.xsd">

    <context:component-scan base-package="com.bsg5.chapter3.mem03"
                            resource-pattern="*Normalizer.class"/>
</beans>
```

Here we see the `resource-pattern` annotation for `<context:component-scan />`. This tag is a filter for the classes being scanned. Here, we use `resource-pattern="*Normalizer.class"`, which means that the only classes included in the scan are classes that *end with* `Normalizer` – thus, our `SimpleNormalizer` and `CapLeadingNormalizer` classes.

Why are we using `resource-pattern` here? Well, what we're really doing is saying to scan only **specific** classes in the `com.bsg5.chapter3.mem03` package. If we didn't limit the scan to only the normalization classes, we'd be importing the `MusicService3` too, and we don't want to include that class in a configuration that's supposed to be limited to, well, normalizers only.

The expression used here is a Java regular expression and includes the *entire* resource name – by default it's `**/*.class`, meaning "any file in the entire package tree beginning at the package specified in `base-package` that ends with `.class`."

71

In the `normalizers.xml` configuration, however, it's limited to "any file in the current package that ends with `Normalizer.class`", with the package set to `com.bsg5.chapter3.mem03`, so it will only pick up our two `Normalizer` implementations.

Now we get to see our "master configuration" in use, showing the use of the two `<import />` tags. This creates a "flattened configuration," such that anything that loads `config-04.xml` is going to see every component loaded by not only `config-04.xml` but anything loaded by `normalizers.xml` and `musicservicetest.xml` as well.

Listing 3-26. `chapter3/src/test/resources/config-04.xml`

```xml
<?xml version="1.0" encoding="UTF-8"?>

<!-- chapter3/src/test/resources/config-04.xml -->

<beans xmlns="http://www.springframework.org/schema/beans"
       xmlns:xsi="http://www.w3.org/2001/XMLSchema-instance"
       xmlns:context="http://www.springframework.org/schema/context"
       xsi:schemaLocation="http://www.springframework.org/schema/beans
         http://www.springframework.org/schema/beans/spring-beans.xsd
         http://www.springframework.org/schema/context
         http://www.springframework.org/schema/context/spring-context.xsd">

    <import resource="/normalizers.xml" />
    <import resource="/musicservicetest.xml"/>
    <context:component-scan base-package="com.bsg5.chapter3.mem04" />
</beans>
```

In fact, let's prove this, by writing a quick test that validates that the beans we expect to have in our configuration are available. As usual, we'll use a `@DataProvider` to provide a flexible dataset for a parameterized test. We'll do something a little different, in that we'll put both `String` instances and `Class` references into the data provider – and we'll check the type to figure out which `ApplicationContext getBean()` method to use. (There are probably cleaner ways to do this, but honestly, this is a throwaway test. We don't need it to be perfect, we just need it to work for our purposes.[25])

---

[25]It might be handy to have a *failing* condition in this test, but that complicates the data provider greatly, by indicating if a "miss" should fail the test or not. Consider that a quick exercise for the reader.

Listing 3-27. chapter3/src/test/java/com/bsg5/chapter3/TestConfiguratio nImport.java

```java
package com.bsg5.chapter3;

import com.bsg5.chapter3.mem03.CapLeadingNormalizer;
import com.bsg5.chapter3.mem03.SimpleNormalizer;
import org.springframework.beans.factory.annotation.Autowired;
import org.springframework.context.ApplicationContext;
import org.springframework.test.context.ContextConfiguration;
import org.springframework.test.context.testng.
AbstractTestNGSpringContextTests;
import org.testng.annotations.DataProvider;
import org.testng.annotations.Test;

import static org.testng.Assert.assertNotNull;
import static org.testng.Assert.fail;

@ContextConfiguration(locations = "/config-04.xml")
public class TestConfigurationImport extends
AbstractTestNGSpringContextTests {
    @Autowired
    ApplicationContext context;

    @DataProvider
    Object[][] resources() {
        return new Object[][]{
                {"musicServiceTests"},
                {MusicServiceTests.class},
                {"foo"},
                {"bar"},
                {SimpleNormalizer.class},
                {CapLeadingNormalizer.class},
                {"musicService4"}
        };
    }
```

```java
    @Test(dataProvider = "resources")
    public void validateResourceExistence(Object resource) {
        if (resource instanceof String) {
            assertNotNull(context.getBean(resource.toString()));
        } else {
            if (resource instanceof Class<?>) {
                assertNotNull(context.getBean((Class<?>) resource));
            } else {
                fail("Invalid resource type");
            }
        }
    }
}
```

At last, it's time to see our MusicService4, a near-clone of MusicService3 – as all of our MusicService implementations have been. The major change here is that we're going to make our Normalizer references final, and we're going to initialize them through constructor injection. We'll then have one more test class (a near-clone of other tests, referring to config-04.xml instead of the other configurations) to make sure our configuration loads smoothly and correctly (and, for that matter, quickly).

Listing 3-28. chapter3/src/main/java/com/bsg5/chapter3/ mem04/MusicService4.java

```java
package com.bsg5.chapter3.mem04;

import com.bsg5.chapter3.AbstractMusicService;
import com.bsg5.chapter3.Normalizer;
import org.springframework.beans.factory.annotation.Autowired;
import org.springframework.beans.factory.annotation.Qualifier;
import org.springframework.stereotype.Component;

@Component
public class MusicService4 extends AbstractMusicService {
    private final Normalizer artistNormalizer;
    private final Normalizer songNormalizer;
```

```
public MusicService4(@Autowired
                    @Qualifier("bar")
                            Normalizer artistNormalizer,
                    @Autowired
                    @Qualifier("foo")
                            Normalizer songNormalizer) {
    this.artistNormalizer = artistNormalizer;
    this.songNormalizer = songNormalizer;
}

@Override
protected String transformArtist(String input) {
    return artistNormalizer.transform(input);
}

@Override
protected String transformSong(String input) {
    return songNormalizer.transform(input);
}
}
```

Here, we've still got the @Autowired and @Qualifier annotations in use; they're just applied to arguments in the constructor instead of being applied to class attributes. The class attributes themselves are marked private final – because they're not used outside of this class, and because we want to tell the virtual machine to not allow the references to change, once set.

In *this* class, having the references be final is of limited value, mostly because the entire MusicService is of limited value – so far our implementations have been designed purely to show Spring configuration features. With that said, in real components, having values marked final can help the JVM optimize code, and it also makes your intent for the values clear: these are not things to be managed or changed. They're meant to be set and left alone.

Now we have an almost desultory test: it looks exactly like TestMusicService3, except for the configuration file name. We're going to parameterize the configurations later in this chapter, and actually test *every one of our configuration files* in one single test, but let's take a look at XML configuration and programmatic configuration of Spring, first.

Listing 3-29. chapter3/src/test/com/bsg5/chapter3/TestMusicService4.java

```java
package com.bsg5.chapter3;

import org.springframework.beans.factory.annotation.Autowired;
import org.springframework.test.context.ContextConfiguration;
import org.springframework.test.context.testng.
AbstractTestNGSpringContextTests;
import org.testng.annotations.Test;

@ContextConfiguration(locations = "/config-04.xml")
public class TestMusicService4 extends AbstractTestNGSpringContextTests {
    @Autowired MusicService service;
    @Autowired MusicServiceTests tests;

    @Test
    public void testSongVoting() {
        tests.testSongVoting(service);
    }

    @Test
    public void testGetMatchingArtistNames() {
        tests.testMatchingArtistNames(service);
    }

    @Test
    public void testGetSongsForArtist() {
        tests.testSongsForArtist(service);
    }

    @Test
    public void testMatchingSongNamesForArtist() {
        tests.testMatchingSongNamesForArtist(service);
    }

}
```

Our next section will recreate what we've just walked through, except without relying on annotations. We're going to walk through the process of using XML to configure Spring beans and wire them together.

3.4 Configuration Through XML

XML is not *required* to define a configuration, even though we've used it so far to kick-start the process of scanning for components. However, it *is* historically the most common (it's the oldest configuration mechanism), and it also has the benefit of centralizing configuration very easily. (We can see that because in every configuration in this chapter, we've used XML to do component scanning.)

What we'd like to do is demonstrate the basic XML wiring capabilities, by replicating our annotation-based examples, except with XML. The only exceptions will be the test classes themselves, which will continue to use annotations for injection; this is because the AbstractTestNGSpringContextTests class (and its JUnit equivalent) specifically implements a process by which annotation injection is applied. Therefore, there'd be no point to explicitly using XML to wire the test class' dependencies; the annotations are already being scanned and processed.

3.4.1 Declaring a Bean with `<bean />`

To declare a component in XML, one uses the `<bean />` tag, as shown in Listing 3-30.

Listing 3-30. `chapter3/src/test/resources/musicservicetest.xml`

```
<bean id="musicServiceTests" class="com.bsg5.chapter3.MusicServiceTests" />
```

This is a simple and straightforward usage of `<bean/>`, but there are a *lot* of attributes that can be used here. We're going to cover the most common ones in this chapter, with others covered in Chapter 4. There are more attributes than are being covered in this table, but the ones that aren't included here are rare.

Attribute	Meaning	Description
name	The qualified name of the bean.	If no name is provided, the bean name is derived from the class name.
class	The fully qualified class of the bean.	There are cases where this is actually unnecessary, but they're rare and not covered in a book for Spring beginners.
scope	The lifetime of the bean component.	This determines if getBean() will return the same instance on every invocation (thus keeping the component as a singleton) or if Spring will create a new instance on every call to getBean(). The default is the singleton mode (with the attribute value being singleton, if you can imagine). If a prototype is desired, the attribute value is prototype.
lazy-init	When in the context's lifecycle, a bean should be created.	If set to true, the bean will be instantiated when it's requested, rather than on container startup. The default is false so the Spring beans are created immediately and eagerly.
autowire	Controls the autowiring behavior for this bean.	Spring will not autowire references created via XML by default; this setting allows programmers to fine-tune autowiring behavior. It can be set to no, which means "no autowiring," byName and byType which means autowiring is based on the attribute name (so foo will match a component with the name foo) or by reference type, and constructor, which is like byType except for constructor arguments.
dependson	A list of beans that must be initialized before this one.	This is a comma-separated list of dependency references that must be fully initialized before this one is initialized. This is not normally required; Spring can determine if bean foo depends on bar or not, so this is only if the default dependency mechanism fails thanks to static references or something like that. In general, if you need this, you've done something wrong.

Other attributes to look for, particularly in Chapter 4, include init-method, destroy-method, factory-method, and factory-bean.

So what we see in Listing 3-31 is a simple Spring bean, called `musicServiceTests`, of type `com.bsg5.chapter3.MusicServiceTests`. It will be created as soon as the configuration is loaded (since `lazy-init` is left to the default, which is `false`), and it will be a singleton (only one instance loaded per `ApplicationContext`), since we let the scope to its default value, which is `singleton`.

This is, of course, the simplest type of bean to create, a bean that has no attributes to manage. It's entirely self-contained. What happens if we want to set other attributes – as we do with our `Normalizer` instances? Well, first, let's create a `normalizers-na.xml` configuration. We're going to use `normalizers-na.xml` because `normalizers.xml` uses annotations for configuration, and we want to be explicit[26]; our beans will still be named `foo` and `bar` but we want to create them explicitly. Note that the beans are the `Normalizer` classes from the `mem03` package – and we're going to reuse `MusicService3` as well, just without the annotations being processed.

Listing 3-31. `chapter3/src/test/resources/normalizers-na.xml`

```
<?xml version="1.0" encoding="UTF-8"?>

<!-- chapter3/src/test/resources/normalizers.xml -->

<beans xmlns="http://www.springframework.org/schema/beans"
       xmlns:xsi="http://www.w3.org/2001/XMLSchema-instance"
       xsi:schemaLocation="http://www.springframework.org/schema/beans
        http://www.springframework.org/schema/beans/spring-beans.xsd">

    <bean id="bar" class="com.bsg5.chapter3.mem03.SimpleNormalizer" />
    <bean id="foo" class="com.bsg5.chapter3.mem03.CapLeadingNormalizer" />
</beans>
```

3.4.2 Wiring Components Together with `<property />`

Now that we've declared a set of configurations with, well, a set of Spring beans, we need to figure out how to use these beans in our `MusicService3`; if you paid any attention to Chapter 2, of course, you know: we're going to use `<property />` to set the references.

---

[26]We're using "na" to mean "no annotations."

The property tag has the following attribute values and meanings.

Attribute	Meaning	Description
name	This is the name of the property to set.	This is required.
value	This is the value of the argument, which must be easily coerced into the type.	This cannot coexist with ref.
ref	This is a reference to another named Spring bean, by name.	This cannot coexist with value.

In this case, we have two Normalizer references available, provided we import normalizers-na.xml – and we will – so we're going to use ref to set the values. Here's our config-05.xml, which declares a MusicService (with a type of com. bsg5.chapter3.mem03.MusicService3) and then calls setArtistNormalizer() and setSongNormalizer() with the appropriate references, looking them up by name.

Listing 3-32. chapter3/src/test/resources/config-05.xml

```
<?xml version="1.0" encoding="UTF-8"?>

<!-- chapter3/src/test/resources/config-05.xml -->

<beans xmlns="http://www.springframework.org/schema/beans"
       xmlns:xsi="http://www.w3.org/2001/XMLSchema-instance"
       xsi:schemaLocation="http://www.springframework.org/schema/beans
        http://www.springframework.org/schema/beans/spring-beans.xsd">

    <import resource="/normalizers-na.xml" />

    <bean name="musicService" class="com.bsg5.chapter3.mem03.MusicService3">
        <property name="artistNormalizer" ref="foo" />
        <property name="songNormalizer" ref="bar" />
    </bean>
</beans>
```

Of course, it's all well and good to have nice, convenient, modular configuration files… but they don't *do* anything. Astute readers know what's coming next: a test!

This test is going to be *very* similar to our other tests, with one difference: we're going to load multiple configuration files in our @ContextConfiguration annotation. (Our tests don't use the XML configuration, nor should they, really.) Other than the usage of an *array* of configuration files, this test is identical to TestMusicService4. Each configuration file is loaded into a single ApplicationContext, so this is a handy way for us to modularize for tests, where beans like our MusicServiceTests don't need to be part of the "main configuration," our config-05.xml file.

Listing 3-33. chapter3/src/test/com/bsg5/chapter3/TestMusicService5.
java

```
package com.bsg5.chapter3;

import org.springframework.beans.factory.annotation.Autowired;
import org.springframework.test.context.ContextConfiguration;
import org.springframework.test.context.testng.
AbstractTestNGSpringContextTests;
import org.testng.annotations.Test;

@ContextConfiguration(locations = {"/config-05.xml","/musicservicetest.xml"})
public class TestMusicService5 extends AbstractTestNGSpringContextTests {
    @Autowired
    MusicService service;
    @Autowired
    MusicServiceTests tests;

    @Test
    public void testSongVoting() {
        tests.testSongVoting(service);
    }

    @Test
    public void testGetMatchingArtistNames() {
        tests.testMatchingArtistNames(service);
    }
```

```
    @Test
    public void testGetSongsForArtist() {
        tests.testSongsForArtist(service);
    }

    @Test
    public void testMatchingSongNamesForArtist() {
        tests.testMatchingSongNamesForArtist(service);
    }
}
```

3.4.3 Wiring Components Together with `<constructor-arg />`

Our next example will replicate what we *just* did, but just as we saw in the series of annotation-based examples, this one will use constructor injection. Just as we did with `TestMusicService5` (which reused `MusicService3`), we're going to reuse `MusicService4` with another configuration and another test.

First, the configuration. This one will use `<constructor-arg />` instead of `<property />`. The `<constructor-arg />` node has the following attributes available.

Attribute	Meaning	Description
type	This is the type of the argument, if it cannot be derived from the value.	Must match the type hierarchy.
value	This is the value of the argument, which must be easily coerced into the `type`.	This cannot coexist with `ref`.
ref	This is a reference to another named Spring bean, by name.	This cannot coexist with `value`.
name	This is the name of the argument, as in the constructor's source code.	This cannot coexist with `index`.
index	This is the index of the argument being set.	This cannot coexist with `name`.

So let's take a look at our `config-06.xml`, which does the same thing as `config-05.xml`, except with the constructor-only version of the `MusicService`.

Listing 3-34. `chapter3/src/test/resources/config-06.xml`

```xml
<?xml version="1.0" encoding="UTF-8"?>

<!-- chapter3/src/test/resources/config-06.xml -->

<beans xmlns="http://www.springframework.org/schema/beans"
       xmlns:xsi="http://www.w3.org/2001/XMLSchema-instance"
       xsi:schemaLocation="http://www.springframework.org/schema/beans
        http://www.springframework.org/schema/beans/spring-beans.xsd">

    <import resource="/normalizers-na.xml" />

    <bean name="musicService" class="com.bsg5.chapter3.mem04.MusicService4">
        <constructor-arg name="artistNormalizer" ref="foo" />
        <constructor-arg name="songNormalizer" ref="bar" />
    </bean>
</beans>
```

And we'd be breaking a habit if we didn't include *yet another* test, another copy of an earlier test, except this time referring to `config-06.xml` instead of, well, anything else.

Listing 3-35. `chapter3/src/test/com/bsg5/chapter3/TestMusicService6.java`

```java
package com.bsg5.chapter3;

import org.springframework.beans.factory.annotation.Autowired;
import org.springframework.test.context.ContextConfiguration;
import org.springframework.test.context.testng.
AbstractTestNGSpringContextTests;
import org.testng.annotations.Test;

@ContextConfiguration(locations = {"/config-06.xml","/musicservicetest.xml"})
public class TestMusicService6 extends AbstractTestNGSpringContextTests {
    @Autowired
    MusicService service;
```

```
    @Autowired
    MusicServiceTests tests;

    @Test
    public void testSongVoting() {
        tests.testSongVoting(service);
    }

    @Test
    public void testGetMatchingArtistNames() {
        tests.testMatchingArtistNames(service);
    }

    @Test
    public void testGetSongsForArtist() {
        tests.testSongsForArtist(service);
    }

    @Test
    public void testMatchingSongNamesForArtist() {
        tests.testMatchingSongNamesForArtist(service);
    }

}
```

We're now going to take a look at a *third* way to configure an ApplicationContext: Java configuration.

3.5 Configuration Through Java

With programmatic configuration, you have a few options: one is to define a Java class and mark it as a @Configuration, providing methods to return Spring beans internally. This is (mostly) *static* configuration.

Another way to configure Spring programmatically is to grab an ApplicationContext and manually register components in it. This is *dynamic* configuration. The latter is very flexible, but uncommon, so we're going to focus on static configuration in this section.

With static configuration, you declare a class with methods that return components; mark the methods that return Spring beans with @Bean, and mark the *class* with

@Configuration, and you're done, although of course you have the capability to fine-tune the annotations. If the methods have arguments, then Spring tries to use a resolution mechanism similar to constructor-based injection.

3.5.1 Declaring Components with @Bean

Let's see a simple configuration in action. This configuration will mirror what we did with the MusicService1 in Listing 3-11 – a simple component with no dependencies.

Listing 3-36. chapter3/src/test/com/bsg5/chapter3/Configuration7.java

```
package com.bsg5.chapter3;

import com.bsg5.chapter3.mem01.MusicService1;
import org.springframework.context.annotation.Bean;
import org.springframework.context.annotation.Configuration;

@Configuration
public class Configuration7 {
    @Bean
    MusicService musicService() {
        return new MusicService1();
    }
}
```

Our eagle-eyed readers will notice that we have Configuration7, leaving out configurations one through six. This is deliberate. This is the seventh configuration in this chapter, so rather than restarting the sequence, we just continued where we left off. Good eye, though, readers.

This configuration would contribute one Spring bean to an ApplicationContext, whose name would be derived from the method – so create a reference to a MusicService called musicService, with an instance reference of type MusicService1. (We'll show how you can name the references differently in a later example.)

Let's create another configuration class, one that creates a `MusicServiceTests` reference, which we'll use in a test we'll see after we walk through the other configuration possibilities.

Listing 3-37. chapter3/src/test/com/bsg5/chapter3/TestConfiguration.java

```java
package com.bsg5.chapter3;

import org.springframework.context.annotation.Bean;
import org.springframework.context.annotation.Configuration;

@Configuration
public class TestConfiguration {
    @Bean
    MusicServiceTests musicServiceTests() {
        return new MusicServiceTests();
    }
}
```

3.5.2 Using a Programmatic Configuration for `ApplicationContext`

We've seen how to load configurations with `ClassPathXmlApplicationContext` (from Chapter 2), but that class accepts XML file locations as arguments; here, we have no XML at all. In order to use this kind of configuration, we need to use `AnnotationConfigApplicationContext`, passing it a reference to the `Class<?>` that represents the configuration. We can pass in as many configuration classes as we need. In practice, a runnable application might look something like Listing 3-38, which loads our two configuration classes and dumps every managed Spring bean's name to the console.

Listing 3-38. chapter3/src/test/com/bsg5/chapter3/MusicServiceRunner.java

```java
package com.bsg5.chapter3;

import org.springframework.context.ApplicationContext;
import org.springframework.context.annotation.
AnnotationConfigApplicationContext;

public class MusicServiceRunner {
```

```
    public static void main(String[] args) {
        Class<?>[] configurations = new Class<?>[]
                {Configuration7.class, TestConfiguration.class};
        ApplicationContext context =
                new AnnotationConfigApplicationContext(configurations);
        for(String name:context.getBeanDefinitionNames()) {
            System.out.println(name);
        }
    }
}
```

If it's run without changes, the output looks like Listing 3-39.

Listing 3-39. Output of `MusicServiceRunner`

```
org.springframework.context.annotation.
internalConfigurationAnnotationProcessor
org.springframework.context.annotation.internalAutowiredAnnotationProcessor
org.springframework.context.event.internalEventListenerProcessor
org.springframework.context.event.internalEventListenerFactory
configuration7
testConfiguration
musicService
musicServiceTests
```

You can see in this output how there's a reference to `musicService` and `musicServiceTests`. (We're going to walk through a few more configuration examples before using this – and the rest of our configurations, *all* of them – in a test.)

3.5.3 Wiring Components Together with `@Autowired` with Static Configuration

References marked with `@Autowired` are still candidates for injection, of course. What's more, the rules for injection hold even with programmatic configuration. In the second configuration (`config-02.xml`), we had a single `Normalizer` in the configuration, automatically wired into a `MusicService2`. Listing 3-40 shows what that same configuration looks like, using Java for configuration instead of XML.

Listing 3-40. `chapter3/src/test/com/bsg5/chapter3/Configuration8.java`

```java
package com.bsg5.chapter3;

import com.bsg5.chapter3.mem02.MusicService2;
import com.bsg5.chapter3.mem02.SimpleNormalizer;
import org.springframework.context.annotation.Bean;
import org.springframework.context.annotation.Configuration;

@Configuration
public class Configuration8 {
    @Bean
    Normalizer normalizer() {
        return new SimpleNormalizer();
    }

    @Bean
    MusicService musicService() {
        return new MusicService2();
    }
}
```

3.5.4 Using `@Qualifier` to Select Specific Components for Wiring

For `MusicService3`, we had multiple `Normalizer` references. Again, the resolution works out exactly the same; the injected reference is qualified by name if no other candidate exists, and in the programmatic configuration, the name of the bean defaults to the name of the method that returns a given class instance. (Thus, in Listing 3-40, the beans are named `musicService` and `normalizer`.)

In our next example, we have two methods that produce `Normalizer` references: `foo()` and `capNormalizer()`. If they're both marked solely with `@Bean`, the Spring beans' names will be, logically enough, `foo` and `capNormalizer`, respectively, but that would yield a missing reference for the autowired attribute in `MusicService3`, which is looking for a component named `bar`.

We can name references explicitly, by using the `name` attribute in the `@Bean` annotation. Our next configuration shows this in action.

Listing 3-41. chapter3/src/test/com/bsg5/chapter3/Configuration9.java

```java
package com.bsg5.chapter3;

import com.bsg5.chapter3.mem03.CapLeadingNormalizer;
import com.bsg5.chapter3.mem03.SimpleNormalizer;
import com.bsg5.chapter3.mem03.MusicService3;
import org.springframework.context.annotation.Bean;
import org.springframework.context.annotation.Configuration;

@Configuration
public class Configuration9 {
    @Bean
    Normalizer foo() {
        return new SimpleNormalizer();
    }

    @Bean(name="bar")
    Normalizer capNormalizer() {
        return new CapLeadingNormalizer();
    }

    @Bean
    MusicService musicService() {
        return new MusicService3();
    }
}
```

3.5.5 Constructor Injection with Static Configuration

Our last example corresponds to our examples that leverage constructor injection. We have a few options here: we could construct the references manually (thus, new MusicService4(new SimpleNormalizer(), new SimpleNormalizer())), but this violates the principle of allowing Spring to manage the references.

We can actually have the bean construction method *itself* accept arguments (with names that resolve to bean components or set explicitly via @Qualifier). Spring will then do argument matching based on type or name, allowing us to use those references in the construction of the new component.

Listing 3-42. chapter3/src/test/com/bsg5/chapter3/Configuration10.java

```java
package com.bsg5.chapter3;

import com.bsg5.chapter3.mem03.CapLeadingNormalizer;
import com.bsg5.chapter3.mem03.SimpleNormalizer;
import com.bsg5.chapter3.mem04.MusicService4;
import org.springframework.beans.factory.annotation.Qualifier;
import org.springframework.context.annotation.Bean;
import org.springframework.context.annotation.Configuration;

@Configuration
public class Configuration10 {
    @Bean
    Normalizer foo() {
        return new SimpleNormalizer();
    }

    @Bean
    Normalizer bar() {
        return new CapLeadingNormalizer();
    }

    @Bean
    MusicService musicService(Normalizer bar,
                              @Qualifier("foo")
                                    Normalizer baz) {
        return new MusicService4(bar, baz);
    }
}
```

The advantage provided here is not only that of *flexibility* but *management*. Only one instance of a SimpleNormalizer, for example, is created; it's a singleton.

3.5.6 Testing Every Configuration with a DataProvider

We haven't seen most of these configurations in use, and the only use we've seen is that of a poor excuse for a test. Let's write a test that actually exercises *every* configuration we've presented so far. This class has some fairly significant oddities to it, so we'll present two methods it contains and explain what these methods do, then we'll see the entire class, with the method in context.

Listing 3-43. chapter3/src/test/com/bsg5/chapter3/TestMusicService10.java

```java
private void runMethod(Object config, Consumer<MusicService> method) {
    ApplicationContext context;
    if (config instanceof String) {
        context = new ClassPathXmlApplicationContext(config.toString());
    } else {
        if (config instanceof Class<?>) {
            context = new AnnotationConfigApplicationContext((Class<?>)
            config);
        } else {
            throw new RuntimeException("Invalid configuration argument: " +
            config);
        }
    }
    MusicService service = context.getBean(MusicService.class);
    method.accept(service);
}

@Test(expectedExceptions = RuntimeException.class)
public void testRunMethod() {
    runMethod(Boolean.TRUE, tests::testSongVoting);
}
```

The runMethod() method is internal to our test, and what it does is pretty simple but might seem odd to some readers: it accepts a configuration object of some kind as well as a method reference that accepts an ApplicationContext. The config object is looked into, to see if it's a Class or a String; if it's a String, the ApplicationContext is loaded from XML, and if it's a Class, it's loaded from a programmatic configuration. (If it's not one of those, an exception is thrown. Our other method tests this out.)

Once the context is loaded, it grabs a `MusicService` from the context and then invokes the method passed in as the second argument with the `MusicService`. A failure in the method being invoked – an exception or assertion failure – is bubbled up to the caller of `runMethod()`. Therefore, we can accept a configuration of some kind – either a `String` or a `Class` – and invoke a method with a properly constructed `ApplicationContext` at will.

We've seen this in our `MusicServiceTests`, by the way – we're just going one level higher and compositing method invocation twice instead of once.

So let's take a look at the *entire* test class, `TestMusicService10.java`. It's going to use a data provider method (called `configurations()`) to create a list composed of references to *every* configuration this chapter contains, and in every method that refers to the data provider, it will call `runMethod()` with the provided configuration reference and a method reference from `MusicServiceTests`. Any failures will show up as test failures.

Listing 3-44. chapter3/src/test/com/bsg5/chapter3/TestMusicService10. java

```
package com.bsg5.chapter3;

import org.springframework.beans.factory.annotation.Autowired;
import org.springframework.context.ApplicationContext;
import org.springframework.context.annotation.
AnnotationConfigApplicationContext;
import org.springframework.context.support.ClassPathXmlApplicationContext;
import org.springframework.test.context.ContextConfiguration;
import org.springframework.test.context.testng.
AbstractTestNGSpringContextTests;
import org.testng.annotations.DataProvider;
import org.testng.annotations.Test;

import java.util.function.Consumer;

@ContextConfiguration(classes = {TestConfiguration.class})
public class TestMusicService10 extends AbstractTestNGSpringContextTests {
    @Autowired
    MusicServiceTests tests;
```

```
@DataProvider
Object[][] configurations() {
    return new Object[][]{
            {"/config-01.xml"},
            {"/config-02.xml"},
            {"/config-03.xml"},
            {"/config-04.xml"},
            {"/config-05.xml"},
            {"/config-06.xml"},
            {Configuration7.class},
            {Configuration8.class},
            {Configuration9.class},
            {Configuration10.class}
    };
}
// tag::runMethod[]
private void runMethod(Object config, Consumer<MusicService> method) {
    ApplicationContext context;
    if (config instanceof String) {
        context = new ClassPathXmlApplicationContext(config.toString());
    } else {
        if (config instanceof Class<?>) {
            context = new AnnotationConfigApplicationContext((Class<?>)
            config);
        } else {
            throw new RuntimeException("Invalid configuration argument:
            " + config);
        }
    }
    MusicService service = context.getBean(MusicService.class);
    method.accept(service);
}
```

```
@Test(expectedExceptions = RuntimeException.class)
public void testRunMethod() {
    runMethod(Boolean.TRUE, tests::testSongVoting);
}
// end::runMethod[]

@Test(dataProvider = "configurations")
public void testSongVoting(Object config) {
    runMethod(config, tests::testSongVoting);
}

@Test(dataProvider = "configurations")
public void testGetMatchingArtistNames(Object config) {
    runMethod(config, tests::testMatchingArtistNames);
}

@Test(dataProvider = "configurations")
public void testGetSongsForArtist(Object config) {
    runMethod(config, tests::testSongsForArtist);
}

@Test(dataProvider = "configurations")
public void testMatchingSongNamesForArtist(Object config) {
    runMethod(config, tests::testMatchingSongNamesForArtist);
}
}
```

Some interesting observations from this test's successful conclusion:

1. On the author's machine, this test runs in 1.6 seconds, with the
    most significant times being spent on warmup (as the code is
    first seen by the JVM). The XML-based test configurations tended
    to run slightly slower than the programmatic configurations
    (as one might expect), but even the slowest runs in around
    50 milliseconds, although readers' results may vary slightly
    depending on a number of factors.

2. More significantly, we're demonstrating rather different
    components, all referred to by the same interface, all used
    identically from the calling code. Our test runs through
    ten different configurations, with four fairly differentiated
    implementation classes, and there's absolutely no change in
    how classes are acquired from the Spring context. There's no
    real performance difference; there's some time spent initializing
    the contexts, but it's not significant, because most contexts are
    retained for far longer than a single test.

3.6 Next Steps

In Chapter 4, we're going to explore some of the lifecycle options in Spring, where we
have even more control over how beans are created (through constructors, as we've
done in this chapter, or factories), as well as how we invoke methods when Spring beans
are created or destroyed. We're also going to see how to create new Spring beans such
that they're not singleton objects.

CHAPTER 4

Lifecycle

In this chapter, we'll expand on our sample application and learn about the lifecycle options in Spring. We'll introduce how to invoke methods when Spring beans are created or destroyed and how to do so via multiple configurable options either using the Spring XML file, annotations, or the programmatic configurations, all of which were used in Chapter 3.

4.1 Introduction of Lifecycle

Every object has a lifecycle in the Java Virtual Machine. When an object is created, it's got a series of initialization stages (at the class level, then the instance level), then the class' constructor is called. When (and if) the object becomes unreachable by program code, the object might be cleaned up by the garbage collector, which might itself call specially named methods so that the object can clear out any allocated resources, a process known as finalization.[1]

Dependency Injection frameworks add extra control to the lifecycle of objects, by adding callbacks for lifecycle events or offering hooks that the dependency context will call when certain things have been accomplished. Spring also provides scope within a given context, to control whether the resources are considered to be singletons or not.

Let's look at scope, first.

---

[1]Finalization has long been known to be a good way to wreck your application's performance, but sometimes it was the only tool available that allowed classes to know when to force-remove allocated resources. Since Java 9, though, there's an alternative: the `java.lang.ref.Cleaner` class, which isn't entirely trivial but is far more safe to use.

© Joseph B. Ottinger and Andrew Lombardi 2019

J. B. Ottinger and A. Lombardi, *Beginning Spring 5*, https://doi.org/10.1007/978-1-4842-4486-9_4

4.1.1 Scope

Spring provides two basic scopes for objects in the standard `ApplicationContext` – `singleton` and `prototype`.

An object set to `singleton` scope – the default – is created and destroyed **once** in a given application context. If you retrieve an object multiple times, you will receive the same object reference each time.

An object set to `prototype` scope is constructed on retrieval, and every time you get an object of this type from the context, you will receive a unique object; Spring acts like a builder[2] in this case. You might use this scope if you have an object whose state is mutated but, once changed, the object isn't useful for any other process.

A builder is actually an excellent example of this kind of pattern. With many instances of the builder pattern, one creates the builder, then adds data to it. When the data is considered "complete," you'd call the `build()` method – or some analog – that yields a completed object from the builder. The builder isn't useful for building anything else once it's delivered what it's built, because it contains state that's unique to the object being built; you'd then discard the builder, and if you needed another object, you'd create a new builder to create it. In Spring terms, builders would be ideal prototypes.

There **are** actually other scopes available through Spring's web module, but we'll discuss them in Chapter 6, where they're more appropriate.

Let's take a look at a trivial example showing the scopes in action. We're going to create a project for this chapter (called `chapter4`, because we're quite original in this book), and we're going to write a quick test that demonstrates how we can define object scopes and also what the effect of those scopes might be.

First, we need to create our directory structure, starting in the overall project directory (Listing 4-1).

---

[2]The builder pattern is a pattern described by *Design Patterns: Elements of Reusable Object-Oriented Software*, by Gamma, Helm, Johnson, and Vlissides. It's a pattern that refers to how objects are created consistently; see `https://en.wikipedia.org/wiki/Builder_pattern` for more.

Listing 4-1. Creating the directory structure with POSIX

```
mkdir -p chapter4/src/main/java/com/bsg5/chapter4
mkdir -p chapter4/src/test/java/com/bsg5/chapter4
mkdir -p chapter4/src/test/resources
```

We also need a `build.gradle` and `settings.gradle`, neither of which add anything new or spectacular to our build so far. Remember that things like `$springFrameworkVersion` were defined in Chapter 2, in our top-level project. (If the current versions of any of these dependencies change, you can change it in the top-level `build.gradle` and have those changes reflected throughout the entire project.)

Listing 4-2. `chapter4/build.gradle`

```
dependencies {
    compile "org.springframework:spring-core:$springFrameworkVersion"
    compile "org.springframework:spring-context:$springFrameworkVersion"
    compile "org.springframework:spring-test:$springFrameworkVersion"
    compile "javax.annotation:javax.annotation-api:1.3.2"
}
```

Now it's time to get more interesting. Let's create an abstract class to hold a single piece of data – called `HasData` – and we'll extend it with multiple classes embedded with our test code. We can get away with this because we're not actually creating classes for the purpose of anything other than demonstrating lifecycle, and these aren't public classes.[3]

Listing 4-3. `chapter4/src/main/java/com/bsg5/chapter4/HasData.java`

```
package com.bsg5.chapter4;

import java.util.Objects;

abstract class  HasData {
    String datum = "default";
```

---

[3]Java's source rules specify that a file **must** be named the same as a single public class contained in that file. In this case, we have **no** public classes, which limits their use to inside the package in which they exist.

```
public String getDatum() {
    return datum;
}

public void setDatum(String datum) {
    this.datum = datum;
}

@Override
public boolean equals(Object o) {
    if (this == o) return true;
    if (!(o instanceof HasData)) return false;
    HasData hasData = (HasData) o;
    return Objects.equals(getDatum(), hasData.getDatum());
}

@Override
public int hashCode() {
    return Objects.hash(getDatum());
}
}
```

The equals() method is slightly more complex than it might have been, because it has to accept subclasses of HasData (and, in fact, it has no choice; since HasData is abstract, you'll never have an actual instance of HasData). It's also worth noting that IDEs can (and did) generate these methods; every method was generated automatically by IDEA. (For what it's worth, Eclipse would have generated equivalent code; it just so happens that your authors used IDEA here.)

Why would equals() need to accept subclasses? Well, it really depends on the use case. Here, we have no choice but to accept things that aren't the same class as HasData, because HasData is abstract – there will never be a valid instance of this type, unless the definition changes. However, if we're talking about **concrete** types, then you still might want to accept subclasses – because many frameworks like Hibernate (https://hibernate.org) will generate proxies as subclasses for entities, such that they look exactly like the entity classes but have code to interact with the database as needed. HasData isn't particularly likely to become an entity for Hibernate, but it's good practice to do the right thing when you can.

To set an object to be a prototype, we simply add the scope attribute to the configuration. (We're going to show XML configuration first, as it's more flexible and explicit than the annotations when it comes to fine-grained control of events.) The two values are – surprisingly – prototype and singleton, although singleton is the default and therefore isn't necessary at all.

We are defining two beans – foo and bar – both of the same type, because we can retrieve objects by name, with different scopes.

Listing 4-4. chapter4/src/test/resources/config-01.xml

```xml
<?xml version="1.0" encoding="UTF-8"?>

<!-- chapter4/src/test/resources/config-01.xml -->

<beans xmlns="http://www.springframework.org/schema/beans"
       xmlns:xsi="http://www.w3.org/2001/XMLSchema-instance"
       xsi:schemaLocation="http://www.springframework.org/schema/beans
         http://www.springframework.org/schema/beans/spring-beans.xsd">

    <!--
    note that "singleton" scope is the default, so this declaration is
    unnecessary.
    -->
    <bean name="foo"
          class="com.bsg5.chapter4.FirstObject"
          scope="singleton"/>
    <bean name="bar"
          class="com.bsg5.chapter4.FirstObject"
          scope="prototype"/>
</beans>
```

In our test, we have a data provider that refers to the reference names themselves, as well as a flag to tell the test whether the types are to be considered distinct or not. Our test grabs a single instance of the specified type by name, then mutates it from its original state. It then gets another instance with the same name.

If the type is specified to be a singleton, the objects should be the same **instance** (i.e., o1 == o2), and setting the data in one should also be reflected in the other (in other words, there's both instance equality and data equality).

If the type is specified to be a *prototype* instead, then the objects should **not** be the same instance, and setting the data in one should leave the other in its default state.

Listing 4-5. chapter4/src/test/java/com/bsg5/chapter4/TestLifeCycle01.java

```
package com.bsg5.chapter4;

import org.springframework.beans.factory.annotation.Autowired;
import org.springframework.context.ApplicationContext;
import org.springframework.test.context.ContextConfiguration;
import org.springframework.test.context.testng.AbstractTestNGSpringContextTests;
import org.testng.annotations.DataProvider;
import org.testng.annotations.Test;

import java.util.UUID;

import static org.testng.Assert.*;

class FirstObject extends HasData {
}

@ContextConfiguration(locations = "/config-01.xml")
public class TestLifecycle01 extends AbstractTestNGSpringContextTests {
    @Autowired
    ApplicationContext context;

    @DataProvider
```

```java
    Object[][] getReferences() {
        return new Object[][]{
                {"foo", true},
                {"bar", false}
        };
    }

    @Test(dataProvider = "getReferences")
    public void testReferenceTypes(String name, boolean singleton) {
        HasData o1 = context.getBean(name, HasData.class);

        String defaultValue = o1.getDatum();
        o1.setDatum(UUID.randomUUID().toString());

        HasData o2 = context.getBean(name, HasData.class);
        if (singleton) {
            assertSame(o1, o2);
            assertEquals(o1, o2);
            assertNotEquals(defaultValue, o2.getDatum());
        } else {
            assertNotSame(o1, o2);
            assertNotEquals(o1, o2);
            assertEquals(defaultValue, o2.getDatum());
        }
    }
}
```

4.1.2 Calling Constructors

In Chapter 3 we saw how we can specify constructor arguments for Spring beans, either by naming arguments or using the argument index. (The most straightforward technique is to use named arguments, if many exist, although perhaps using @Autowired references is even simpler. But we're sticking to XML in this section.) Chapter 3 walks through most of this fairly well, but we'll offer a short example here just for completeness' sake.

Listing 4-6. `chapter4/src/test/resources/config-02.xml`

```xml
<?xml version="1.0" encoding="UTF-8"?>

<!-- chapter4/src/test/resources/config-02.xml -->

<beans xmlns="http://www.springframework.org/schema/beans"
       xmlns:xsi="http://www.w3.org/2001/XMLSchema-instance"
       xsi:schemaLocation="http://www.springframework.org/schema/beans
        http://www.springframework.org/schema/beans/spring-beans.xsd">

    <bean name="foo" class="com.bsg5.chapter4.SecondObject">
        <constructor-arg name="initialValue"
                          value="Initial Value"/>
    </bean>
</beans>
```

Note the use of the `name` attribute in the `constructor-arg` directive – it maps to the actual parameter named `initialValue`.

And now a test that utilizes that configuration is shown in Listing 4-7.

Listing 4-7. `chapter4/src/test/java/com/bsg5/chapter4/TestLifeCycle02.java`

```java
package com.bsg5.chapter4;

import org.springframework.beans.factory.annotation.Autowired;
import org.springframework.context.ApplicationContext;
import org.springframework.test.context.ContextConfiguration;
import org.springframework.test.context.testng.
AbstractTestNGSpringContextTests;
import org.testng.annotations.Test;

import static org.testng.Assert.assertEquals;

class SecondObject extends HasData {
    SecondObject(String initialValue) {
        setDatum(initialValue);
    }
}
```

```
@ContextConfiguration(locations = "/config-02.xml")
public class TestLifecycle02 extends AbstractTestNGSpringContextTests {
    @Autowired
    ApplicationContext context;

    @Test
    public void validateConstruction() {
        HasData o1 = context.getBean(HasData.class);
        assertEquals(o1.getDatum(), "Initial Value");
    }
}
```

Our test here is simpler, because all we need to do is make sure the object built by Spring has the expected data value.

4.1.3 Calling Methods After Construction and Before Destruction

We can also call methods after object construction and, oddly, before the context drops all references it is managing. This is done in XML with the init-method and destroy-method attributes.

The destroy-method is not the same as a Java finalizer, although it can serve **some** of the same roles; if the ApplicationContext is able to be closed (through the well-named close() method, first seen in ConfigurableApplicationContext in the class hierarchy), the context will call these methods **before the context closes**. This is not the same as finalization; if the classes have finalizers or utilize Java 9's Cleaner facility, those methods will be called before garbage collection occurs.

Note that destroy-method only applies to Spring beans that are **singletons**. Prototypes are created by Spring and then are considered to be unmanaged, once retrieved; Spring will construct them and pass them to your code, and then forget such instances exist. Therefore, the method indicated by destroy-method will not be called on prototyped instances; this is **probably** all right because destroy-method should be rarely used in any event, as one rarely closes Spring contexts in the first place.

In other words, `destroy-method` is present to allow you to finely control when something **might** happen to a Spring bean, but it's unlikely to be useful in ordinary development. That won't stop us from demonstrating it, though!

For both methods, there's a contract the methods need to follow. They can be named anything valid (since we specify which methods are to be called), but the methods must not have a return value (they have to be declared of type `void`) and they cannot have method parameters.

Here's a configuration that shows the methods being specified.

Listing 4-8. `chapter4/src/test/resources/config-03.xml`

```xml
<?xml version="1.0" encoding="UTF-8"?>

<!-- chapter4/src/test/resources/config-03.xml -->

<beans xmlns="http://www.springframework.org/schema/beans"
       xmlns:xsi="http://www.w3.org/2001/XMLSchema-instance"
       xsi:schemaLocation="http://www.springframework.org/schema/beans
        http://www.springframework.org/schema/beans/spring-beans.xsd">

    <bean name="foo"
          class="com.bsg5.chapter4.ThirdObject"
          init-method="init"
          destroy-method="dispose"
    />
</beans>
```

What this means is that when Spring creates the `ThirdObject`, it will call `init()` after all construction has been finished, just as if the following code snippet were run.

Listing 4-9. A code snippet replicating `init-method`

```java
ThirdObject foo=new ThirdObject();
foo.init();
```

Our test source will define `ThirdObject` and create a static reference, called semaphore. (It's not **truly** a semaphore, but it… could be?) This reference is set **only** by the `init` method; therefore, we can verify that the proper initialization methods are being followed. We also define a `destroy` method that sets the `semaphore` reference to null; it's not a true semaphore, but it's sort of acting like one for our test.

The actual test itself uses a ConfigurableApplicationContext instead of an ApplicationContext, because we want to explicitly close the context after we've retrieved an object from it. The ApplicationContext interface does not define close(), whereas the ConfigurableApplicationContext implements Closeable (as well as ApplicationContext and Lifecycle, for that matter). The method visibility is the **only** reason we're using ConfigurableApplicationContext – if it weren't for close() not being defined on ApplicationContext, it would serve well for this test.

The test method grabs a bean from the application context and then runs two simple verifications: one is that the bean **instance** looks correct (i.e., it has data matching what we expect), and the other is that the semaphore is populated.

We then close the context and check the semaphore reference again – which, if dispose() has been called, will be set to null.

Listing 4-10. chapter4/src/test/java/com/bsg5/chapter4/TestLifeCycle03. java

```
package com.bsg5.chapter4;

import org.springframework.beans.factory.annotation.Autowired;
import org.springframework.context.ConfigurableApplicationContext;
import org.springframework.test.context.ContextConfiguration;
import org.springframework.test.context.testng.
AbstractTestNGSpringContextTests;
import org.testng.annotations.Test;

import static org.testng.Assert.*;

class ThirdObject extends HasData {
    static Object semaphore = null;

    public void init() {
        semaphore = new Object();
    }
    public void dispose() {
        semaphore = null;
    }
}
```

```
@ContextConfiguration(locations = "/config-03.xml")
public class TestLifecycle03 extends AbstractTestNGSpringContextTests {
    @Autowired
    ConfigurableApplicationContext context;

    @Test
    public void testInitDestroyMethods() {
        ThirdObject o1 = context.getBean(ThirdObject.class);
        assertNotNull(ThirdObject.semaphore);
        assertEquals(o1.getDatum(), "default");
        context.close();
        assertNull(ThirdObject.semaphore);
    }
}
```

4.1.4 Lifecycle Listeners

There are more options for listening to lifecycle events, too: the InitializingBean and DisposableBean interfaces. These interfaces define afterPropertiesSet() and destroy(), respectively, and these methods will be called at the proper times (i.e., after construction and all properties are set, and before the context releases the reference to the bean). Functionally it's exactly the same as with the init-method and destroy-method attributes in the XML configuration; the main difference is that these interfaces bind you directly to Spring's interfaces, whereas theoretically the init-method and destroy-method references do not.[4]

As with our other tests, here's a configuration file describing a FourthObject. Note the lack of lifecycle methods being described.

Listing 4-11. `chapter4/src/test/resources/config-04.xml`

```
<?xml version="1.0" encoding="UTF-8"?>

<!-- chapter4/src/test/resources/config-04.xml -->
```

---

[4]This is sophistry, really. A method specified with init-method would have to be manually called, as would a method specified with destroy-method, to make sense; these methods exist primarily in the context of Spring lifecycles, and which one you choose is really up to you, although you're probably best off using annotations – covered later in this chapter – to accomplish similar effects.

```
<beans xmlns="http://www.springframework.org/schema/beans"
       xmlns:xsi="http://www.w3.org/2001/XMLSchema-instance"
       xsi:schemaLocation="http://www.springframework.org/schema/beans
         http://www.springframework.org/schema/beans/spring-beans.xsd">

    <bean name="foo"
          class="com.bsg5.chapter4.FourthObject"
    />
</beans>
```

Now, our test. The actual test itself is functionally equivalent to the TestLifecycle03 test, with the main difference being the class type being used, which is FourthObject instead of ThirdObject. The FourthObject class itself implements both InitializingBean and DisposableBean and therefore replaces ThirdObject's init and dispose methods with afterPropertiesSet and destroy, respectively.

Listing 4-12. chapter4/src/test/java/com/bsg5/chapter4/TestLifeCycle04.java

```
package com.bsg5.chapter4;

import org.springframework.beans.factory.DisposableBean;
import org.springframework.beans.factory.InitializingBean;
import org.springframework.beans.factory.annotation.Autowired;
import org.springframework.context.ConfigurableApplicationContext;
import org.springframework.test.context.ContextConfiguration;
import org.springframework.test.context.testng.
AbstractTestNGSpringContextTests;
import org.testng.annotations.Test;

import static org.testng.Assert.*;

class FourthObject extends HasData
        implements InitializingBean, DisposableBean {
    static Object semaphore = null;

    @Override
    public void afterPropertiesSet() throws Exception {
        semaphore = new Object();
    }
```

```
    @Override
    public void destroy() throws Exception {
        semaphore = null;
    }
}

@ContextConfiguration(locations = "/config-04.xml")
public class TestLifecycle04 extends AbstractTestNGSpringContextTests {
    @Autowired
    ConfigurableApplicationContext context;

    @Test
    public void testLifecycleMethods() {
        FourthObject o1 = context.getBean(FourthObject.class);
        assertNotNull(FourthObject.semaphore);
        assertEquals(o1.getDatum(), "default");
        context.close();
        assertNull(FourthObject.semaphore);
    }
}
```

4.2 Lifecycle with JSR-250 Annotations

Annotations provide most – but not **quite** all – features that the XML configuration
provides. The main difference is in construction; most other lifecycle features are either
identical (with the InitializingBean and DisposableBean interfaces) or have direct
analogs (e.g., with annotations that contain method names for init-method). Let's step
through our features, one by one, starting with component scope.

4.2.1 Annotated Beans with Scopes

The scopes can be demonstrated with annotations logically enough: simply add the
@Scope annotation with the correct scope name. Our example will be slightly more
contrived than our XML example, because we need two different types such that
they're annotated differently. We're going to use only **one** configuration file for all of the
annotated lifecycle tests, though, and here it is.

Listing 4-13. chapter4/src/test/resources/annotated.xml

```xml
<?xml version="1.0" encoding="UTF-8"?>

<!-- chapter4/src/test/resources/config-04.xml -->

<beans xmlns="http://www.springframework.org/schema/beans"
       xmlns:xsi="http://www.w3.org/2001/XMLSchema-instance"
       xmlns:context="http://www.springframework.org/schema/context"
       xsi:schemaLocation="http://www.springframework.org/schema/beans

         http://www.springframework.org/schema/beans/spring-beans.xsd
         http://www.springframework.org/schema/context
         http://www.springframework.org/schema/context/spring-context.xsd">

    <context:component-scan base-package="com.bsg5.chapter4"/>
</beans>
```

Here's a working test with two annotated component types, `FifthObject` and `SixthObject`. It's very nearly the same as our `TestLifecycle01` class, with the main differences being the component classes themselves, and we also use the component classes to look up references instead of named references.

Listing 4-14. chapter4/src/test/java/com/bsg5/chapter4/TestLifeCycle05. java

```java
package com.bsg5.chapter4;

import org.springframework.beans.factory.annotation.Autowired;
import org.springframework.beans.factory.config.ConfigurableBeanFactory;
import org.springframework.context.ApplicationContext;
import org.springframework.context.annotation.Scope;
import org.springframework.stereotype.Component;
import org.springframework.test.context.ContextConfiguration;
import org.springframework.test.context.testng.
AbstractTestNGSpringContextTests;
import org.testng.annotations.DataProvider;
import org.testng.annotations.Test;
```

```java
import java.util.UUID;

import static org.testng.Assert.*;

@Component
@Scope(ConfigurableBeanFactory.SCOPE_SINGLETON)
class FifthObject extends HasData {
}

@Component
@Scope(ConfigurableBeanFactory.SCOPE_PROTOTYPE)
class SixthObject extends HasData {
}

@ContextConfiguration("/annotated.xml")
public class TestLifecycle05 extends AbstractTestNGSpringContextTests {
    @Autowired
    ApplicationContext context;

    @DataProvider
    Object[][] getReferences() {
        return new Object[][]{
                {FifthObject.class, true},
                {SixthObject.class, false}
        };
    }

    @Test(dataProvider = "getReferences")
    public void testReferenceTypes(Class<HasData> clazz, boolean singleton) {
        HasData o1 = context.getBean(clazz);

        String defaultValue = o1.getDatum();
        o1.setDatum(UUID.randomUUID().toString());

        HasData o2 = context.getBean(clazz);
        if (singleton) {
            assertSame(o1, o2);
            assertEquals(o1, o2);
            assertNotEquals(defaultValue, o2.getDatum());
```

```
    } else {
        assertNotSame(o1, o2);
        assertNotEquals(o1, o2);
        assertEquals(defaultValue, o2.getDatum());
    }
  }
}
```

4.2.2 Constructors with Annotated Classes

Here's where things diverge from the XML configuration: annotated classes will be invoked with as much information as is available, and the objects will be constructed in an order that satisfies dependencies as much as possible. This mirrors things we've seen in Chapter 3; if a constructor has a parameter marked with `@Autowired`, Spring will look for a class that matches the parameter's type and qualifier, if any, and inject it into the constructor call. As such, there's not really anything to show here that wouldn't mirror what we've already seen in Chapter 3 (see 3.3 for a full discussion and example of constructor injection with annotations).

4.2.3 Calling Methods After Construction and Before Destruction

Here's where things get interesting. Instead of naming methods for `init-method` and `destroy-method`, we have two annotations available to us through the `javax.annotation-api` artifact, imported from our `build.gradle` file: `@PostConstruct` and `@PreDestroy`. Methods marked with these annotations will be called at the appropriate spots in the object's and context's lifecycle, as we can see in Listing 4-15.

Listing 4-15. `chapter4/src/test/java/com/bsg5/chapter4/TestLifeCycle06.java`

```
package com.bsg5.chapter4;

import org.springframework.beans.factory.annotation.Autowired;
import org.springframework.context.ConfigurableApplicationContext;
import org.springframework.stereotype.Component;
import org.springframework.test.context.ContextConfiguration;
```

```java
import org.springframework.test.context.testng.AbstractTestNGSpringContext
Tests;
import org.testng.annotations.Test;

import javax.annotation.PostConstruct;
import javax.annotation.PreDestroy;

import static org.testng.Assert.*;

@Component
class SeventhObject extends HasData {
    static Object semaphore = null;

    @PostConstruct
    public void initialize() throws Exception {
        semaphore = new Object();
    }

    @PreDestroy
    public void dispose() throws Exception {
        semaphore = null;
    }
}

@ContextConfiguration("/annotated-06.xml")
public class TestLifecycle06 extends AbstractTestNGSpringContextTests {
    @Autowired
    ConfigurableApplicationContext context;

    @Test
    public void testInitDestroyMethods() {
        EighthObject o1 = context.getBean(EighthObject.class);
        assertNotNull(EighthObject.semaphore);
        assertEquals(o1.getDatum(), "default");
        context.close();
        assertNull(EighthObject.semaphore);
    }

}
```

Careful readers will notice the use of `annotated-06.xml` as the configuration file. This file is identical to `annotated.xml` – with the **only** difference being the name. This isn't something required by the test in and of itself, but if you run every test in this chapter in a single build (as with `gradle build` or `gradle test`), the `context.close()` will interfere with other tests' completions. Using a unique file name for this and for the next test (which uses `annotated-07.xml`) avoids this problem.[5]

Listing 4-16. Copying `annotated.xml` for other tests

```
cp chapter4/src/test/resources/annotated.xml \
  chapter4/src/test/resources/annotated-06.xml
cp chapter4/src/test/resources/annotated.xml \
  chapter4/src/test/resources/annotated-07.xml
```

We also still have the callback interfaces themselves to rely on, `InitializingBean` and `DisposableBean`. The class' annotated status changes nothing about these callbacks, as shown in yet another test (Listing 4-17).

Listing 4-17. `chapter4/src/test/java/com/bsg5/chapter4/TestLifeCycle07.java`

```
package com.bsg5.chapter4;

import org.springframework.beans.factory.DisposableBean;
import org.springframework.beans.factory.InitializingBean;
import org.springframework.beans.factory.annotation.Autowired;
import org.springframework.context.ConfigurableApplicationContext;
import org.springframework.stereotype.Component;
import org.springframework.test.context.ContextConfiguration;
import org.springframework.test.context.testng.
AbstractTestNGSpringContextTests;
import org.testng.annotations.Test;

import static org.testng.Assert.*;
```

---

[5]This assumes you're not using source code downloaded from `https://apress.com` for this book; if you're using the source code from the book's web site, all of these files will obviously be in the right places already.

```
@Component
class EighthObject extends HasData
        implements InitializingBean, DisposableBean {
    static Object semaphore = null;

    @Override
    public void afterPropertiesSet() throws Exception {
        semaphore = new Object();
    }

    @Override
    public void destroy() throws Exception {
        semaphore = null;
    }
}

@ContextConfiguration(locations = "/annotated-07.xml")
public class TestLifecycle07 extends AbstractTestNGSpringContextTests {
    @Autowired
    ConfigurableApplicationContext context;
    @Test
    public void testLifecycleMethods() {
        EighthObject o1 = context.getBean(EighthObject.class);
        assertNotNull(EighthObject.semaphore);
        assertEquals(o1.getDatum(), "default");
        context.close();
        assertNull(EighthObject.semaphore);
    }
}
```

4.3 Lifecycle with Java Configuration

Annotated beans are all well and good, but annotating the beans makes their configuration *global* – if you set an annotated bean's name, it's set for every instance of that class in the current classpath; compare that to XML, where you can have multiple beans of the same class, with different names and different property values.

We've demonstrated how to set beans to different scopes with XML and annotations; there's also the ability to use a configuration class as well, and scope applies here just like it does elsewhere. The advantage of a configuration class is that you can have multiple configuration classes present on the classpath at any time, which gives you the power and cleanliness of the annotated approach, with the flexibility of the XML approach.

Let's take one more look at a test. This one will create another object type extending HasData – this time, named NinthObject – but the configuration will be stored in a local class called Config08. In it, there are two methods declared, foo() and bar(), and these methods are both marked with @Bean – which means that foo() will describe how to create a bean named foo, and bar() will describe how to name a bean named bar. We could, of course, provide annotation directives to rename the beans instead of using the method names, but that's something we've already seen in Chapter 3.

Just as with our annotation example, we can add @Scope("prototype") to our methods, which tells Spring the appropriate scope to use for beans with that name.

We're also changing the @ContextConfiguration for the test class, to refer to Config08.class instead of a named configuration file. Past that, though, everything looks similar (and acts the same) as what we saw in TestLifecycle05.java – we have a data provider that tells the test whether the class should be a singleton or not and validates the instance references and instance data appropriately.

Listing 4-18 shows the test source.

Listing 4-18. chapter4/src/test/java/com/bsg5/chapter4/TestLifeCycle07. java

```
package com.bsg5.chapter4;

import org.springframework.beans.factory.DisposableBean;
import org.springframework.beans.factory.InitializingBean;
import org.springframework.beans.factory.annotation.Autowired;
import org.springframework.context.ConfigurableApplicationContext;
import org.springframework.stereotype.Component;
import org.springframework.test.context.ContextConfiguration;
import org.springframework.test.context.testng.
AbstractTestNGSpringContextTests;
import org.testng.annotations.Test;
```

```java
import static org.testng.Assert.*;

@Component
class EighthObject extends HasData
        implements InitializingBean, DisposableBean {
    static Object semaphore = null;

    @Override
    public void afterPropertiesSet() throws Exception {
        semaphore = new Object();
    }

    @Override
    public void destroy() throws Exception {
        semaphore = null;
    }
}

@ContextConfiguration(locations = "/annotated-07.xml")
public class TestLifecycle07 extends AbstractTestNGSpringContextTests {
    @Autowired
    ConfigurableApplicationContext context;

    @Test
    public void testLifecycleMethods() {
        EighthObject o1 = context.getBean(EighthObject.class);
        assertNotNull(EighthObject.semaphore);
        assertEquals(o1.getDatum(), "default");
        context.close();
        assertNull(EighthObject.semaphore);
    }
}
```

4.4 Additional Scopes

Spring, being a maze of twisty passages, all alike, naturally adds more to scopes (the `prototype` and `singleton` scopes) than this chapter discusses – mostly because the additional scopes exist in context of Spring Web, covered in Chapter 6. The rules for scoping don't change, but the names and reachability do; a component can be marked such that it exists as a singleton in the context of a single HTTP request, for example, or in the context of a user session. These scopes will be explored in more detail in the appropriate chapter (which is, as mentioned, Chapter 6). Chapter 5 introduces the servlet API and a simple way of accessing a Spring context from HTTP endpoints, but that method is too simple to provide the full capability of Spring.

4.5 Next Steps

In Chapter 5, we're going to switch gears and talk about integrating Spring with Jakarta EE. Spring has been a driving force in the enterprise environment space since its early days, and we'll introduce some of the terminology and APIs, as well as a fairly archaic and simple approach to integrating Spring, in preparation for something far more useful in Chapter 6.

CHAPTER 5

Spring and Jakarta EE

Spring can certainly be used in a standalone environment, but the most common environment for Spring has historically been in an enterprise environment, powering web applications and backend services in a managed server. This chapter will demonstrate some aspects of integration in a Jakarta EE container (formerly known as Java EE, or J2EE, or maybe even just "Tomcat" depending on your level of exposure, currency, and experience).

This chapter also introduces submodules to our projects, as well as intermodule dependencies. We're going to create a `chapter5common` module (where we will store some classes that will be the same through the other modules), a `chapter5anno` module (which will use annotation-based configuration), and a `chapter5xml` module (which will use, of all things, XML for configuration). We're not going to use a Java configuration because we wouldn't learn anything new through the process. (We'll be shifting to using Java-based configurations heavily once we hit Chapter 6, though.)

5.1 Introduction to Jakarta EE

Jakarta EE is a set of specifications covering most, if not all, enterprise architectural patterns for applications written on the Java platform. For example, if you have a request/response interaction model for your application, there's a specification that covers it – the Servlet specification. If you have a message-oriented architecture, there's the Java Message Service. If you need a remote invocation architecture, Jakarta EE has a few specifications for that, too, starting with the Enterprise Java Bean specification. There's even a Context and Dependency Injection (CDI) specification that looks an awful lot like Spring does.

121

© Joseph B. Ottinger and Andrew Lombardi 2019
J. B. Ottinger and A. Lombardi, *Beginning Spring 5*, https://doi.org/10.1007/978-1-4842-4486-9_5

There are, of course, reference implementations for the specifications. GlassFish (`https://javaee.github.io/glassfish/`) is the current reference implementation for the Servlet and the Java Message Service specifications, for example; Weld (`http://weld.cdi-spec.org/`) is the reference implementation for CDI, even though it's very arguable that Spring inspired the specification in the first place.

Jakarta EE, incidentally, is a fairly recent name for what used to be called Java Enterprise Edition ("JavaEE") and, before being known as "Java EE," was "Java 2, Enterprise Edition," or "J2EE." In 2018, Java EE was released by Oracle to the Eclipse Foundation to be managed by the open source community, which renamed it "Jakarta EE" because of copyright issues around the name "Java." It's yet more branding confusion around Java – which has suffered from branding, naming, and version confusion from Day Paisley (or, as humans refer to it, "day one"), but hopefully the management of Jakarta EE by an open source community will help stabilize names and versions for the future.[1]

What this chapter will do is show you some basics around the most commonly used enterprise specification, the Servlet specification, using arguably the most common servlet container, Apache Tomcat. Be warned: Jakarta EE isn't simple. Jakarta EE implementations run as nested applications inside of other applications, with consequences to classpaths and resource availability, and even *writing* about it can be confusing because there are so many different and successful approaches to solving each given problem.

This chapter is actually going to serve mostly to introduce concepts that future chapters will rely on, and illustrate a fairly archaic way of integrating Spring into Jakarta EE – mostly serving as an easy on-ramp to more complex and complete solutions.

5.1.1 The Servlet API

As previously stated, the servlet API is designed for services that follow a request/response lifecycle: a request comes in, and a response goes out. Ultimately, requests map to a single class that implements a known interface, `javax.servlet.Servlet`, but servlets can chain (or `forward`) calls to other servlets. The API also defines filters that can execute before or after servlet invocation as well as listeners that can watch for events emitted by the container (like application startup or shutdown).

---

[1]Java has always had confusion around names and versions: for example, there used to be a release called J2SE 4, which was "Java 2, Standard Edition," version *1.4*. The 1.4 edition was also edition 4... and most people without a lot of exposure to Java spent a lot of time wondering what versions referred to what components. This was something that plagued Sun, the company that created Java, and has never really gone away.

Servlet containers establish network listeners on specific ports; how this is done is very dependent on the servlet container in question. They typically use HTTP – the HyperText Transfer Protocol, one version of which can be found at `https://tools.ietf.org/html/rfc2616` – but they don't *have* to.

A servlet has a `service()` method along with a servlet context[2] and some lifecycle methods (including `init()` and `destroy()`). The `service()` method receives `ServletRequest` and `ServletResponse` references, both of which are interfaces themselves. The `ServletRequest` interface references information about the request (the protocol, attributes of the request, parameters, etc.), and the `ServletResponse` provides mechanisms by which a servlet can build a response matching the request.

Filters can be defined in a manner similar to servlets; there's a general `javax.servlet.Filter` interface with a single primary entry point (called `doFilter()`, of all things, although `Filter` has other methods associated with filter lifecycles); this method receives the request and response objects created by the servlet container, as well as a `FilterChain` reference. The filter can do almost anything it wants with the request and response, although usually filters will either set up data for delegated services or decorate responses.

Again, most servlets work with HTTP. As a protocol, HTTP maps Uniform Resource Locators – URLs – to data. HTTP also specifies verbs in relation to these URLs, such as `GET`, `POST`, `DELETE`, and `HEAD`. (There are others; check the specification[3] for the full list.)

Each HTTP verb has implicit semantic meanings.

Roy T. Fielding wrote a dissertation back in 2000 called *Architectural Styles and the Design of Network-based Software Architectures*. You can find it at `www.ics.uci.edu/~fielding/pubs/dissertation/top.htm`; it describes an architectural approach called "REST," for "Representational State Transfer." REST

---

[2]Wait, there's the word "context" again. Spring application contexts aren't quite the same as Jakarta EE application contexts, but they're similar; they just don't have the same roles at all. Remember, we warned you that this could get interesting.

[3]There are multiple HTTP specifications, because HTTP can do a lot and in a lot of different ways. A useful reference for the "basic HTTP specification" as everyone thinks of it is HTTP 1.1: see `https://tools.ietf.org/html/rfc2616` – but note that that's *definitely* not the final word on HTTP.

is a *big deal* in HTTP-based applications; it took some of the implications of the HTTP protocol and formalized them. If you **really** want to know how to use the HTTP verbs and how URLs work on the modern Web, check out REST – which we'll be using to create our application services in Chapters 6 and 7.

- GET is a request for a resource whose location is known, and URLs used with GET are traditionally able to be bookmarked. This is by far the most common type of HTTP request.

- POST is a request to store data into a known location (although how this location is determined depends on the implementation).

- PUT is another type of storage request, although where POST means "store," PUT implies "store or update if the object already exists."

- HEAD means to return data **about** the resource without returning the resource itself; this can be used to determine if a resource has been updated, for example.

- DELETE requests that a resource referred to by the URL is removed somehow.

One usually speaks of the verbs in context of the URL itself; thus, one might say to issue a GET `http://localhost/foo/bar` – or, in the context of a specific host already, you might say to simply GET `/foo/bar`.

In `HttpServlet`, the `service()` method is overridden to dispatch the request type to methods specifically named for each verb, and with parameter types that cater to HTTP[4]; thus, GET in HTTP is handled by the `doGet()` method, POST in HTTP is handled by the `doPost()` method, and so forth and so on.

It's useful to understand how Servlets work and what they are actually doing, in order to make future endpoints easier to conceptualize. We're eventually going to leverage resource handlers provided by Spring itself, and those handlers will dispatch requests into methods of our choosing, with arguments parsed by the framework and not manually as we'll be doing in this chapter.

---

[4]Servlet has a `service(ServletRequest, ServletResponse)`; `HttpServlet` overrides this method to delegate to a `service(HttpServletRequest, HttpServletResponse)` method, which – if not overridden itself – will delegate to `doGet()`, `doPost()`, and so forth.

5.1.2 Modern Web Application Design Principles

It used to be that web applications were built to be monolithic, or "complete": they would include all static resources necessary for server-side rendering of content, for example. This hasn't been the preferred practice for quite some time now, with the use of rich clients being very much the norm. A web application will refer to Javascript libraries like JQuery or Vue.js that request resources in JSON or XML[5] and render that content appropriately.

There's nothing preventing coders from using the older, monolithic approach, and there's nothing inherently wrong with it, although it's difficult to say whether there are any actual advantages to rendering a full page instead of sending data client-side to be rendered on demand. The server-side rendering means that it's nicer on lower-powered clients, as long as they have bandwidth to spare; the client-side rendering is better on bandwidth but uses more CPU power on the browser's machine. (In practice, users have idle CPU cycles to use for client-side rendering, and a busy server is a more finite resource, so this approach makes a lot of cost-effective sense, although some applications' needs may vary.)

For the purposes of this book, we're going to use the modern approach, because it allows us to focus on the server-side technologies in use, rather than how rich clients work. We'll use simple command line tools to issue HTTP requests where necessary, instead of using Javascript embedded in a web page.

5.2 Module Structure

We're going to create three modules in this chapter: chapter5common, chapter5anno, and chapter5xml. We do this because Gradle wants to address each module by name, and nesting modules tends to make this process more obscure. With a simpler, flatter structure, Gradle is able to build a graph of what needs to run more easily and quickly.

The suggestion of a flat structure for Gradle comes courtesy of James Nelson (https://github.com/jamesxnelson), after some headaches were incurred thanks to trying to replicate how Maven would have built the project.

---

[5]JSON ("JavaScript Object Notation") and XML are both structured data formats, with XML being a formal data format and JSON being far more convenient for both humans and, well, Javascript to read.

5.2.1 The Common Module

Our first module will be a simple common module. It will contain two servlets, matching services that we'll want in our music gateway application.[6]

To create our directory structure, we need to create chapter5common/src/main/java/com/bsg5/chapter5.

Listing 5-1. Creating the directory structure with POSIX

```
mkdir -p chapter5common/src/main/java/com/bsg5/chapter5
```

We'll also want a build.gradle.

Listing 5-2. chapter5common/build.gradle

```
dependencies {
    compileOnly 'javax.servlet:javax.servlet-api:4.0.1'

    compile "org.springframework:spring-core:$springFrameworkVersion"
    compile "org.springframework:spring-context:$springFrameworkVersion"
    compile "com.fasterxml.jackson.core:jackson-databind:$jacksonVersion"

    compile project(':chapter3')
}
```

This is all fairly straightforward, although we're adding a resource for the servlet API, set to compileOnly, which means that it's available for the compiler (we can compile using classes from the servlet API, which is rather important when compiling servlets), but it's not a transitive dependency. It *shouldn't* be a transitive dependency, remember; servlets run in a container like Tomcat, which will have its own copy of the servlet API, so our application should actually make sure that it has no dependency that would duplicate what the container would provide.

---

[6]They will not, however, survive this chapter. They're written with manual servlet processes in mind, which is what programmers used to have to do back before Facebook was a thing. Spring has a better way; we'll see what that is in Chapter 6. In the meantime, these servlets will help us validate what we're learning in this chapter. With that said, we're going to be writing equivalents over and over again.

We also have a transitive dependency on the `chapter3` module, with `compile project(':chapter3')`, meaning that projects that use our `common` module will also need to include `chapter3`. The transitive dependency means that a dependency on `chapter5common` carries with it another dependency on `chapter3` – as well as dependencies on anything else that `chapter5common` or `chapter3` depends on.[7] We are going to use one of the `MusicService` implementations from Chapter 3 in some of our examples here, because we don't want to have to rebuild a working example when we have fully working interfaces and implementations already written.

This way, we can have an intermodule dependency without having to copy our module outputs into a known repository.

Now it's time to see our servlets. Both of them will have the exact same structure:

1. Grab a Spring application context from the servlet context.

2. Get a `MusicService` from the Spring application context.

3. Create a `Gson` reference to prepare to generate JSON output.

4. Get servlet parameters from the `HttpServletRequest`.

5. Validate parameters.

6. Generate output from the `MusicService`, using Gson's `toJson()` method to convert to JSON.

The first servlet is the `VoteForSongServlet`. We won't get a chance to see this in action until we finish either the `anno` or `xml` modules, but note the `@WebServlet(urlPatterns="/vote")`, which tells us part of the URL this servlet will be attached to. (The other parts of the URL are the protocol, host, the port the server is listening on, and the application name itself – so when we run the `anno` project, by default, this servlet will be available at `http://localhost:8080/anno/vote`.)

---

[7]The management of transitive dependencies is one of the things that make build tools in Java like Maven or Gradle so *absolutely necessary*. Without transitive dependencies, programmers would have to chase down the entire dependency tree for every library they used. The transitive dependency mechanism built into the tools is far, far, far better.

Listing 5-3. chapter5common/src/main/java/com/bsg5/chapter5/
VoteForSongServlet.java

```java
package com.bsg5.chapter5;

import com.bsg5.chapter3.MusicService;
import com.fasterxml.jackson.databind.ObjectMapper;
import org.springframework.context.ApplicationContext;

import javax.servlet.annotation.WebServlet;
import javax.servlet.http.HttpServlet;
import javax.servlet.http.HttpServletRequest;
import javax.servlet.http.HttpServletResponse;
import java.io.IOException;

@WebServlet(urlPatterns = "/vote")
public class VoteForSongServlet extends HttpServlet {
  @Override
    public void doGet(HttpServletRequest req, HttpServletResponse resp)
            throws IOException {
        ApplicationContext context = (ApplicationContext) req
                .getServletContext()
                .getAttribute("context");
        MusicService service = context.getBean(MusicService.class);
        ObjectMapper mapper = new ObjectMapper();

        String artist = req.getParameter("artist");
        String song = req.getParameter("song");

        if (artist == null || song == null) {
            log("Missing data in request: requires artist and song
            parameters");
            resp.setStatus(500);
        } else {
            log("Voting for artist " + artist + ", song " + song);
            service.voteForSong(artist, song);
```

```
                resp.setStatus(200);
                resp.getWriter().println(
                        mapper.writeValueAsString(service.getSong(artist, song))
                );
            }
        }
}
```

Note how we get the ApplicationContext. A ServletRequest has a ServletContext associated with it by the container; we're going to store a reference to an ApplicationContext as an attribute into the ServletContext. The two servlets we're showing here are going to grab the Spring context from the Servlet context.

Our next servlet – the GetSongsForArtistServlet – follows the exact same pattern.

Listing 5-4. chapter5common/src/main/java/com/bsg5/chapter5/ GetSongsForArtistServlet.java

```java
package com.bsg5.chapter5;

import com.bsg5.chapter3.MusicService;
import com.bsg5.chapter3.model.Song;
import com.fasterxml.jackson.databind.ObjectMapper;
import org.springframework.context.ApplicationContext;

import javax.servlet.annotation.WebServlet;
import javax.servlet.http.HttpServlet;
import javax.servlet.http.HttpServletRequest;
import javax.servlet.http.HttpServletResponse;
import java.io.IOException;
import java.util.List;

@WebServlet(urlPatterns = "/songs")
public class GetSongsForArtistServlet extends HttpServlet {
  @Override
    public void doGet(HttpServletRequest req, HttpServletResponse resp)
            throws IOException {
        ApplicationContext context = (ApplicationContext) req
                .getServletContext()
                .getAttribute("context");
```

```
MusicService service = context.getBean(MusicService.class);
ObjectMapper mapper = new ObjectMapper();

String artist = req.getParameter("artist");

if (artist == null ) {
    log("Missing data in request: requires artist parameter");
    resp.setStatus(500);
} else {
    List<Song> data=service.getSongsForArtist(artist);

    resp.setStatus(200);
    resp.getWriter().println(
            mapper.writeValueAsString(data)
    );
}
    }
}
```

Fascinating stuff, and archaic, but it's necessary in order to save ourselves from copying source files back and forth. It's time we looked at an actual web application, first with a non-Spring-related "Hello, World" servlet, and then we'll see how we can create a Spring context for use by our common module's servlets.

5.2.2 The Annotation-Based Web Application

Let's see how we can do two things: one, build a working web application, and two, use a Spring context that programmatically scans packages for Spring-annotated classes, for use by our servlets. This application is going to be called anno, not because we're fond of Latin words for periods of time, but because it's much shorter to type than "annotation" or other variants that might be more descriptive.

Let's write our "hello world" servlet first, because it allows us to get all of our pieces in place to integrate Spring for our second and third servlets.

Gradle has plugins that can conveniently build artifacts designed for web containers, called "web archives," or – more colloquially – "wars."[8] It **also** has a convenient plugin to run a web application inside a container, which we'll see in a few paragraphs.

First, we need to create the anno directory itself.

Listing 5-5. Creating the directory structure with POSIX

```
mkdir -p chapter5anno/src/main/java/com/bsg5/chapter5
mkdir -p chapter5anno/src/main/webapp/WEB-INF/templates/jtwig
```

The source layout is nearly identical to our other projects' source layout, with one additional directory: src/main/webapp, which contains static resources that get processed directly by the container: stylesheets, images, static files, configuration files for the container, and such. (This is differentiated from src/main/resources in that things in src/main/resources get located in the artifact's **classpath**.) In our application's case, we know we have a template that we want in the WEB-INF directory (which our "hello world" servlet will use), so we can go ahead and create that structure.

Our build.gradle is where things start to get interesting. Note the addition of the extra things in the plugins section, and note also the additional dependencies:

- The servlet API itself, as in the common module.

- See also spring-web for web application–specific bits of Spring.

- A templating library, Jtwig.[9]

- A dependency on the code from Chapter 3 (compile project(':chapter5common')) which we'll use to do the actual work in this chapter.

- Lastly, the org.gretty plugin, which gives Gradle a convenient way to run Tomcat with our application deployed in it.

---

[8]So now, if anyone ever asks you what war is good for, you can tell them with a straight face that wars are good for deploying web applications built in Java. Everyone wins, but be careful: this might get a cup of coffee thrown at you.

[9]Jtwig, found at https://Jtwig.org/, bills itself as a "modern template engine for Java." For our purposes, it's handy because it's simple to bootstrap. As our chapter continues and we build services rather than a user interface, Jtwig will become less important for us.

Listing 5-6. `chapter5anno/build.gradle`

```
plugins {
    id 'war'
    id 'org.gretty' version '2.2.0'
}

dependencies {
    compileOnly 'javax.servlet:javax.servlet-api:4.0.1'
    compile "org.springframework:spring-web:$springFrameworkVersion"
    compile 'org.jtwig:jtwig-web:5.87.0.RELEASE'

    compile project(':chapter5common')
}
```

Our First Standalone Working Servlet

Now it's time for us to create our first *working* Servlet[10] – an endpoint that will accept a request from a web browser and generate a response for it. It's not very long, but it shows us how to accept a GET request (again, the most common request type) from a browser and how to render output via Jtwig (a skill that's useful to have, but not one that's horrendously useful for this chapter).

Listing 5-7. `chapter5anno/src/main/java/com/bsg5/chapter5/ FirstHelloServlet.java`

```
package com.bsg5.chapter5;

import org.jtwig.web.servlet.JtwigRenderer;

import javax.servlet.ServletException;
import javax.servlet.annotation.WebServlet;
import javax.servlet.http.HttpServlet;
import javax.servlet.http.HttpServletRequest;
```

---

[10]We've already shown two Servlets, but they don't run properly – because we haven't shown how to populate the Servlet context with a Spring context yet. The Servlet here is a "hello, world" servlet, something to make sure our project is working properly. Once we know that we're able to run a servlet container and interact with it, we'll have validated our process and we won't need to go back over it – only replicate it.

```java
import javax.servlet.http.HttpServletResponse;
import java.io.IOException;

@WebServlet(urlPatterns = "/hello1")
public class FirstHelloServlet extends HttpServlet {
    /**
     *
     */
    private static final long serialVersionUID = -4427011101374936594L;
    private final JtwigRenderer renderer = JtwigRenderer.defaultRenderer();

    @Override
    protected void doGet(HttpServletRequest request, HttpServletResponse
    response)
            throws ServletException, IOException {
        renderer.dispatcherFor("/WEB-INF/templates/jtwig/hello.jtwig.html")
                .with("name", "world")
                .render(request, response);
    }
}
```

In this servlet – identified with an annotation and available at a relative URL path of /hello1 – we have a lot of boilerplate to handle imports, and we also declare a JtwigRenderer instance, which is our handy entry point into Jtwig. We also have a doGet() method – which handles GET requests over HTTP – which does nothing more than render a Jtwig template (held in "/WEB-INF/templates/Jtwig/hello.Jtwig.html", shown in Listing 5-8) with a variable name that has a static value of "world". As promised, let's take a look at our Jtwig template.

Listing 5-8. chapter5anno/src/main/webapp/WEB-INF/templates/Jtwig/ hello.Jtwig.html

```html
<!DOCTYPE html>
<html>
<head>
    <title>Hello, {{ name }}</title>
</head>
```

```
<body>
<p>
    Hello, {{ name }}
</p>
</body>
</html>
```

Without going too far into too much detail (see the Jtwig web site), this template is simply an HTML5 document, with placeholders for a value called name. The renderer (the JtwigRenderer, of course) will replace {{ name }} with the value of name passed into the render() method, if any.

All this is well and good, but it's a little bit abstract: how do we *run* it? How can we get our Servlet to actually achingly and finally greet the world, which surely has been waiting with bated breath?[11]

We do it with Gradle and the aforementioned gretty plugin, of course, by executing the following command in the top-level project directory, the one that contains chapter3 and chapter5.

Listing 5-9. Starting the servlet container

```
$ gradle :chapter5anno:tomcatStartWar
```

After some churning to download the appropriate resources and compile our servlet, Gradle informs us that – among other things – Tomcat is running on port 8080 and our code is available at http://localhost:8080/chapter5anno.

Listing 5-10. Some of the log output from the servlet container

```
INFO: Starting ProtocolHandler ["http-nio-8080"]
20:11:56 INFO  Tomcat 8.0.51 started and listening on port 8080
20:11:56 INFO  chapter5 runs at:
20:11:56 INFO  http://localhost:8080/chapter5anno
```

If you recall the @WebServlet annotation we used on FirstHelloServlet, you'll remember that we have a relative URL path of /hello1. This is added to the web application's root URL – which is, as shown, http://localhost:8080/chapter5anno – giving our servlet

---

[11]It's "bated" breath and not "baited," no matter how much your authors wanted to seem as if they'd been eating fish.

an endpoint of `http://localhost:8080/chapter5anno/hello1`. If we open up a web browser and go to that location, we will be showered with glory and praise as our browser window triumphantly displays `Hello, world` and all of our dreams come true.

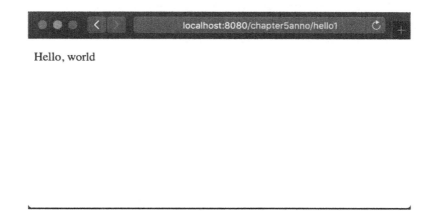

We can also test with a command line application, `curl`,[12] which we'll be doing for our other servlets.

Listing 5-11. The output from a successful HTTP request

```
$ curl http://localhost:8080/chapter5anno/hello1
<?doctype html5?>
<html>
<head>
    <title>Hello, world</title>
</head>
<body>
<p>
    Hello, world
</p>
</body>
</html>

$
```

---

[12]Curl can be found at `https://curl.haxx.se/` – if it's not already installed on your OS, convenient downloads can be found at that site.

It's exciting stuff, but as with other "hello, world" mechanisms, it mostly makes sure all of the plumbing is in place so that we can start working on more interesting bits.

Adding a Spring Context for Our Servlets

There are a few ways to use Spring in servlets: we could use a Spring module like Spring Web (which has a servlet that serves as a dispatcher to service objects written with Spring in mind,[13] and which we're actually including as a dependency here) or Spring Boot (which actually has its own servlet engine embedded), or we could have a web application instantiate a Spring context and access it as a resource from within traditional servlets. Most Spring experts would probably lean toward Spring Boot, with Boot's trivial development and deployment model, but Spring Boot is a subject for Chapter 7, not Chapter 5, and Spring Web is a subject for later chapters (Chapter 6) as well... which means we get to get our feet wet with more basic approaches.

When we look at Spring Web and Spring Boot (again, Chapters 6 and 7, respectively), we'll find simpler ways to accomplish what we'll see here – but this chapter will give us insight into what's happening behind the scenes in the later chapters, too.

So now that we've talked about this being a "basic approach," and so forth – what **is** the approach?

We're going to add a `ServletContextListener` to our two web applications, and in this `ServletContextListener` we'll instantiate a Spring `WebApplicationContext` and store it in the application scope for the entire web application. When we need resources from the Spring context, we'll grab them from the `ServletContext` – somewhat like the traditional JNDI model in Jakarta EE, as we saw in our servlets in the `common` module. (When we look at Spring Web and Spring Boot, we'll see easy ways to autowire dependencies.)

Let's look at the `ServletContextListener`, which we're going to name `AnnotationContextListener`.

Listing 5-12. `chapter5anno/src/main/java/com/bsg5/chapter5/`
`AnnotationContextListener.java`

```
package com.bsg5.chapter5;

import org.springframework.context.ApplicationContext;
```

---

[13]We'll be introducing `@Controller` and other such annotations in Chapter 6.

```
import org.springframework.web.context.
        support.AnnotationConfigWebApplicationContext;

import javax.servlet.ServletContextEvent;
import javax.servlet.ServletContextListener;
import javax.servlet.annotation.WebListener;

@WebListener
public class AnnotationContextListener implements ServletContextListener {
    @Override
    public void contextInitialized(ServletContextEvent event) {
        ApplicationContext context = buildAnnotationContext();
        event.getServletContext().setAttribute("context", context);
    }

    private ApplicationContext buildAnnotationContext() {
        AnnotationConfigWebApplicationContext context =
                new AnnotationConfigWebApplicationContext();
        context.scan("com.bsg5.chapter3.mem03");
        context.refresh();
        return context;
    }

    @Override
    public void contextDestroyed(ServletContextEvent sce) {
    }
}
```

For the most part, this class is very simple. It uses @WebListener on the entire class –
which tells the servlet container to use an instance of this class **where appropriate** –
and, given that it implements ServletContextListener, it will receive context-related
events. There are only two: contextInitialized (called when the application is started)
and contextDestroyed (called when the application is destroyed, if possible).

We don't care about the contextDestroyed() event – not in this case, at least – so we
simply provide an empty implementation to satisfy the interface's contract. However, we
want to create our Spring context in the contextInitialized event.

The `AnnotationConfigWebApplicationContext`, as its name implies, provides us the ability to scan for available components, as with the `<context:component-scan />` tag we've seen in earlier chapters. With this class, we can programmatically tell the Spring context which packages to scan for available annotations, which is exactly what the `buildAnnotationContext()` method does.[14] Once we have the `AnnotationConfigWebApplicationContext`, we need to tell it where to look to find candidate classes – and in this case, we're reusing one of the Chapter 3 memory-based implementations, so we provide it a single package name, `com.bsg5.chapter3.mem03`. This method actually accepts an array of package names, and it's a variadic function[15]; it just so happens that we only need to scan one package for our purposes here, but we could have provided a comma-delimited list of as many packages as we needed scanned.

Note that this isn't quite the same as a Java configuration. If we were using a Java configuration instead of building our configuration, we could have marked with it `@ComponentScan` – which would have done the same thing as we're doing here with `@AnnotationConfigWebApplicationContext` and `<context:component-scan />`. We'll see it used in later chapters, when we actually do switch over to using Java-based configuration.

It's usually wise to scan *exactly* what you need, rather than adding entire trees of packages. Scanning is fairly slow; you won't do it often (only on application startup), but it's still fairly heavy on the Java runtime. If you don't have a lot of classes you're actually interested in, consider programmatic configuration with a class annotated with `@Configuration` rather than scanning packages. We're scanning here mostly because it's a few less lines of code than the Java configuration, which requires a class with its own boilerplate.

However, simply telling the context where it **should** scan doesn't make it actually perform the scan. That's the role of `context.refresh()`. After we've done **that**, we get the `ServletContext` from the `ServletContextEvent` and store the Spring context into

---

[14]It actually scans entire package *trees* – so any packages that have the scanned packages as their roots will be scanned as well. We could also use the Java configuration approach, and not scan at all; see Chapter 3 for how to do this.

[15]This means that it takes a variable number of arguments. In the method declaration, this is often shown by using something like "String ... args", where `args` is actually a typed array.

the Servlet context as a named attribute[16]; we name it "context" for simplicity. Once we've done that, any executable code in the entire web application can grab the Spring context from the Servlet context, by name.

When we use the Spring context in this manner (with an explicit load of the Spring context into the servlet context), we don't get autowiring of Spring resources into our servlets. We get them from the Spring context instead. (The beans that are retrieved **from** the Spring context, however, will have autowiring in place – and the particular `MusicService` we use requires and demonstrates this.) Since we have full control over instance lifecycle (see Chapter 4), we have fine-grained control over what gets created, and when.

All that's incredibly useful[17]; we can now grab our `MusicService` from Spring, as shown in the servlets from the `common` module, but how do we demonstrate it?

By doing the same thing we did with our "hello, world" servlet, of course.

Our `anno` application includes the `common` module, as we've shown (and mentioned multiple times, in case readers weren't paying attention). When we include the `common` module, those servlets are automatically set to respond to the URL patterns specified by the `@WebServlet` annotation – which means `/vote` and `/songs`. That means when we run our `anno` application with `tomcatStartWar`, those servlets are already active – although they aren't going to work correctly unless we have our `ServletContextListener` in place.

We can test this by using a command line application such as `curl`. After starting the application, issue a curl command.

Listing 5-13. Testing the application manually

```
$ curl "http://localhost:8080/chapter5anno/vote?artist=Therapy+Zeppelin&
song=Medium"
{"name":"Medium","votes":1}
$ curl "http://localhost:8080/chapter5anno/vote?artist=Therapy+Zeppelin&
song=Medium"
{"name":"Medium","votes":2}
$ curl http://localhost:8080/chapter5anno/songs?artist=Therapy+Zeppelin
[{"name":"Medium","votes":2}]
```

---

[16]So many contexts!

[17]It's "incredibly useful," so to speak: Chapter 6 will show us how to get around pretty much **all** of this. But this is basically what's happening behind the scenes.

Wise readers might wonder why we're not testing this automatically (as part of the build process), as we've done elsewhere in the book. The answer is pretty simple: it's hard to do! Cranking up a compliant servlet container in a test is doable, but the best way to do it is with something like Arquillian (`https://arquillian.org/`) – which is unfortunately not trivial to explain. There's a ton of plumbing that goes into recreating the proper infrastructure, and it's largely outside the scope of this book. Plus, this form of building applications is, as already said multiple times, a bit archaic – our next chapter will use Spring Web, which not only makes our endpoints far easier to write, but it also makes them inherently *testable* without all of the effort we'd have to go through for *this* chapter's rather basic technique.

We promise, we're not trying to shortchange you, readers! We're actually just not wasting effort showing you a testing process you're not really going to need, but you *will* want to have a basic understanding of what the Servlet API is and how it works, in order to construct decent endpoints for your own applications. Check out the next chapter. It touches on all of this, and does it properly, and then in later chapters we do it *even better*.

5.2.3 The XML-Based Spring Context Application

Here, everything is **almost** identical to our annotation-based application – which was, of course, the whole point of creating the `common` module. We're not going to bother with the "hello world" servlet, so this web application will contain our `ServletContextListener` and an XML configuration file (along with the servlets we wrote in our `common` module). With our instructions for Gradle, we have four files.

First, the directory structure, starting from the `chapter5xml` directory itself.

Listing 5-14. Creating the directory structure with POSIX

```
mkdir -p chapter5xml/src/main/java/com/bsg5/chapter5
mkdir -p chapter5xml/src/main/webapp/WEB-INF
```

Our `build.gradle` is effectively identical to the `build.gradle` from the `chapter5anno` module, with the only real difference being that we no longer need Jtwig (as the "hello world" servlet was the only class where Jtwig was used).

Listing 5-15. `chapter5xml/build.gradle`

```
plugins {
    id 'war'
    id 'org.gretty' version '2.2.0'
}

dependencies {
    compileOnly 'javax.servlet:javax.servlet-api:4.0.1'
    compile "org.springframework:spring-web:$springFrameworkVersion"
    compile project(":chapter5common")
}
```

The `ServletContextListener` creates an `XmlWebApplicationContext` instead of an `AnnotationConfigWebApplicationContext`, which means we'll need to have an XML file in the application, but apart from that, everything should be very familiar.

Listing 5-16. `chapter5xml/src/main/java/com/bsg5/chapter5/` `XMLContextListener.java`

```java
package com.bsg5.chapter5;

import org.springframework.context.ApplicationContext;
import org.springframework.web.context.support.XmlWebApplicationContext;

import javax.servlet.ServletContext;
import javax.servlet.ServletContextEvent;
import javax.servlet.ServletContextListener;
import javax.servlet.annotation.WebListener;

@WebListener
public class XMLContextListener implements ServletContextListener {
    @Override
    public void contextInitialized(ServletContextEvent event) {
        ApplicationContext context =
                buildXmlContext(event.getServletContext());
        event.getServletContext().setAttribute("context", context);
    }
```

```
    private ApplicationContext buildXmlContext(ServletContext sc) {
        XmlWebApplicationContext context = new XmlWebApplicationContext();
        context.setServletContext(sc);
        context.refresh();
        return context;
    }

    @Override
    public void contextDestroyed(ServletContextEvent sce) {
    }
}
```

Note that when we build an XmlWebApplicationContext, we also set a reference to the current ServletContext. This is primarily used in different environments than the one we're creating; it's useful when Spring dispatches requests to resources itself, which we're not using here. When we get into Chapter 6, this sort of thing will happen behind the scenes and we won't have to worry about it, but here it's just making sure the Spring Context is set up as it expects.

And of course we need the configuration file itself.

Listing 5-17. chapter5xml/src/main/webapp/WEB-INF/applicationContext.xml

```xml
<?xml version="1.0" encoding="UTF-8"?>

<!-- chapter5/xml/src/main/webapp/WEB-INF/applicationContext.xml -->

<beans xmlns="http://www.springframework.org/schema/beans"
       xmlns:xsi="http://www.w3.org/2001/XMLSchema-instance"
       xmlns:context="http://www.springframework.org/schema/context"
       xsi:schemaLocation="http://www.springframework.org/schema/beans
         http://www.springframework.org/schema/beans/spring-beans.xsd
         http://www.springframework.org/schema/context
         http://www.springframework.org/schema/context/spring-context.xsd">

    <context:component-scan base-package="com.bsg5.chapter3.mem03" />

</beans>
```

This is a near-exact copy of one of the XML configurations from Chapter 3, just renamed to match the default location searched by XmlWebApplicationContext. (We can provide a resource to the context to read its configuration, but by default it searches the web application's local resources – in this case, /WEB-INF/aplicationContext.xml, as shown.)

If we run the xml module with Gradle, via gradle :chapter5:xml:tomcatStartWar, we can exercise the application in the exact same technique we used with the anno app, changing only the application name from anno to xml.

Listing 5-18. Testing the application manually

```
$ curl "http://localhost:8080/chapter5xml/vote?artist=Therapy+Zeppelin&
song=Medium"
{"name":"Medium","votes":1}
$ curl "http://localhost:8080/chapter5xml/vote?artist=Therapy+Zeppelin&
song=Medium"
{"name":"Medium","votes":2}
$ curl "http://localhost:8080/chapter5xml/songs?artist=Therapy+Zeppelin"
[{"name":"Medium","votes":2}]
```

Our excitement should know no boundaries! – but seriously, we've actually done a lot so far in this chapter. It just so happens that Spring provides easier ways to accomplish the same things, which we'll see in the next chapter.

5.3 Next Steps

In this chapter, we saw what goes on behind the curtains in a web application, with raw servlets, template rendering with Jtwig, and resource requisition from manually populated Spring contexts. We also got to see how submodules can be applied in Gradle. Chapter 6 will show us how to build a more fully featured band gateway application, by removing all of the manual invocations and conversions (and servlets) from our application, leading us to a more streamlined and modern web application development process, including automated testing.

CHAPTER 6

Spring Web

6.1 Introduction to Spring MVC

Spring Web is a framework that provides a Model View Controller (MVC) architecture to develop applications with Spring for the Web. In the previous chapter, we built out several servlets running within the Spring framework, but aside from the beans and other management aspects you get baked into Spring, we were still using regular servlets in the previous chapter. And as we saw in the previous chapter, nothing stops you from doing this; however as we'll hopefully be able to show, using this module will save you loads of time.

6.2 MVC

The web module of Spring organizes components using a paradigm known as MVC – an acronym that stands for Model View Controller. The architecture can be used to develop applications that are more flexible and loosely coupled than what we saw in the previous chapter. (We also get to stop managing the configuration so carefully.) We can easily separate the business logic and input and front-end logic into separate components and use Spring to wire them together.

In MVC, a **model** holds the data for our application which allows us to separate our business logic from how we deal with the data. In the Java world, this is a POJO or Plain Old Java Object which we're all pretty used to at creating many times daily.

The **view** is responsible for taking model data and showing it in some way to the front end. In this chapter we will show renderers for both HTML and JSON. With HTML we'll be focused on rendering templates using a more human-readable format, and with JSON we'll be showing the result of an API call.

© Joseph B. Ottinger and Andrew Lombardi 2019
J. B. Ottinger and A. Lombardi, *Beginning Spring 5*, https://doi.org/10.1007/978-1-4842-4486-9_6

The **controller** is used to interface with the user. In a web-based interaction, this consists of user requests, form submissions, and what view to show from a business logic perspective. It is also responsible for how the model gets passed around.

6.3 Hello, World with MVC

In this chapter we're going to keep the module structure really simple compared to what we did for chapter5. It will be a return to the infinitely simple structure we had prior, just like Java, simple, not verbose at all.[1]

First, we need to create our directory structure, starting in the overall project directory.

Listing 6-1. Creating the directory structure with POSIX

```
mkdir -p chapter6/src/main/java/com/bsg5/chapter6
mkdir -p chapter6/src/webapp/WEB-INF/templates
mkdir -p chapter6/src/test/java/com/bsg5/chapter6
```

As with previous chapters, we will need our Gradle configuration file, build. gradle. There's nothing too special about it other than the addition in dependencies of our spring-web, spring-webmvc, and the hamcrest library (http://hamcrest. org/JavaHamcrest/) which adds a more flexible assert_that functionality along with interchangeable matchers that make testing more flexible and extensible with error messages that make sense. We'll use the preceding code to help with testing our controllers. The rest has been dutifully copied from previous incarnations in chapter5 and earlier which gave us the ability to run a Jetty instance with a simple Gradle target.

Listing 6-2. chapter6/build.gradle

```
plugins {
    id 'war'
    id 'org.gretty' version '2.2.0'
}
```

---

[1] I'm laughing at writing this because Spring has offenders like the super simple, not-verbose-at-all SimpleBeanFactoryAwareAspectInstanceFactory, which, uh... yeah.

```
dependencies {
    compileOnly 'javax.servlet:javax.servlet-api:4.0.1'

    compile "org.springframework:spring-core:$springFrameworkVersion"
    compile "org.springframework:spring-context:$springFrameworkVersion"
    compile "org.springframework:spring-web:$springFrameworkVersion"
    compile "org.springframework:spring-test:$springFrameworkVersion"
    compile "org.springframework:spring-webmvc:$springFrameworkVersion"
    compile "org.jtwig:jtwig-web:5.87.0.RELEASE"
    compile "org.jtwig:jtwig-spring:5.87.0.RELEASE"
    compile "com.fasterxml.jackson.core:jackson-databind:$jacksonVersion"
    compile "com.fasterxml.jackson.core:jackson-annotations:$jacksonVersion"
    compile "ch.qos.logback:logback-classic:1.2.3"
    compile project(":chapter3")

    testCompile 'org.hamcrest:hamcrest-all:1.3'
}
```

In previous chapters we've gone into some depth on the XML configuration, so in this chapter and subsequent ones, we'll forego that and focus on annotations for all our instrumentation needs. Why you may ask? Plainly the Java-based configuration is much easier and more standard across the Java ecosystem, and we tend to like removing verbosity if it doesn't add anything of value. In Listing 6-3 we'll take a simple controller which will output a common tutorial phrase to the end user once the endpoint is hit.

Listing 6-3. chapter6/src/main/java/com/bsg5/chapter6/GreetingController.java

```
package com.bsg5.chapter6;

import org.springframework.http.HttpStatus;
import org.springframework.http.MediaType;
import org.springframework.http.ResponseEntity;
import org.springframework.stereotype.Controller;
import org.springframework.web.bind.annotation.GetMapping;
import org.springframework.web.bind.annotation.ResponseBody;

@Controller
```

```
public class GreetingController {

    @GetMapping(path = "/greeting", produces = {MediaType.TEXT_PLAIN_VALUE})
    @ResponseBody
    public ResponseEntity<String> greeting() {
        return new ResponseEntity<>("Hello, World!", HttpStatus.OK);
    }

}
```

There is a fair bit happening in the snippet that we haven't talked about, so let's unpack it. We've introduced a GET request mapping using the annotation @GetMapping. This annotation is a more specific form of the base @RequestMapping. We'll talk more about HTTP methods when we touch on REST, but suffice to say that there is an annotation for each HTTP method you'd like to map to your controllers. A String is a simple type and requires no conversion, and in more complex cases, Spring MVC will use Jackson to convert an entity to whatever type your method is expected to return. As we can see from our @GetMapping, it *produces* a type of text/plain. Our method returns a ResponseEntity of type String, which makes sense given that we're returning a simple plain text item. The simple return is one of Hello, World! with a status of OK or HTTP 200. Spring MVC will do a check on start to ensure you don't have any conflicting mappings.

It's always a good idea to ensure that your controller actually works and does the thing you expect, so let's create a test to validate our assumptions.

Listing 6-4. chapter6/src/test/java/com/bsg5/chapter6/ TestGreetingController.java

```
@Test
@WebAppConfiguration
@ContextConfiguration(classes = GatewayAppWebConfig.class)
public class TestGreetingController extends
AbstractTestNGSpringContextTests {

  @Autowired
  private WebApplicationContext wac;

  private MockMvc mockMvc;
```

```
@Test
public void greetingTest() throws Exception {
  this.mockMvc = MockMvcBuilders.webAppContextSetup(this.wac).build();
  this.mockMvc.perform(get("/greeting")
      .accept(MediaType.ALL))
      .andExpect(status().isOk())
;
  }
```

The preceding test is a fairly simple test ensuring that our controller is handling things that we expect it to. We are using the MockMvc class which fakes the HTTP call for the web layer so that we can keep this test quick, and we're purposefully not starting up a web container here as that will be covered more in Chapter 7 with the TestRestTemplate. With the test we can ensure the contract is being fulfilled and our code is doing what it's supposed to, which is exactly what you'd want to see in a test.

If you'd like to run the web server and test it manually (always a fine idea), you can run the command line to start tomcat with gradle :chapter6:tomcatStart, hit the endpoint http://localhost:8080/chapter6/greeting, and be greeted with a simple text string Hello, World!.

So far we've introduced a simple GET request. In the examples that follow, we will continue showing off portions of Spring MVC and follow REST as closely as we can in each. Given that this is the first time we're talking about REST in the book, it's probably appropriate for us to discuss some of the architectural concepts inherent in using this paradigm which we'll do in the next section.

6.3.1 REST Concepts

One of the guiding API design strategies of the last few decades has been REST, or Representational State Transfer.[2] It was developed by Roy T. Fielding in the late 1990s in parallel with the development of HTTP 1.1 and based on existing designs of the HTTP 1.0.

---

[2]You can find more info about REST at https://en.wikipedia.org/wiki/Representational_state_transfer. If you'd like to read Dr. Fielding's actual dissertation, it's online, too, at www.ics.uci.edu/~fielding/pubs/dissertation/top.htm- it can be fascinating reading if only for history's sake.

When comparing the SOAP protocol[3] to the architectural principles specified by REST, we see a larger focus on reducing overall complexity and discoverability by using the concepts baked into the HTTP protocol.

The following two things should be followed as a base implementation of a RESTful API. There are many others, but these are the most prevalent:

- A base URI, for example, `http://api.bandgateway.com/songs/` which specifies the collection (songs in this case), which you'll be operating under using the actions specified using HTTP methods.

- Use the HTTP methods appropriately, the most often used are `GET`, `POST`, `PUT`, and `DELETE`. Others like `PATCH`, `OPTIONS`, and `HEAD` are used less often but still important. In REST, they are used as actions operating on your collections or entities.

We're not suggesting that the other tenets of the REST architectural style aren't useful – they are. But they're also out of scope for **this** book.

The preceding tenets should get you a good portion of the way toward a less complicated API. Let's talk a bit about what we mean about using HTTP methods appropriately.

Using HTTP Methods Appropriately

They say there's no wrong way to eat a Reese's, and the same can be said of using HTTP methods. There is, however, a **prescribed** way of using the HTTP methods to follow the REST architectural style.

REST splits things into member resources and collection resources. It bills itself as a paradigm because it doesn't fit every possible API out there but does a very good job at representing most patterns you can think of. Later we'll expand on some of this, but if your API feels like it needs something a bit different, that's fine; it's not a perfect abstraction so focus on getting the job done rather than building out the perfect API. For the purposes of our simple API, we'll talk about a single level of both resources **and** collections, but just know that nesting is possible and simple enough to achieve

---

[3]SOAP stands for Simple Object Access Protocol and is a standardized way of exchanging information with XML; you can read more about it at `https://en.wikipedia.org/wiki/SOAP`. Unfortunately, it's named rather ironically: it's actually not that simple to use.

with Spring MVC. If you're dealing with a collection of resources, you'd be looking at a URL like `http://api.bandgateway.com/songs/`. For a member resource, we will specify an identifier of some kind so your URL structure will look more like `http://api.bandgateway.com/songs/42`.

Warning: Jargon ahead!

The list of HTTP verbs often refers to a concept of "idempotency." A call is "idempotent" when you can make multiple calls with the exact same data and produce the **same** result. Operations that are read-only – like GET – are idempotent by nature; for other verbs, it can get a little more complicated. If a call changes the application state but does so consistently, it's considered to be idempotent, like what would happen if you turned a light switch to "on" multiple times – it's just going to stay on. In reality, of course, it's a little more complicated.

Abstractions are nice, but not perfect. Back to our text!

- GET is used to retrieve a resource. A request of this nature has no side effects,[4] meaning that they are safe because the state of the resource is never changed.

- POST is used to create new resources and will use the collection resource URL structure. The primary differences with PUT are that it is not idempotent as multiple calls to POST will create new resources and it uses the collection resource URL structure. (It's not idempotent because each call will create new object state, and the new state will have its own identifiers, and so forth.)

- PUT is used primarily to update an existing resource in full. If the resource does not exist, the origin server must use the HTTP 201 (Created) response code, and if it is an update, a HTTP status code 200 if returning the entity, or an HTTP status code 204 if the choice is made to not return the entity.

---

[4]Side effects may include dizziness, nausea, headache, bloat, and abdominal pain. Or that could just be this writing.

- PUT requests are idempotent[5] which means that it will produce the same result if executed once or multiple times, which ensures repeated/retried calls to a PUT will not cause unintended effects (thus, idempotency.) In addition a PUT request is operated on an individual resource rather than the collection since it's intended to be an update in most cases.

- DELETE is used to remove a resource identified by the Request URI. As with PUT, a DELETE operation is idempotent which means repeatedly calling the DELETE API on that resource will not change the outcome but a second time will return a 404 assuming the delete was successful.

- OPTIONS is generally used for CORS requests.[6] A deeper look at CORS is beyond the scope of this book; it is a security-based mechanism implemented via HTTP headers that tells a browser to allow an application running at one origin to have permission to access selected resources from a different origin. A common vector of web-based attack is injecting malicious JavaScript code which may hit other domains you have desired access to. A best practice is to limit the scope of external code that is allowed to hit your API to an approved list of domains.

The preceding list is a good primer on useful methods with HTTP and REST so let's put them into action next with our first REST endpoint.

6.4 Developing Our First Endpoint with MVC

Now that we've explained a bit more about the concepts involved with REST, let's start building out some endpoints. The easiest to explain is a simple GET request. The following snippet will handle any requests going to a URI like `http://api.bandgateway.com/songs?artist=threadbare%20loaf`.

---

[5]Idempotency problems? Ask your doctor if PUT requests are right for you.
[6]For an explanation of CORS, you can visit `https://spring.io/understanding/cors` for more detail.

When Spring returns the query parameter, it will be URL decoded so
threadbare%20loaf will turn into threadbare loaf with an ASCII space in between.
With a URI there are specific allowed characters to allow easier transport. These
characters are defined by RFC 3986 Section 2 (https://tools.ietf.org/html/
rfc3986) and generally include US-ASCII alphanumeric characters along with
several reserved characters which have meaning in a URI string. If a character being
represented doesn't fall within the specification, they are percent-encoded with the
US-ASCII code representing that character.

Listing 6-5. chapter6/src/main/java/com/bsg5/chapter6/
GetSongsController.java

```java
package com.bsg5.chapter6;

import com.bsg5.chapter3.MusicService;
import com.bsg5.chapter3.model.Song;
import org.springframework.beans.factory.annotation.Autowired;
import org.springframework.http.HttpStatus;
import org.springframework.http.ResponseEntity;
import org.springframework.stereotype.Controller;
import org.springframework.web.bind.annotation.GetMapping;
import org.springframework.web.bind.annotation.PathVariable;
import org.springframework.web.bind.annotation.RequestParam;
import org.springframework.web.bind.annotation.ResponseBody;

import java.net.URLDecoder;
import java.nio.charset.StandardCharsets;
import java.util.List;

@Controller
public class GetSongsController {

    @Autowired

        return new ResponseEntity<>(song, HttpStatus.OK);
    }

    @GetMapping("/songs")
    @ResponseBody
```

```
    public ResponseEntity<List<Song>> getSongsByArtist(
            @RequestParam(name="artist") String artist
    ) {
        System.out.println(artist);
        List<Song> data = service.getSongsForArtist(artist);
```

In Listing 6-5 we have a class GetSongsController, and in order to tell Spring MVC that we intend this to be a class that will respond to methods of some fashion, we annotate it with @Controller. This annotation is basically a more specific form of @Bean or @Component that we've seen in earlier chapters and we'll use a lot more throughout this chapter and the book. We want to be able to pull in our MusicService so we use the annotation @Autowired on the declaration which we learned about back in Chapter 5. As we move through the chapters, we'll continue to use services from previous chapters so we can expand on concepts building on what we already know.

As in the GreetingController earlier in the chapter, we've annotated our getSongsByArtist method with a @GetMapping annotation which means any GET request to /songs will hit this method.

Our getSongsByArtist method is set up to return a list of Song objects as a JSON array. In order to do this, we need to accept a query parameter artist. Since we're down the road of annotation land already, we preface our method parameter with @RequestParam which maps it to a web parameter.

A @RequestParam maps to query parameters, form data, and parts in multipart requests. While not required, any of the @*Mapping annotations will accept a params attribute so you can be more explicit about which params map to your method. For the @RequestParam, it can have the following parameters, all of which are also optional.

Parameter	Description
name	This is the name of the query parameter in the URI.
required	Default is true, safe to ignore if that fits your requirements, otherwise specify the opposite.
defaultValue	Used in the event a value is not specified so you can operate on the default.

We're going to return a JSON array of Songs, so we're going to implement a bit of magic and return a `ResponseEntity` object which is commonly used in Spring MVC as the return value for a `@Controller` method. What `ResponseEntity` adds to the response is a status code. In order for Spring to know that it should use the return value and bind it to the response body, we use our last annotation in this example `@ResponseBody`.

The other method handling requests in `GetSongsController` is listed later. It shows the use of another method of accepting user input. We don't currently have any unique identifier to use as lookup, so we're going to depend on two key pieces of information that make up a song, the artist and song name. If you'll remember in Chapter 1, a song name is not enough to make up a unique identifier given that there have been examples of duplicate song names over the years.

A `@PathVariable` maps to a pattern in the mapping definition annotation and can have the following optional parameters.

Parameter	Description
name	This is the name of the path parameter in the URI.
required	Default is true, safe to ignore if that fits your requirements, otherwise specify the opposite.

Listing 6-6 shows what our `getSong` method looks like given the preceding information. We won't bore you with reexplaining any detail on the annotations that we've previously explained in the `@RequestParam` explanations.

Listing 6-6. `chapter6/src/main/java/com/bsg5/chapter6/` `GetSongsController.java`

```
package com.bsg5.chapter6;

import com.bsg5.chapter3.MusicService;
import com.bsg5.chapter3.model.Song;
import org.springframework.beans.factory.annotation.Autowired;
import org.springframework.http.HttpStatus;
import org.springframework.http.ResponseEntity;
import org.springframework.stereotype.Controller;
import org.springframework.web.bind.annotation.GetMapping;
```

```
import org.springframework.web.bind.annotation.PathVariable;
import org.springframework.web.bind.annotation.RequestParam;
import org.springframework.web.bind.annotation.ResponseBody;

import java.net.URLDecoder;
import java.nio.charset.StandardCharsets;
import java.util.List;

@Controller
public class GetSongsController {

    @Autowired
    MusicService service;

    @GetMapping("/artists/{artist}/songs/{name}")
    @ResponseBody
    public ResponseEntity<Song> getSong(
            @PathVariable("artist") final String artist,
            @PathVariable("name") final String name
    ) {
        String artistDecoded = URLDecoder.decode(artist, StandardCharsets.
        UTF_8);
        String nameDecoded = URLDecoder.decode(name, StandardCharsets.UTF_8);
        Song song = service.getSong(artistDecoded, nameDecoded);

        return new ResponseEntity<>(song, HttpStatus.OK);
    }

}
```

Our GET request here accepts two @PathVariable parameters and passes those into our method. The URI will look something like the following: http://api.bandgateway. com/artists/threadbare+loaf/songs/someone+stole+the+flour. In the case of path parameters unlike our query parameter earlier, this will NOT be automatically URL decoded by Spring. In our controller method since we're looking for "threadbare loaf" not "threadbare+loaf," we will use the URLDecoder class available in the Java standard library to get at a decoded version of the artist and name.

Spring also has its own encoder and decoder. Which one should you use?

It really doesn't matter. Both libraries will do the same thing, and they're both available to you. In the next chapter, we'll use the Spring encoder and decoder, and we won't notice a difference.

Now that we have these two endpoints, we need to test them just like our GreetingController. We'll do the same song and dance with our tests here and show you how to mock and ensure that your endpoints are processing the inputs and delivering the outputs in the way you expect.

Listing 6-7. chapter6/src/test/java/com/bsg5/chapter6/
TestGetSongsController.java

```
package com.bsg5.chapter6;

import org.springframework.beans.factory.annotation.Autowired;
import org.springframework.http.MediaType;
import org.springframework.test.context.ContextConfiguration;
import org.springframework.test.context.testng.
AbstractTestNGSpringContextTests; import org.springframework.test.context.
web.WebAppConfiguration;
import org.springframework.test.web.servlet.MockMvc;
import org.springframework.test.web.servlet.setup.MockMvcBuilders;
import org.springframework.web.context.WebApplicationContext;
import org.testng.annotations.Test;

import static org.springframework.test.web.servlet.request.
MockMvcRequestBuilders.get;
import static org.springframework.test.web.servlet.result.
MockMvcResultMatchers.status;

@Test
@WebAppConfiguration
@ContextConfiguration(classes = GatewayAppWebConfig.class)
public class TestGetSongsController extends
AbstractTestNGSpringContextTests {
```

```
    @Autowired
    private WebApplicationContext wac;

    private MockMvc mockMvc;

    @Test
    public void getSongControllerTest() throws Exception {
        this.mockMvc = MockMvcBuilders.webAppContextSetup(this.wac).build();

            this.mockMvc.perform(get("/songs")
                    .param("artist", "van halen")
                    .param("name", "jump")
                    .accept(MediaType.ALL))
                    .andExpect(status().isOk());
    }

    @Test
    public void getSongsTestWithoutParameters() throws Exception {
        this.mockMvc = MockMvcBuilders.webAppContextSetup(this.wac).build();

        this.mockMvc.perform(get("/songs")
                .accept(MediaType.ALL))
                .andExpect(status().is4xxClientError());

    }

    @Test
    public void getSongsByArtistTest() throws Exception {
        this.mockMvc = MockMvcBuilders.webAppContextSetup(this.wac).build();

        this.mockMvc.perform(get("/songs").param("artist", "van halen")
                .accept(MediaType.ALL))
                .andExpect(status().isOk());
    }

}
```

We chose using a mock here to make test writing simple and fast. With our usage of hamcrest and the extensible matchers it provides, it makes writing these assertions a breeze. In Chapter 7 we will expand on this and use more tooling in the testing space.

The more astute reader will look at the preceding code or have entered it all into their codebase and wonder how to map the template with our controller. Let's set up our initializer and config which will show how this is done.

6.5 Configuration

We're getting very used to annotation-based configuration, and so we'll expand by showing some configuration classes and how they're used.

First up is the GatewayAppInitializer which requires us to override two of its methods getRootConfigClasses and getServletConfigClasses. We'll override a third, getServletMappings, which identifies what the root mappings will be for Spring's DispatcherServlet to listen to. The one we care about the most is getServletConfigClasses which returns our GatewayAppWebConfig class.

Listing 6-8. chapter6/src/main/java/com/bsg5/chapter6/
GatewayAppInitializer.java

```java
package com.bsg5.chapter6;

import org.springframework.web.servlet.support.
AbstractAnnotationConfigDispatcherServletInitializer;
public class GatewayAppInitializer extends
AbstractAnnotationConfigDispatcherServletInitiali
    @Override
    protected Class<?>[] getRootConfigClasses() {
        return new Class[0];
    }

    @Override
    protected Class<?>[] getServletConfigClasses() {
        return new Class[]{GatewayAppWebConfig.class};
    }

    @Override
    protected String[] getServletMappings() {
        return new String[]{"/"};
    }
}
```

Our GatewayAppWebConfig will start with two annotations which should make sense intrinsically, @Configuration and @EnableWebMvc, as this is a configuration class, and we want to enable Spring MVC for the things that we're configuring here.

The next annotation – @ComponentScan – we've seen mentioned in Chapter 5. It pulls in all classes under the specified package structure – in this case, our service and model classes from Chapter 3 com.bsg5.chapter3.mem03 and the classes for Chapter 6 under com.bsg5.chapter6.

Listing 6-9. chapter6/src/main/java/com/bsg5/chapter6/
GatewayAppWebConfig.java

```
package com.bsg5.chapter6;

import org.jtwig.spring.JtwigViewResolver;
import org.springframework.context.annotation.Bean;
import org.springframework.context.annotation.ComponentScan;
import org.springframework.context.annotation.Configuration;
import org.springframework.web.servlet.ViewResolver;
import org.springframework.web.servlet.config.annotation.EnableWebMvc;
import org.springframework.web.servlet.config.annotation.
ViewResolverRegistry;
import org.springframework.web.servlet.config.annotation.WebMvcConfigurer;

@Configuration
@EnableWebMvc
@ComponentScan(basePackages = {"com.bsg5.chapter6", "com.bsg5.chapter3.mem03"})
public class GatewayAppWebConfig implements WebMvcConfigurer {
    @Override
    public void configureViewResolvers(ViewResolverRegistry registry) {
        registry.viewResolver(jtwigViewResolver());
    }

    @Bean
    public ViewResolver jtwigViewResolver() {
        JtwigViewResolver viewResolver = new JtwigViewResolver();
        viewResolver.setPrefix("web:/WEB-INF/templates/");
```

```
        viewResolver.setSuffix(".jtwig.html");
        return viewResolver;
    }

}
```

In Chapter 5 we introduced using Jtwig for our template rendering, and we'll continue doing that with Spring MVC. The reason to use this library is it provides a very simple and easily understood templating engine. It's a fine option, and if you're looking for something a bit more popular, you can look into Mustache (`https://mustache.github.io/`), FreeMarker (`https://freemarker.apache.org/`), or dispense with any of this and just write RESTful components which return JSON.

In order to use Jtwig, we need to register a new `ViewResolver` and set up where our templates are and what suffix to use when we scan. The `jtwig-spring` package offers a handy `ViewResolver` which we can return to make things easier.

We haven't seen any usage of templates in this chapter yet, so let's move through a simple example where we can put our new configuration into practice!

6.6 Templates and Models

In the preceding section, we've covered pretty nicely the `@Controller` aspect of the Model View Controller paradigm. Let's take a little time to talk about the View and the Model.

There are three classes provided by Spring we can use to move data into our view from our controller classes: `Model`, `ModelMap`, and `ModelAndView`. Let's take a look at our usage of the `Model` class in the next example.

Listing 6-10. `chapter6/src/main/java/com/bsg5/chapter6/`
`GreetingWithModelController.java`

```
package com.bsg5.chapter6;

import org.springframework.stereotype.Controller;
import org.springframework.ui.Model;
import org.springframework.web.bind.annotation.GetMapping;
import org.springframework.web.bind.annotation.PathVariable;
```

```
@Controller
public class GreetingWithModelController {

    @GetMapping("/greeting/{name}")
    public String greeting(@PathVariable(name="name") String name, Model
    model) {
        model.addAttribute("name", name);
        return "greeting";
    }

}
```

In Listing 6-10 we see a controller with a @PathVariable similar to what we've seen earlier accepting a required name field. Our method returns a String here rather than a ResponseEntity because we're going to pass back the name of the template we want to serve this request. Our method accepts a Model class into which we're throwing the value passed into the path name. One of the nice things about a Model is that it will also allow you to merge a Map of String values should you have the need.

You will remember in the configuration section that we set up a ViewResolver for handling Jtwig templates. This is being put into action now with our greeting.jtwig. html template. You can see from our method that we pass back a "greeting" String, and merging that with the configuration we set up with our ViewResolver, we can infer that the template path will be templates/greeting.jtwig.html.

Let's take a look at our template.

Listing 6-11. chapter6/src/main/webapp/WEB-INF/templates/greeting. jtwig.html

```
<!DOCTYPE html>
<html>
<head>
    <title>Hello, {{ name }}</title>
</head>
<body>
```

```
<p>
    Hello, {{ name }}
</p>
</body>
</html>
```

Our template does a variable replacement on a Model attribute called name and effectively does a model.getAttribute("name") to fill in for the {{ name }} snippet in the code. A Model is essentially an interface that gets passed into your method and allows you to add attributes to it.

The second method of passing model data to our view is a ModelMap. This method allows you to chain calls and supports autogenerated attribute names from the values. Let's see a simple example of this:

```
public String greeting(ModelMap map) {
    map.addAttribute("helloWorld");
    map.addAttribute("threadbareLoaf");
    return "greeting";
}
```

In the preceding code, we're using the autogenerate functionality so that our model will have two attribute names, one called "helloWorld" and the other "threadbareLoaf." It's silly, but then life can be pretty silly, can't it? (If it can't, how do we explain some of the text in this book?)

The final method of model data passing is the ModelAndView. It is a convenience class for returning both the model and the view in a single call. The underlying holder of model data is a ModelMap, and the view can be a String view like we've seen previously which needs to be resolved by a ViewResolver class, or a view object can be specified directly.

```
public ModelAndView greeting() {
    Map<String, String> model = new HashMap<>();
    model.put("helloWorld", "helloWorld");
    model.put("threadbareLoaf", "threadbareLoaf");
    return new ModelAndView("greeting", model);
}
```

In the preceding simple example, we have duplicated what we did in the `ModelMap` example, but we're using the `ModelAndView` class now. It may not seem like much of a savings, but it allows us to encapsulate both model and view in a single class, so it affords us quite a lot of power. In the next section, we're going to tackle errors and how to configure and show them on the front end.

6.7 Error Handling

Taking care of error cases when they come up is vital to the building of your web application. With that in mind, let's take a look at some ways in which you can let users of our application know when they have hit an error. Our first order of business is to build a custom exception which will simply extend `RuntimeException` and expose one of the methods. Let's take a look at that now.

Listing 6-12. `chapter6/src/main/java/com/bsg5/chapter6/ArtistNotFoundException.java`

```
package com.bsg5.chapter6;

public class ArtistNotFoundException extends RuntimeException {

    /**
     *
     */
    private static final long serialVersionUID = 1462190646166272903L;

    public ArtistNotFoundException(String message) {
        super(message);
    }

}
```

Listing 6-12 is pretty standard stuff, and you can definitely customize to your heart's content with error codes or other data should you feel it necessary. The way this comes into action, though, given that we're firmly on the side of using annotations everywhere, is with the `@ExceptionHandler` annotation. In our snippet in Listing 6-13, we're showing a handler for our custom exception `ArtistNotFoundException`, and this is going to tell Spring that the view we're looking for when something like that is thrown should be handled here.

Let's take a look at some code to show how this is done.

Listing 6-13. chapter6/src/main/java/com/bsg5/chapter6/
GetArtistsExceptionController.java

```
@Controller
public class GetArtistsExceptionController {

    @Autowired
    MusicService service;

    @ExceptionHandler(ArtistNotFoundException.class)
    public ModelAndView handleCustomException(ArtistNotFoundException ex) {

        ModelAndView model = new ModelAndView("error");
        model.addObject("message", ex.getMessage());
        model.addObject("statusCode", 404);
        return model;

    }

}
```

This will handle a very specific exception that can be thrown in a controller method. It uses the ModelAndView object that we learned about in the previous section and prefills in the 404 status code since this is a "Not Found" exception. What happens when something else happens, though, and it's an exception we haven't accounted for? We can define a catch-all exception like the code snippet in Listing 6-14.

Listing 6-14. chapter6/src/main/java/com/bsg5/chapter6/
GetArtistsExceptionController.java

```
@Controller
public class GetArtistsExceptionController {

    @Autowired
    MusicService service;

    @ExceptionHandler(Exception.class)
    public ModelAndView handleAllExceptions(Exception ex) {
```

```
        ModelAndView model = new ModelAndView("error");
        model.addObject("message", ex.getMessage());
        model.addObject("statusCode", 500);
        return model;
    }

}
```

This will default to returning a 500 since it may have been thrown somewhere outside of our code, and this is probably a legitimate server error that we can tell the user about.

Our next method is going to be a little silly, since we're using service methods from Chapter 3, and they don't throw exceptions or return nulls, we've just got a controller method that will respond with any GET /artists/{artist} with the 404.

Listing 6-15. chapter6/src/main/java/com/bsg5/chapter6/ GetArtistsExceptionController.java

```
@Controller
public class GetArtistsExceptionController {

    @Autowired
    MusicService service;

    @GetMapping("/artists/{artist}")
    @ResponseBody
    public ResponseEntity<Artist> getSong(
            @PathVariable("artist") final String artist
    ) {
        throw new ArtistNotFoundException("Artist with name " + artist + "
        not found");
    }
}
```

Our ModelAndView definitions in the two exception handler methods of our controller reference a view named "error." Let's take a look at our error template.

Listing 6-16. chapter6/src/main/webapp/WEB-INF/templates/error.jtwig.html

```
<!DOCTYPE html>
<html>
<head>
    <title>Error {{ statusCode }}</title>
</head>
<body>
<p>
    An error has occurred with status: {{ statusCode }} and message: {{
    message }}
</p>
</body>
</html>
```

The preceding template is simple; it perfectly encapsulates a simple error page and pulls data from our controller in the event something goes wrong.

6.8 Next Steps

In this chapter, we saw how to build a more fully featured band gateway application, by removing all of the manual invocations and conversions (and servlets) from our application, leading us to a more streamlined and modern web application development process, including automated testing. The next chapter will focus on the Spring Reactive framework...

CHAPTER 7

Spring Boot

So far, we've looked at Dependency Injection and various configuration approaches, and we've explored deploying some web services into Apache Tomcat. Along the way we've used a small set of Spring modules, picking and choosing as needed. It's time for us to switch gears and look at Spring Boot, which is a project structure generally aimed at **microcontainers**; Spring Boot gives us an easier way to get larger feature sets out of Spring and offers an integrated set of services aimed at deploying running applications without having to rely on traditional Jakarta EE services like Apache Tomcat.

Microcontainers have multiple definitions, but in context, it's a self-contained application, representable as a single artifact, deployed in a virtual machine. That sounds a little odd in the context of Java, which runs in a virtual machine itself; wouldn't every application qualify as a "microcontainer," then?

The answer is "... maybe." However, the more common use of a "microcontainer" is an application with a single purpose, like "run the band gateway application," running inside its own virtual machine (therefore, a virtual machine running inside another virtual machine) such as a Docker container.

7.1 What Is Spring Boot?

Spring Boot can be defined in many ways, just like Spring can be defined in many ways.

At its heart, it's a project that combines many of the most commonly used bits of Spring into a single cohesive unit such that dependencies are easier to manage, as well as an executable environment to make deployment without a container quite doable.

© Joseph B. Ottinger and Andrew Lombardi 2019
J. B. Ottinger and A. Lombardi, *Beginning Spring 5*, https://doi.org/10.1007/978-1-4842-4486-9_7

We haven't really run into enough correlated dependencies to give ourselves a headache with trying to chase down **problems** in our dependencies, although as we've progressed we've added more and more modules to our chapter projects. So far we've been laser-focused on each chapter's topics such that we've been able to keep dependency lists to a fair minimum. Even so, there are a few issues we've encountered – although we haven't needed to address them, because they're so minor, and our tools actually fix them for us.

Namely, in Chapter 6, we used `jtwig-spring` for rendering our "Hello, World" content. This library actually has transitive dependencies itself, on `spring-webmvc`, `guava`, `jtwig-web`, `slf4j-api`, and `commons-lang`. The "issue" – note scare quotes! – is that the dependency on `spring-webmvc` contained by the `jtwig-spring` artifact is actually on version `4.2.3.RELEASE` and not the Spring 5 version of `spring-webmvc`. Gradle actually allows us to override the versions easily; when we declare the dependency ourselves, Gradle assumes that we want the specific version we are referring to instead of a transitive dependency, and thus it overrides the transitive dependency with the right version.

With the Spring Boot parent project, we coalesce many of the Spring dependencies into one reference list and thus eliminate a host of potential problems in one fell swoop. This has implications for our library declarations and testing, since almost everything is made available by magic.[1]

But there's more.

Spring Boot is designed to give you the ability to make your projects executable *without* a container like Apache Tomcat. You can still write your controllers and Spring beans the exact same way, but instead of starting a Tomcat instance and deploying your web application into it (a process we are more or less pretending to do when we use `gradle tomcatStartWar`), Spring Boot can be executed as a regular executable Jar file. It embeds a web container itself (Tomcat, by default) and manages it; it also manages logging, database connections (and database setup), configurations, metrics, and other things.

It can be horribly convenient.

---

[1]True story: There was a chapter in which testing was such a pain without Spring Boot that your authors decided to move the chapter to be **after** the Spring Boot chapter so that Boot's tooling could be used.

7.2 Setting Up a Project

Actually setting up a Spring Boot project is rather easy. In Gradle, it involves a single plugin and a single initial dependency (with the option of configuring an executable jar) – after which everything more or less works through convention, **including** a basic configuration. Let's walk through yet another "Hello, World" application just to show the parts we need – and note that we'll be adding pieces as we go through the chapter.

First, of course, we need to create the source structure and build.gradle itself. The source structure mirrors every other chapter we've seen so far, with a main and test directory; our main contains a java directory and a resources directory. (We'll be using resources later in the chapter to add static content just to illustrate how we can create a "user interface" – a term being applied very loosely in this book's case.)

Listing 7-1. Creating the directory structure with POSIX

```
mkdir -p chapter7/src/main/java/com/bsg5/chapter7
mkdir -p chapter7/src/main/resources
mkdir -p chapter7/src/test/java/com/bsg5/chapter7
```

Our build.gradle is fairly bland – a good thing in a build script. Things to note are

1. The declaration of the org.springframework.boot plugin, which provides version information for subsequent dependencies

2. The **use** of the io.spring-dependency-management plugin

3. The spring-boot-starter-web dependency, whose version comes from the boot plugin – so we don't have to (or want to, normally) specify anything (it's pulled from the plugin)

4. The bootJar section, which tells Spring Boot how to package our application into an executable jar file, in this case rather inventively named bsg5-chapter7 – so our actual executable jar's name will be bsg5-chapter7-1.0.0.jar

This four-part structure (the plugins reference, the applied plugin, the dependency, and bootJar) is very, very common with Spring Boot applications – you could probably cut and paste this as a starter for Spring Boot projects if you wanted. (For the record, we're going to alter this script later in the chapter to add some features our tests will need.)

For the record, this isn't special information or tribal knowledge of any kind –
Spring Boot's own documentation shows you nearly the exact same thing, as will
nearly any other Spring Boot reference.

Listing 7-2. `chapter7/build.gradle`

```
plugins {
    id 'org.springframework.boot' version '2.1.3.RELEASE'
}

apply plugin: 'java'
apply plugin: 'io.spring.dependency-management'

dependencies {
    compile 'org.springframework.boot:spring-boot-starter-web'
    testCompile 'org.springframework.boot:spring-boot-starter-test'
    testCompile 'org.testng:testng:6.14.3'
}

bootJar {
    baseName = 'bsg5-chapter7'
    version =  '1.0.0'
}

sourceCompatibility = 11
targetCompatibility = 11

test {
    useTestNG()
}
```

7.3 Checking the Foundation

Now that we have our project structure set up, we can create our entry point, which
we're going to call `Chapter7Application`. It will have no specific code to execute in
and of itself – it will load a configuration (via the `@SpringBootApplication` annotation,

which has special meanings as we'll see in a few more paragraphs) – and crank up a web container as well as creating a lot of beans for us, for metrics, and other services. What our application will do is simple: declare beans and controllers and make sure they're visible to the application class (by virtue of being in the same package tree, so having a package that starts with `com.bsg5.chapter7`, including any packages **under** `com.bsg5.chapter7`). Those services will be automatically made available to whatever needs them, as we'll see.

7.3.1 Building the Application

Listing 7-3. `chapter7/src/main/java/com/bsg5/chapter7/` `Chapter7Application.java`

```
package com.bsg5.chapter7;

import org.springframework.boot.SpringApplication;
import org.springframework.boot.autoconfigure.SpringBootApplication;

@SpringBootApplication
public class Chapter7Application {

    public static void main(String[] args) {
        SpringApplication.run(Chapter7Application.class, args);
    }
}
```

7.3.2 Building Our Transport Object

Of course, this isn't useful without an actual controller to serve as an HTTP endpoint somewhere, so let's also create a simple greeting service, to make sure the parts all work together. First, we'll create a `Greeting` – an object containing content – that we can serve from a REST endpoint.

Note the use of methods like `Objects.equals()` and `Objects.hash()` – these are utility methods introduced in Java 1.7 to help generate hash codes and determine equality.

If you skipped the ideas behind REST in Chapter 6, this might be a good time to go back and review. If you don't want to do that, it's okay – basically, we're hosting a resource behind an HTTP GET request.

Listing 7-4. chapter7/src/main/java/com/bsg5/chapter7/Greeting.java

```java
package com.bsg5.chapter7;

import java.util.Objects;

public class Greeting {
    String message;

    public Greeting(String message) {
        this.message = message;
    }

    public Greeting() {
    }

    public String getMessage() {
        return message;
    }

    public void setMessage(String message) {
        this.message = message;
    }

    @Override
    public boolean equals(Object o) {
        if (this == o) return true;
        if (!(o instanceof Greeting)) return false;
        Greeting greeting = (Greeting) o;
        return Objects.equals(getMessage(), greeting.getMessage());
    }

    @Override
    public int hashCode() {
        return Objects.hash(getMessage());
    }
}
```

7.3.3 Actually Saying "Hello"

Now that we have an object to pass around, let's create our `GreetingController`, in concept incredibly similar to the `GreetingController` from Chapter 6.[2] We'll add a special case or two: for one thing, we'll have a generalized greeting in case no name is provided, and for another, we'll have our controller not recognize the name of the Invisible Man ("Jack Griffin," in the 1933 horror film).

Listing 7-5. `chapter7/src/main/java/com/bsg5/chapter7/`
`GreetingController.java`

```java
package com.bsg5.chapter7;

import org.springframework.web.bind.annotation.PathVariable;
import org.springframework.web.bind.annotation.RequestMapping;
import org.springframework.web.bind.annotation.RestController;

@RestController
public class GreetingController {
    @RequestMapping(value = {"/greeting/{name}", "/greeting"})
    Greeting greeting(@PathVariable(required = false) String name) {
        String object = name != null ? name : "world";

        /* Jack Griffin is the name of the "Invisible Man." */
        if (object.equalsIgnoreCase("jack griffin")) {
            return new Greeting("I don't know who you are.");
        } else {
            return new Greeting("Hello, " + object + "!");
        }
    }
}
```

---

[2]We could have used Chapter 6's classes in this chapter, but Chapter 6 doesn't use Spring Boot and this chapter **does**, obviously enough. This means Chapter 6's classes would imply dependency management issues that we're trying to avoid here, so we're going to rewrite the classes for clarity's sake, as well as illustrating some different concepts.

A few things to point out:

- @RequestMapping means that this endpoint will handle the responses for multiple HTTP methods, so we can issue a POST to this endpoint as well as a GET and it should respond the same. If we wanted to restrict the HTTP method, we could use @GetMapping or @PostMapping, for example.

- We have multiple locations specified – one with {name}, and one without. That's to handle the situation where no name is provided, so we can respond to /greeting/World and /greeting with the same endpoint. This is not particularly wise, as POST accepts different kinds of data and we're pretending all HTTP requests are treated the same.

- We map the parameter type with a @PathVariable annotation, where we specify that it's not required (because being required is the default). If we didn't tell Spring that it was optional, we'd get an exception when the value was not provided.

7.3.4 Testing with Spring Boot

Of course, there's no point in having a controller or service if we don't know that it works, so let's create a test for it that runs a few sample inputs with their expected outputs. There are actually two approaches we can take here; one approach to testing is that we can test the controller directly, by issuing method calls directly against the endpoint method. However, that avoids a lot of the functionality of the endpoint itself. Let's take a quick look at that code, just to see what we're talking about.

Listing 7-6. chapter7/src/test/java/com/bsg5/chapter7/
TestGreetingController.java

```
@Test(dataProvider = "greetingData")

public void testDirectGreeting(String name, String greeting) {
    assertEquals(
            greetingController.greeting(name).getMessage(),
}
```

This is fine code, I suppose, and it actually verifies that the Java code for the controller is doing what it's supposed to. However, what we'd like to do is issue a call over HTTP, to make sure our parameter conversion and URL mappings are working properly, and that we're getting our objects back in the right form. We can do this, provided we allow Spring Boot to wire in an object to issue REST calls in a test, along with building the actual endpoint. To issue the call, we use a `TestRestTemplate`, which will allow us to get a `ResponseEntity<Greeting>` back from our endpoint. The `ResponseEntity` allows us to check the actual results of the REST call – HTTP codes, and the like – as well as returning an object we can examine as in our prior test. It means that we have more code to actually validate the results of the call, but that's okay; we're actually interested in such things. (If we weren't interested in the HTTP status, we could use `TestRestTemplate.getForObject()` instead, which would return the `Greeting` itself and ignore the `ResponseEntity` wrapper.) Here's the complete, functioning `TestGreetingController` class, to show what's going on.

Listing 7-7. `chapter7/src/test/java/com/bsg5/chapter7/TestGreetingController.java`

```
package com.bsg5.chapter7;

import org.springframework.beans.factory.annotation.Autowired;
import org.springframework.boot.test.context.SpringBootTest;
import org.springframework.boot.test.web.client.TestRestTemplate;
import org.springframework.boot.web.server.LocalServerPort;
import org.springframework.http.HttpStatus;
import org.springframework.http.ResponseEntity;
import org.springframework.test.context.testng.
AbstractTestNGSpringContextTests;
import org.testng.annotations.DataProvider;
import org.testng.annotations.Test;

import static org.testng.Assert.assertEquals;
```

```
@SpringBootTest(webEnvironment = SpringBootTest.WebEnvironment.RANDOM_PORT)
public class TestGreetingController extends
AbstractTestNGSpringContextTests {
    @Autowired
    private GreetingController greetingController;
    @LocalServerPort
    private int port;
    @Autowired
    private TestRestTemplate restTemplate;

    @DataProvider
    Object[][] greetingData() {
        return new Object[][]{
                new Object[]{null, "Hello, world!"},
                new Object[]{"World", "Hello, World!"},
                new Object[]{"Andrew", "Hello, Andrew!"},
                new Object[]{"Jack Griffin", "I don't know who you are."}
        };
    }

    @Test(dataProvider = "greetingData")
    public void testRestGreeting(String name, String greeting) {
        String url = "http://localhost:" + port + "/greeting/" +
            (name != null ? name : "");
        ResponseEntity<Greeting> result =
            restTemplate.getForEntity(url, Greeting.class);
        assertEquals(result.getStatusCode(), HttpStatus.OK);
        assertEquals(result.getBody().getMessage(), greeting);
    }

    @Test(dataProvider = "greetingData")
    public void testDirectGreeting(String name, String greeting) {
        assertEquals(
                greetingController.greeting(name).getMessage(),
                greeting);
    }
}
```

We can actually run a test **now** and have the four tests run; now we know our controller is working properly.

7.3.5 Configuration in Spring Boot

To finish up, then, do we need to create any additional configuration of some kind?

As it turns out, we don't. (Not yet, at least.) The `@SpringBootApplication` annotation actually implies autoconfiguration (so wiring happens automatically, and a lot of infrastructure is generated for us), component scanning in the same package (and packages "under" the same package) as the class that has the annotation (so all classes in `com.bsg5.chapter7` are scanned to check whether they're Spring beans or not), and implicitly includes a configuration reference as well – so unless we're doing something out of the ordinary, Spring Boot will automatically see every bean that is referenced somewhere in the current package, including classes that contain a Java configuration. We're actually done with our "Hello, World" web service itself.

We've mentioned package trees a few times so far in this chapter, where we say that scanning happens in `com.bsg5.chapter7` and packages "under" that package, if we had any. It's worth remembering, though, that packages are **named** hierarchically, and it's convenient to think of them as a hierarchy, but they're not actually hierarchical; you can't `import` a package tree, but only a specific package.

You'd have to import each package specifically.

So when we write that scanning happens in a "package tree," note that it's actually walking through packages with a common prefix; it's not actually a tree.

We can build our application into an executable jar file with `gradle :chapter7:bootJar`, which will create our executable jar in `chapter7/build/libs/bsf5-chapter7-1.0.0.jar`. We can **run** this jar trivially.

Listing 7-8. Building and running our "Hello, World" container

```
gradle :chapter7:bootJar
java -jar chapter7/build/libs/bsg5-chapter7-1.0.0.jar
```

After a fairly large amount of logging information on startup (which should take only a few seconds), we can open `http://localhost:8080/greeting/Joe` in a browser and be warmly (perhaps even "affectionately") greeted by our application.

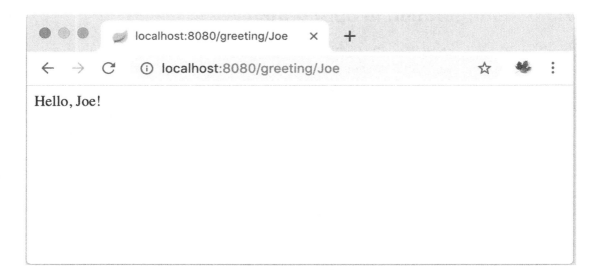

7.3.6 Static Content with Spring Boot

It's also worth noting that we can have Boot serve static content, as long as we locate it in `src/main/resources/static` in our build tree. (It's actually more than that: static content can be served from `/static`, `/public`, `/resources`, or even `/META-INF/resources` by default – and yes, you can alter these as well, although it's not advised. Having **four** "standard locations" is amusing in and of itself, without adding more confusion.)

Let's add a `hello-boot.html` page that will allow us to actually **make** a REST call from an HTML page, just to demonstrate an end-to-end process.

This is not a recommendation for any kind of rich client programming practices. This is pretty much just about as simple a "rich client" as can be made, and readers are advised to read one of Apress' many fine books on HTML user interfaces rather than take this primitive example as advice of proper design and practice.

What our HTML page will have is fairly simple: an HTML form that submits data via a short Javascript function, the Javascript itself, and a placeholder to render results. The Javascript will use JQuery (https://jquery.com/) to issue a REST call against our endpoint, much like our test did, and it will alter the placeholder to render the data from our GreetingController verbatim.

Listing 7-9. chapter7/src/main/resources/static/hello-boot.html

```
<!DOCTYPE html>
<html>
<head>
    <title>Hello, World</title>
    <script
        src="https://ajax.googleapis.com/ajax/libs/jquery/3.3.1/jquery.min.js">

    </script>
    <script>
        function submitForm() {
            $.get('http://localhost:8080/greeting/'+
                $('#helloform input[name=name]').val(),
                function(data) {
                    $("#greeting").text(data.message);
                },
                'json');
        };
    </script>
    <style>
        p#greeting {
            font-family: "Andale Mono",monospace;
        }
    </style>
</head>
<body>
<div>
    <form id="helloform">
        <p>
            Hello, what is your name?
```

```
            <input type="text" name="name"/>
            <input type="button" value="Submit" onclick="submitForm()"/>
        </p>
        <p id="greeting"></p>
    </form>
</div>
</body>
</html>
```

If we run our application (after rebuilding it, and by running `java -jar chapter7/` `build/libs/bsg5-chapter7-1.0.0.jar`), we can interact with our HTML page by opening `http://localhost:8080/hello-boot.html` and entering various names. For this example, we'll identify as the Invisible Man:

7.3.7 Summary of the "Hello, World" Boot Mechanism

We've seen how to build our project structure and create a runnable class for Spring Boot, as well as how to create an executable jar file; we've also seen how to create a REST endpoint (using concepts we discussed in Chapter 6) with a working test, as well as how to embed static resources into our application. It's time for us to go back to our music recommendation application, and show how more of this would tie together in a (slightly) more real-world application.

7.4 Spring Boot and Database Connections

It's time for us to create a better version of our music gateway services. In previous chapters, we've been reusing a memory-only version of the services from Chapter 3, which was convenient because those services had no other dependencies; they didn't use a database or anything that might require configuration. In the interest of demonstrating a more fully featured configuration, let's create a MusicService backed by an embedded database (H2, in this case).

We're still showing you ways to do things that aren't exactly "the most efficient." That's because this chapter is focused on Spring Boot and some of **its** features, not JDBC or other such technologies; we're purposefully not leveraging some of the things we will cover in subsequent chapters. Some of those things, like Spring Boot itself, will make accomplishing some of these programming tasks much easier and with less code.

First, of course, we need to make sure H2 is available to our project. We also will need to make sure that spring-boot-starter-jdbc is in our list of dependencies, in order to – spoiler alert – get Spring Boot to add connection pooling for our database.[3]

Why H2 and not HSQL or Derby? For one thing, H2 is probably the most popular of them; both it and HSQLDB are actively maintained forks of HSQL, but H2 is maintained by HSQL's original author. Derby is actually surprisingly capable, being nearly a Java version of IBM's DB2 and maintained by Apache, but it's also heavier on system resources than H2 or HSQLDB.

Listing 7-10. chapter7/build.gradle with H2 included

```
plugins {
    id 'org.springframework.boot' version '2.1.3.RELEASE'
}
```

---

[3]Be careful about dependencies here. There's an org.springframework:spring-jdbc dependency as well, but it will use an embedded database url by design, overriding any database connection properties you might set manually.

```
apply plugin: 'java'
apply plugin: 'io.spring.dependency-management'

dependencies {
    compile 'com.h2database:h2'
    compile 'org.springframework.boot:spring-boot-starter-web'
    compile 'org.springframework.boot:spring-boot-starter-jdbc'
    testCompile 'org.springframework.boot:spring-boot-starter-test'
    testCompile 'org.testng:testng:6.14.3'
}

bootJar {
    baseName = 'bsg5-chapter7'
    version =  '1.0.0'
}

sourceCompatibility = 11
targetCompatibility = 11

test {
    useTestNG()
}
```

What's neat here is that for three embedded databases for Java – H2, HSQLDB, and
Derby – Spring Boot can **autoconfigure** our databases for us. All we have to do is include
the dependencies, and Boot does the rest. That doesn't mean we won't **want** to configure
the databases, but for early development and testing, it's rather convenient, as are
many of Spring Boot's features. In the interest of best practices, however, we're going to
manually configure the database connection.

7.4.1 Initializing Data with Spring Boot

Spring Boot also runs SQL for us on application startup. It starts by executing the SQL
commands contained in files named schema.sql and data.sql (in that order) from the
classpath (so we can locate these files, e.g., in our source tree at src/main/resources). It
also will run database-specific scripts based on a platform property – which we'll show –
so that we can have generalized schema setup and then fine-tune the configuration for
whichever database we might choose, if we happen to use features that aren't based

on the SQL standard. (In other words, if our schema requires features for a specific database, using that database's custom SQL, we can locate the custom SQL in a file named specifically for that database.)

Note that our startup scripts are designed for our testing requirements, not for live deployment. We forcibly reset the data to match what our tests require, which is something a live application would not want to do.

We've now mentioned autoconfiguration of the database connection pool and a "platform" property. These come from a simple property file in the classpath, called `application.properties`. In our case, we want to set up a simple database connection, with a JDBC URL, a username, a password, and a database driver name. We don't actually **need** all of these – or any of them, really – but it's good practice to set them for when you'll want to change them to something more robust than an embedded database.[4]

Our `application.properties` file for now is shown in Listing 7-11.

Listing 7-11. `chapter7/src/main/resources/application.properties`

```
spring.datasource.url=jdbc:h2:./chapter7;DB_CLOSE_ON_EXIT=FALSE
spring.datasource.username=sa
spring.datasource.password=
spring.datasource.driver-class-name=org.h2.Driver

spring.datasource.platform=h2
```

With this, we're creating a database in the user's current directory when the application is run, with a database username of `sa` and an empty password (which happens to match the default H2 user profile); we are also explicitly setting the driver class name to `org.h2.Driver`. Lastly, we're setting the platform to be `h2` as well, so

---

[4]There's nothing **wrong** with an embedded database, but note that embedded databases are fast but not typically scalable. If your application gets enough traffic that a single application container gets overwhelmed, you'd need to rebuild the database to point to an external database. It's not a high-priority thing to think about, but it **is** important to be aware. Embedded databases are great, because of how easy they are to use, but they're certainly not a "one stop solution."

Spring Boot will first attempt to run `schema.sql`, and then `schemah2.sql`, after which it will run `data.sql` and `data-h2.sql`.

Why would one have database-specific scripts? Well, SQL is generally going to be the same across every database platform, but not quite. Some databases will have nonstandard datatypes or ways to define primary keys or table relationships; sadly, for as common and as powerful as SQL is, it's terribly common to require database-specific scripting to accomplish certain tasks – and defining the schema is one of the areas that this is most true.

If you recall our data model in Chapter 3, you'll note that we have two entities to manage: `Artist` and `Song`. This sounds like a suggestion that we have two tables that correspond to those entity names, and we could do that, but we're not going to.

The reason is rather simple: this chapter is already covering a lot of ground, and covering both `Artist` and `Song` services would take too long and add relatively little (once you understand what's going on with services related to `Artist`, the services related to `Song` wouldn't make much difference – but it'd take a lot more room). We're going to revise how we access data in the next chapter, so it makes more sense for us to focus on the full feature set of services in Chapter 8 and not here in Chapter 7. We're going to include the data descriptions here – as SQL comments – just to show you where it would go, but then we're going to pretend that `Song` doesn't exist until we hit Chapter 8.

Listing 7-12. `chapter7/src/main/resources/schema-h2.sql`

```
DROP INDEX IF EXISTS artist_name;
DROP TABLE IF EXISTS artists;

CREATE TABLE IF NOT EXISTS ARTISTS
(
  id   IDENTITY,
  name VARCHAR(64) NOT NULL
);
CREATE UNIQUE INDEX IF NOT EXISTS artist_name
  ON ARTISTS(name);
```

```
--CREATE TABLE IF NOT EXISTS SONGS
--(
--  id        IDENTITY,
--  artist_id INT,
--  name      VARCHAR(64) NOT NULL,
--  votes     INT DEFAULT 0,
--  FOREIGN KEY (artist_id) REFERENCES ARTISTS (id)
--    ON DELETE CASCADE
--    ON UPDATE CASCADE
--);
--CREATE UNIQUE INDEX IF NOT EXISTS song_artist
--  ON SONGS (artist_id, name);
```

We also want data in our database when our application starts. In testing, we might clear out the data (and often) so that we know in what condition the database is for a given test. Here's our data.sql file – note that we don't need a platform-specific version of this file, because the SQL we're using is standard and should work on nearly every SQL database out there. (If we happen to use a database for which this SQL does not work, we'd be better off creating a platform-specific file **for that database**.)

Listing 7-13. chapter7/src/main/resources/data.sql

```
INSERT INTO ARTISTS (ID, NAME)
VALUES (1, 'Threadbare Loaf');
INSERT INTO ARTISTS (ID, NAME)
VALUES (2, 'Therapy Zeppelin');
INSERT INTO ARTISTS (ID, NAME)
VALUES (3, 'Clancy In Silt');

--INSERT INTO SONGS (ID, ARTIST_ID, NAME, VOTES)
--VALUES (1, 1, 'Someone Stole the Flour', 4);
--INSERT INTO SONGS (ID, ARTIST_ID, NAME, VOTES)
--VALUES (2, 1, 'What Happened to Our First CD?', 17);
--INSERT INTO SONGS (ID, ARTIST_ID, NAME, VOTES)
--VALUES (3, 2, 'Medium', 4);
--INSERT INTO SONGS (ID, ARTIST_ID, NAME, VOTES)
--VALUES (4, 3, 'Igneous', 5);
```

7.4.2 Building an ArtistService

Now we need to start populating our services – which means, as usual, creating a set of files. We need a way to represent artists – so we'll create a class, `com.bsg5.chapter7.Artist`, logically enough. We'll also want a service – a `Repository`, actually, something that actually does the work of interacting with a database – and we'll call that one `com.bsg5.chapter7.ArtistRepository`. Lastly, we'll need something to connect the service to the web layer – a controller – so, naturally, we'll create a `com.bsg5.chapter7.ArtistController`.

> If you remember Chapter 3 well, you'll recall that we used a `MusicService` class there, which handled all of the things we needed to do with our data model. Here, we're splitting things out, as we said we were going to do back in Chapter 3. The reason: expediency. We chose to build the in-memory service in Chapter 3 as we did because it was far easier to have a single point of control for our data model, contained in a set of data structures. Here, we have an actual "system of record" – the database – and it makes sense for us to split the interactions out into smaller chunks, because we don't have to worry about artists messing around with songs, in terms of our data management.

The `Artist` class is a simple POJO, with everything that implies: a no-argument constructor (a default constructor), private fields, a constructor that will initialize the private fields, accessors and mutators,[5] an implementation of `equals()` and `hashCode()`, and a simple implementation of `toString()` as well. Almost every bit of it was generated by an IDE once the fields were put into the class; there's nothing special or unique about this implementation at all. (The exceptions: `compareTo()`, which ignores case for the artist names, and `equals()` was modified to do the same thing.) It's a long class, compared to what it does – it's simply a container for artist references, after all – but that's the beauty of Java.

---

[5]Accessors and mutators are commonly called "getters" and "setters," respectively, in case you don't recall us mentioning this – but this author still finds the use of "getter" and "setter" rather unacceptable in polite company.

Listing 7-14. chapter7/src/main/java/com/bsg5/chapter7/Artist.java

```java
package com.bsg5.chapter7;

import java.util.Objects;
import java.util.StringJoiner;

public class Artist implements Comparable<Artist> {
    private int id;
    private String name;

    public Artist() {
    }

    public Artist(int id, String name) {
        this.id = id;
        this.name = name;
    }

    public int getId() {
        return id;
    }

    public void setId(int id) {
        this.id = id;
    }

    public String getName() {
        return name;
    }

    public void setName(String name) {
        this.name = name;
    }

    @Override
    public String toString() {
        return new StringJoiner(", ",
            Artist.class.getSimpleName() + "[", "]")
                .add("id=" + id)
```

```
                .add("name='" + name + "'")
                .toString();
    }

    @Override
    public boolean equals(Object o) {
        if (this == o) return true;
        if (!(o instanceof Artist)) return false;
        Artist artist = (Artist) o;
        return getId() == artist.getId() &&
                Objects.equals(
                    getName().toLowerCase(),
                    artist.getName().toLowerCase()
                );
    }

    @Override
    public int hashCode() {
        return Objects.hash(getId(), getName());
    }

    @Override
    public int compareTo(Artist o) {
        return o.getName().toLowerCase().compareTo(getName().toLower
        Case());
    }
}
```

The ArtistService needs a little more explanation.

First, remember that we're trying to implement the following services, as listed in Chapter 3 that relates to artists:

- Retrieve a list of artist names (for use in autocompletion operations)

The implication is that the other four services we listed in Chapter 3 are related to songs instead, even though artists are involved, and this is indeed the case.

The thing is, the other services also imply something about artists as well. Remember that we would want to record that a song exists, as well as vote for one, in our full set of requirements – these are song-related services, to be sure, but the songs also need to be related to artists. Therefore, we should add some basic services to our list of requirements:

- Get an artist by id

- Get artists by name

- Save an artist

The structure of each one of these functions looks a little odd, too. We actually will want two versions of each function: one that accepts just the parameters we need for the function (e.g., an `id` if we're getting an `Artist` by `id`), and another that adds a `Connection` object to those parameters. We'll do this because we want to be able to compose our methods, and we want the composition to not require a unique database connection for every call. For example, saving an artist might look up the artist by name first; we want to use a single `Connection` for both operations, because that gives us the ability to use one database transaction instead of two. (We'll see this done later on in this chapter.)

As with so many other things in this chapter, we're … not actually using database transactions explicitly. We'll get more into transaction isolation features in Chapter 8. In this chapter, though, maintaining transaction state would be distracting.

Let's take a look at the first two of our `ArtistService` methods, `findArtistById()`. These methods are simple enough: retrieve an `Artist` whose primary key matches the one supplied as an argument.

Listing 7-15. `chapter7/src/main/java/com/bsg5/chapter7/services/` `ArtistService.java` excerpt

```
        return findArtistById(conn, id);
    }
}
```

```java
private Artist findArtistById(Connection conn, int id) {
    String sql = "SELECT * FROM artists WHERE id=?";
    try (PreparedStatement ps = conn.prepareStatement(sql)) {
        ps.setInt(1, id);
        try (ResultSet rs = ps.executeQuery()) {
            if (rs.next()) {
                return new Artist(id, rs.getString("name"));
            } else {
                throw new ArtistNotFoundException(id +
                    " not found in artist database");
            }
        }
    } catch (SQLException e) {
        throw new ArtistNotFoundException(e);
    }
}

public Artist saveArtist(String name) throws SQLException {
```

What we see is a simple enough mechanism: if we call the findArtistById(int), we allocate a Connection with Java's try-with-resources (which means that when exiting the try block, the Connection will get closed properly without us having to write explicit code for that purpose), and then, inside the try block, delegate to an overloaded method of the same name, with that Connection.

The overloaded method simply creates a PreparedStatement and uses it to query the database for a matching Artist. If it finds one, it constructs an Artist with the data from the query and returns it. If one isn't found, it throws a custom exception – ArtistNotFoundException.

7.4.3 Handling Exceptions in Spring Boot

We create custom exceptions because we want to handle the different paths in different ways. A generic exception would work, but a custom exception allows us to assign semantic meaning to the exception and handle it precisely. In fact, now that we've mentioned the exception, we should take a quick look at it before looking at the rest of ArtistService.java.

Listing 7-16. `chapter7/src/main/java/com/bsg5/chapter7/`
`ArtistNotFoundException.java`

```
package com.bsg5.chapter7;

import org.springframework.http.HttpStatus;
import org.springframework.web.bind.annotation.ResponseStatus;

@ResponseStatus(HttpStatus.NOT_FOUND)
public class ArtistNotFoundException extends RuntimeException {
    /**
     *
     */
    private static final long serialVersionUID = -7888061245862993240L;

    public ArtistNotFoundException(String message) { super(message);
      }

      public ArtistNotFoundException(Exception e) {
          super(e);
      }
}
```

This is a very vanilla exception class, with one line that we really want to notice:
`@ResponseStatus(HttpStatus.NOT_FOUND)`. This tells a Spring `@Controller` that
this exception should map to a specific HTTP status code – in this case, it's 404,
corresponding to "not found," as the name clearly implies. If we don't set an explicit
response status, the exceptions will be considered service errors, which corresponds to
HTTP status 500. Using the precise HTTP error code means that if this exception gets
returned from a `Controller`, it should be treated as a "resource not found" – which, from
the name, is **exactly** what it represents. (This feels obvious, but we'd have been remiss if
we didn't point it out.)

It's also worth pointing out that it inherits from `RuntimeException`. This is typical for
exceptions in Spring, as it means we don't have to specify thrown exceptions in method
signatures, keeping our code cleaner. There are many ways of looking at this practice,
but **most** languages don't have an analog to Java's explicit error mechanisms, even on
the Java Virtual Machine, and most programmers seem to be okay with writing less
verbose code.

Now we can look at the rest of the `ArtistRepository`. Once we understand the method overloading being used, it's really pretty simple, despite the length of the class. Also worth noting is the use of `@Repository` on the class, and its construction with a `DataSource`. Marking it as a `@Repository` describes its specific architectural role (it encapsulates behavior that interacts with a data storage system) and enables its participation in translating some exception types (a feature we're not going to describe in this chapter).

7.4.4 The Actual Implementation of **ArtistService** and Its Little **Controller**, Too

Listing 7-17. chapter7/src/main/java/com/bsg5/chapter7/
ArtistRepository.java

```
package com.bsg5.chapter7;

import org.springframework.stereotype.Repository;

import javax.sql.DataSource;
import java.sql.Connection;
import java.sql.PreparedStatement;
import java.sql.ResultSet;
import java.sql.SQLException;
import java.util.ArrayList;
import java.util.List;

@Repository
public class ArtistRepository {
    private DataSource dataSource;

    public ArtistRepository(DataSource dataSource) {
        this.dataSource = dataSource;
    }
```

```
public Artist findArtistById(int id) throws SQLException {
    try (Connection conn = dataSource.getConnection()) {
        return findArtistById(conn, id);
    }
}

private Artist findArtistById(Connection conn, int id) {
    String sql = "SELECT * FROM artists WHERE id=?";
    try (PreparedStatement ps = conn.prepareStatement(sql)) {
        ps.setInt(1, id);
        try (ResultSet rs = ps.executeQuery()) {
            if (rs.next()) {
                return new Artist(id, rs.getString("name"));
            } else {
                throw new ArtistNotFoundException(id +
                    " not found in artist database");
            }
        }
    } catch (SQLException e) {
        throw new ArtistNotFoundException(e);
    }
}

public Artist saveArtist(String name) throws SQLException {
    try (Connection conn = dataSource.getConnection()) {
        try {
            return saveArtist(conn, name);
        } catch (SQLException e) {
            return findArtistByName(conn, name);
        }
    }
}

private Artist saveArtist(Connection conn, String name)
    throws SQLException {
    String sql = "INSERT INTO ARTISTS (NAME) VALUES (?)";
    try (PreparedStatement ps = conn.prepareStatement(sql)) {
```

```java
            ps.setString(1, name);
            ps.executeUpdate();
            try (ResultSet rs = ps.getGeneratedKeys()) {
                rs.next();
                return new Artist(rs.getInt(1), name);
            }
        }
    }

    public Artist findArtistByName(String name) throws SQLException {
        try (Connection conn = dataSource.getConnection()) {
            return findArtistByName(conn, name);
        }
    }

    private Artist findArtistByName(
            Connection conn,
            String name
    ) throws SQLException {
        String sql = "SELECT * FROM artists WHERE LOWER(name)=LOWER(?)";
        try (PreparedStatement ps = conn.prepareStatement(sql)) {
            ps.setString(1, name);
            try (ResultSet rs = ps.executeQuery()) {
                if (rs.next()) {
                    return new Artist(
                            rs.getInt("id"),
                            rs.getString("name")
                    );
                } else {
                    throw new ArtistNotFoundException(name +
                        " not found in artist database");
                }
            }
        }
    }
```

```
public List<Artist> findAllArtistsByName(String name)
    throws SQLException {
    try (Connection conn = dataSource.getConnection()) {
        return findAllArtistsByName(conn, name);
    }
}

private List<Artist> findAllArtistsByName(
        Connection conn,
        String name
) throws SQLException {
    String sql = "SELECT * FROM artists WHERE LOWER(name) LIKE LOWER(?)"
            + " ORDER BY name";
    List<Artist> artists = new ArrayList<>();
    try (PreparedStatement ps = conn.prepareStatement(sql)) {
        ps.setString(1, name + "%");
        try (ResultSet rs = ps.executeQuery()) {
            while (rs.next()) {
                artists.add(new Artist(
                        rs.getInt("id"),
                        rs.getString("name")
                ));
            }
        }
    }
    return artists;
}
}
```

There's nothing spectacular in play in this particular implementation of
ArtistRepository, including the SQL itself.

However, saveArtist could use some explanation – it actually returns a valid
Artist. It does this by first trying to save an Artist to the database – but what if the
data is already there? We'd get an exception (a SQLException, indicating a violation of a
unique key constraint). This method, if it gets that SQLException, assumes the Artist is

already in the database and queries for that Artist data and returns that instead – so we always get a valid "saved" Artist, even if we didn't actually create the Artist data in this specific call.

Note that we're still cheating for the sake of expediency; we're not checking to make sure that the SQLException in question was caused by an index violation, which is the only case in which we'd want to follow this logic.

This class uses wildcard matching to do searches in findAllArtistsByName – pass in foo and it will search for all artists whose names start with foo, by using a parameter value of foo% – and it uses the SQL LOWER() function to remove case significance from the queries. But apart from that (and, of course, try-with-resources [https://docs.oracle.com/javase/tutorial/essential/exceptions/tryResourceClose.html]), it's no different from JDBC code written from the earliest days of JDBC. Naturally, from Spring's perspective, this is inefficient and rather awful – Spring has excellent mechanisms for data access that we're **completely** ignoring here – but again, that's more a subject for the next chapter.

We have one more class we need to see to fulfill our service functionality – the Controller itself, which mostly delegates to the ArtistRepository. It's actually quite short, and thankfully so, simply having four exposed endpoints.

Listing 7-18. chapter7/src/main/java/com/bsg5/chapter7/ ArtistController.java

```java
package com.bsg5.chapter7;

import org.springframework.web.bind.annotation.*;

import java.sql.SQLException;
import java.util.List;

@RestController
public class ArtistController {
    private ArtistRepository service;

    public ArtistController(ArtistRepository service) {
        this.service = service;
    }
```

```java
@GetMapping("/artist/{id}")
Artist findArtistById(@PathVariable int id) throws SQLException {
    return service.findArtistById(id);
}

@GetMapping({"/artist/search/{name}", "/artist/search/"})
Artist findArtistByName(
        @PathVariable(required = false) String name
) throws SQLException {
    if (name != null) {
        return service.findArtistByName(name);
    } else {
        throw new IllegalArgumentException("No artist name submitted");
    }
}

@PostMapping("/artist")
Artist saveArtist(@RequestBody Artist artist) throws SQLException {
    return service.saveArtist(artist.getName());
}

@GetMapping({"/artist/match/{name}", "/artist/match/"})
List<Artist> findArtistByMatchingName(
        @PathVariable(required = false)
                String name
) throws SQLException {
    return service.findAllArtistsByName(name != null ? name : "");
}
}
```

Note the use of specific annotations for HTTP GET and POST methods. For the methods annotated with @GetMapping, the parameters are embedded as part of the URL mapping itself, and these are all fairly simple methods.

The saveArtist() method uses @PostMethod, though, and has a parameter of Artist. This means that an Artist model is expected to be passed to the method in the HTTP content – which is fairly standard for REST services. We don't have to worry about doing any conversions from JSON or XML to our Artist class, though, because Spring takes care of all of that for us, as discussed in Chapter 6.

7.4.5 Testing Our `ArtistController`: Does It Work?

We actually do have one more class we'd like to see, though, and it's pretty important: it's the TestArtistController class, which is actually the longest class in the entire chapter, spanning more than 150 lines.

Listing 7-19. chapter7/src/test/java/com/bsg5/chapter7/ TestArtistController.java

```
package com.bsg5.chapter7;

import org.springframework.beans.factory.annotation.Autowired;
import org.springframework.boot.test.context.SpringBootTest;
import org.springframework.boot.test.web.client.TestRestTemplate;
import org.springframework.boot.web.server.LocalServerPort;
import org.springframework.core.ParameterizedTypeReference;
import org.springframework.http.HttpMethod;
import org.springframework.http.HttpStatus;
import org.springframework.http.ResponseEntity;
import org.springframework.test.context.testng.
AbstractTestNGSpringContextTests;
import org.testng.annotations.DataProvider;
import org.testng.annotations.Test;

import java.util.List;

import static org.testng.Assert.*;

@SpringBootTest(webEnvironment = SpringBootTest.WebEnvironment.RANDOM_PORT)
public class TestArtistController extends AbstractTestNGSpringContextTests
{
    @LocalServerPort
    private int port;
    @Autowired
    private TestRestTemplate restTemplate;
```

```
@DataProvider
Object[][] artistData() {
    return new Object[][]{
        new Object[]{1, "Threadbare Loaf"},
        new Object[]{2, "Therapy Zeppelin"},
        new Object[]{3, "Clancy in Silt"},
        new Object[]{-1, null},
        new Object[]{-1, "Not A Band"}

    };
}

@Test(dataProvider = "artistData")
public void testGetArtist(int id, String name) {
    String url = "http://localhost:" + port + "/artist/" + id;
    ResponseEntity<Artist> response =
        restTemplate.getForEntity(url, Artist.class);
    if (id != -1) {
        assertEquals(response.getStatusCode(), HttpStatus.OK);
        Artist artist = response.getBody();
        Artist data = new Artist(id, name);
        assertEquals(artist, data);
    } else {
        assertEquals(response.getStatusCode(), HttpStatus.NOT_FOUND);
    }
}

@Test(dataProvider = "artistData")
public void testSearchForArtist(int id, String name) {
    String url = "http://localhost:" + port + "/artist/search/" +
        (name != null ? name : "");
    ResponseEntity<Artist> response =
        restTemplate.getForEntity(url, Artist.class);
    if (name != null) {
        if (id == -1) {
            assertEquals(response.getStatusCode(),
                HttpStatus.NOT_FOUND);
```

```
            } else {
                assertEquals(response.getStatusCode(), HttpStatus.OK);
                Artist artist = response.getBody();
                Artist data = new Artist(id, name);
                assertEquals(artist, data);
            }
        } else {
            assertEquals(response.getStatusCode(),
                HttpStatus.INTERNAL_SERVER_ERROR);
        }
    }

    /*
     * This method tries to save an artist that should already
     * exist in the database; this will validate that the
     * Repository's saveArtist() method returns a valid artist
     * in all cases, as it should return the original artist reference.
     */
    @Test
    public void testSaveExistingArtist() {
        String url = "http://localhost:" + port + "/artist";
        Artist newArtist =
            restTemplate.getForObject(url + "/1", Artist.class);

        ResponseEntity<Artist> response =
            restTemplate.postForEntity(url, newArtist, Artist.class);
        assertEquals(response.getStatusCode(), HttpStatus.OK);
        Artist artist = response.getBody();
        assertNotNull(artist);

        int id = artist.getId();
        assertEquals(id, newArtist.getId());
        assertEquals(artist.getName(), newArtist.getName());

        response =
            restTemplate.getForEntity(url + "/" + id, Artist.class);
        assertEquals(response.getStatusCode(), HttpStatus.OK);
```

```
        Artist foundArtist = response.getBody();
        assertNotNull(foundArtist);
        assertEquals(artist, foundArtist);
    }

    @DataProvider
    public Object[][] artistSearches() {
        return new Object[][]{
            new Object[]{"", 3},
            new Object[]{"T", 2},
            new Object[]{"Th", 2},
            new Object[]{"Thr", 1},
            new Object[]{"C", 1},
            new Object[]{"Z", 0}
        };
    }

    @Test(dataProvider = "artistSearches")
    public void testSearches(String name, int count) {
        // this is used to help Spring figure out what types
        // are returned by restTemplate.exchange()
        ParameterizedTypeReference<List<Artist>> type =
            new ParameterizedTypeReference<>() {
            };
        String url = "/artist/match/" + name;
        ResponseEntity<List<Artist>> response = restTemplate.exchange(
            url,
            HttpMethod.GET,
            null,
            type
        );
        assertEquals(response.getStatusCode(), HttpStatus.OK);
        List<Artist> artists = response.getBody();
        assertNotNull(artists);
        assertEquals(artists.size(), count);
    }
```

```
    /*
     * We need this to run AFTER testSearches completes, because
     * testSaveArtist() adds to the artist list and therefore we
     * might get one more artists than we're expecting out of
     * some searches.
     */
    @Test(dependsOnMethods = "testSearches")
    public void testSaveArtist() {
        String url = "http://localhost:" + port + "/artist";
        Artist newArtist = new Artist(0, "The Broken Keyboards");

        ResponseEntity<Artist> response = restTemplate.postForEntity(
            url,
            newArtist,
            Artist.class
        );
        assertEquals(response.getStatusCode(), HttpStatus.OK);

        Artist artist = response.getBody();
        assertNotNull(artist);
        int id = artist.getId();
        assertNotEquals(id, 0);
        assertEquals(artist.getName(), newArtist.getName());

        response =
            restTemplate.getForEntity(url + "/" + id, Artist.class);
        assertEquals(response.getStatusCode(), HttpStatus.OK);
        Artist foundArtist = response.getBody();
        assertNotNull(foundArtist);
        assertEquals(artist, foundArtist);
    }
}
```

Naturally, it looks more difficult than it actually is; it has a series of tests that follow the same pattern that we saw in TestGreetingController, in that they build a request and issue it against the ArtistController endpoint, then check for the expected HTTP response and the expected HTTP entity content (i.e., it makes sure that we get the right

HTTP status, and then we check the data the response contained). Most of the code is built around making assertions based on the data we know our database will contain; `artistData()` (one of our data provider methods) contains the `Artist` names and identifiers, `artistSearches()` keeps track of the number of responses matching the content supplied (if the request contains `"Th"` then artists `Threadbare Loaf` and `Therapy Zeppelin` should be returned, for a record count of 2).

There's one method that needs to take place **after** `testSearches()` – `testSaveArtist()` – because `testSaveArtist()` mutates the database and potentially changes the result of one of the searches. It really wouldn't matter which one executes first, but the order should be deterministic. (Otherwise, the methods won't be able to predict the database state, and that's not a good thing.)

7.5 Next Steps

In this chapter, we introduced Spring Boot – a project that integrates many of Spring's features into a single umbrella project, making dependency management easier and offering many services as convention rather than requiring the developer to pick and choose modules to include. We also demonstrated how to create and configure a microcontainer such that our process from compilation to execution became much simpler.

In the next chapter, we're going to cover one of this chapter's weakest aspects: data access, with Spring Data.

CHAPTER 8

Spring Data Access with JdbcTemplate

It's time we started looking at how we actually access data. Spring has multiple ways of accessing data; here, we're going to look at `JdbcTemplate`, a facade that provides trivial access to common operations, and we're going to address some of Chapter 7's other issues with data access.

8.1 Introduction

Chapter 7 was an "umbrella" chapter, a chapter focused on introducing Spring Boot. We then walked through some of the common things Spring Boot does for us, like handling dependency resolution and providing an easy starting point for features developers use often like trivial web deployment, a conveniently executable archive, and nearly transparent database configuration.

We followed all of that up with database access that most experienced developers – and many inexperienced ones – would describe as, perhaps, "quaint." We also made a slight reference to a crucial problem in our database access code – one that ended up limiting our services to working with one of our two database entities, because solving it in the context of Chapter 7 would be more work than it was worth. Instead, we chose to model simpler things in Chapter 7, to defer proper database access to **this** chapter and the next.

© Joseph B. Ottinger and Andrew Lombardi 2019
J. B. Ottinger and A. Lombardi, *Beginning Spring 5*, https://doi.org/10.1007/978-1-4842-4486-9_8

What do you think the "crucial problem" was in Chapter 7, besides the obvious answer of "There was no reference to a 'Song'"? Spoiler in three… two… one…

Chapter 7 didn't manage transactions at all. There was no way to address coordination of database requests without introducing database abstractions that were out of scope for Chapter 7. Instead, we chose to keep things very simple and lay the groundwork for Chapters 8 and 9, both of which address database access in far more elegant (and correct) ways.

In this chapter, we're going to demonstrate the use of `JdbcTemplate`, which itself serves as a model for many of Spring's simpler data access facilities. JdbcTemplate gives us a single, common workflow model as well as providing easy mechanisms to map from relational data into classes as well as a simple model for exception handling and central logging. We're also going to round out what should have been Chapter 7's feature set, by adding controllers to access all of our data, as well as tests for everything.

8.2 Project Setup

This is a simple, fairly straightforward project. First, let's create our project directory structure.

Listing 8-1. Creating the directory structure with POSIX

```
mkdir -p chapter8/src/main/java/com/bsg5/chapter8
mkdir -p chapter8/src/main/resources
mkdir -p chapter8/src/test/java/com/bsg5/chapter8
mkdir -p chapter8/src/test/resources
```

As always, we need a `build.gradle`. We're going to use the Spring Boot dependency resolution we saw first in Chapter 7 and include four things of particular note. Let's take a look at the `build.gradle` and then we'll look at the dependencies in more detail.

Listing 8-2. chapter8/build.gradle

```
plugins {
    id 'org.springframework.boot' version '2.1.4.RELEASE'
}

apply plugin: 'io.spring.dependency-management'

dependencies {
    compile "com.h2database:h2:1.4.199"
    compile "org.springframework.boot:spring-boot-starter-web"
    compile "org.springframework.boot:spring-boot-starter-jdbc"

    compileOnly "org.projectlombok:lombok"
    // we want the most recent release of lombok, so "1.+"
    annotationProcessor "org.projectlombok:lombok:1.+"

    testCompile "org.springframework.boot:spring-boot-starter-test"
}
```

First, note that we're including spring-boot-starter-jdbc. This will bring in everything Spring needs to make sure we have Spring's JDBC support and ecosystem, which means we get all kinds of goodies like a connection pool (HikariCP[1] by default), test-specific datasources, and data loading features (as described in Chapter 7, with schema.sql and data.sql).

The next dependency we want to make sure we've included is actually the least relevant, because it's one we saw in Chapter 7: spring-boot-starter-web. We're including it here because this chapter will in fact contain a fully working back end for our band gateway.

The last dependency we want to examine is fairly important, because we're going to use it for the rest of the book: Lombok. Lombok is an annotation processor for Java that is *incredibly* useful in generating boilerplate code. It provides annotations for use at class level, attribute level, and method level, depending on what you need. It's probably worth its own section in the Table of Contents, so let's give it one.

---

[1]HikariCP is one of many decent JDBC connection pools available for Java and can be found at https://github.com/brettwooldridge/HikariCP.

8.2.1 Lombok: Eliminating Boilerplate Code

Lombok, as stated, is an annotation processor for Java. You add it to your **compilation** classpath (and, with Gradle, tell it to apply Lombok as an annotation processor as part of the compilation cycle), and it will generate code for javac based on the annotations used and the annotation parameters, if any. The result is that we can use annotations and expect full-blown, standard-issue methods – like equals(), hashCode(), toString(), mutators, accessors, and constructors, which are the most common usage – for classes to be generated for us as if by magic.

Lombok is a **compilation** dependency, not a runtime dependency. You don't need to have Lombok in your classpath at runtime at all.

For example, if we have an attribute called name in an Artist class – and we will, of course – we can declare an accessor for that attribute with Lombok quite simply.

Listing 8-3. Eliminating boilerplate Java code with Lombok

```
class Artist {
  @Getter
  String name;
}
```

This annotation will cause the creation of a standard getName() method[2] in the compiled code. There's also a matching @Setter annotation – so we could have used @Getter @Setter String name; to get both setName(String) and getName() in our generated class.

---

[2]The statement that Lombok generates "standard methods" is a little wrong – in general, Lombok will generate **better** methods than most programmers will. We'll take a look at what Lombok generates for a simple Artist.java in a page or so. It's a little verbose, but by golly, it's generally "more correct" than what your authors would have written on their own for such a simple class.

At the class level, there are a number of very helpful annotations, including but not limited to the following.

Annotation	Description
@ToString	This will create a `toString()` implementation for all of the attributes in this class; can have options to include superclasses' `toString()`as well as other features.
@EqualsAndHashCode	This will create both `equals()` and `hashCode()` for this class. As with @ToString, a superclass' method can be included. There are some truly wiggly bits here for JPA, but Lombok **generally** does the right thing.
@NoArgsConstructor	This will define a, well, no-argument constructor for you, as an inverse analog to @AllArgsConstructor.
@RequiredArgsConstructor	This will create a constructor using all attributes that are "required," with a "required" field being either final or marked with @NonNull (with @NonNull coming from any one of many, many frameworks[a]), nonstatic (i.e., instance level), and not starting with $.
@AllArgsConstructor	This will generate a constructor that includes all properties in the class.
@Data	This annotation implies the use of @ToString, @EqualsAndHashCode, @RequiredArgsConstructor at the class level, and @Getter and @Setter for every attribute of the class. If the class has other constructors specified – such as with @NoArgsConstructor – the @RequiredArgsConstructor is **not** automatically generated. With JPA, you'll usually see @Data and @NoArgsConstructor used for entity types, so it may be required that you include this annotation if you want it included (or, of course, you could write the constructor manually).

[a]*If you're interested in seeing which @NonNull annotations are acceptable for this, see* `https://github.com/rzwitserloot/lombok/blob/master/src/core/lombok/core/handlers/HandlerUtil.java` *and look for* `NONNULL_ANNOTATIONS`*.*

Lombok has a lot of features that aren't being described here; this is a very light and cursory overview that is trying to cover *just* enough that we can benefit from Lombok without feeling like our readers have been thrown into the deep end of a pool. You can read more about Lombok's full feature set at `https://projectlombok.org/features/all`.

To show the usefulness of Lombok, let's take a look at our `Artist` class. First, let's take a look at what we actually wrote – the version that uses Lombok to generate most of the class content. Then we'll take a look at what Lombok actually generates for the compiler.

Listing 8-4. `chapter8/src/main/java/com/bsg5/chapter8/Artist.java`

```
package com.bsg5.chapter8;

import lombok.AllArgsConstructor;
import lombok.Data;
import lombok.NoArgsConstructor;
import lombok.RequiredArgsConstructor;
import org.springframework.lang.NonNull;

@Data
@AllArgsConstructor
@RequiredArgsConstructor
@NoArgsConstructor
public class Artist {
    Integer id;
    @NonNull
    String name;
}
```

Now let's take a look at what Lombok actually feeds to the compiler, as generated by using `delombok` (see `https://projectlombok.org/features/delombok`). This code is actually **more** verbose (and careful) than what most code generators would have produced, and from the standpoint of coding safety and correctness, it's **better** – and it's 95 lines (before formatting for print) compared to 17. Lines of code is a terrible metric to measure productivity, but the savings in time is entirely worth it.

Listing 8-5. The `Artist.java` implementation as generated by Lombok

```java
package com.bsg5.chapter8;

import org.springframework.lang.NonNull;

public class Artist {
    Integer id;
    @NonNull
    String name;

    @java.lang.SuppressWarnings("all")
    public Integer getId() {
        return this.id;
    }

    @NonNull
    @java.lang.SuppressWarnings("all")
    public String getName() {
        return this.name;
    }

    @java.lang.SuppressWarnings("all")
    public void setId(final Integer id) {
        this.id = id;
    }

    @java.lang.SuppressWarnings("all")
    public void setName(@NonNull final String name) {
        if (name == null) {
            throw new java.lang.NullPointerException(
                "name is marked @NonNull but is null"
            );
        }
        this.name = name;
    }

    @java.lang.Override
    @java.lang.SuppressWarnings("all")
```

```java
public boolean equals(final java.lang.Object o) {
    if (o == this) return true;
    if (!(o instanceof Artist)) return false;
    final Artist other = (Artist) o;
    if (!other.canEqual((java.lang.Object) this)) return false;
    final java.lang.Object this$id = this.getId();
    final java.lang.Object other$id = other.getId();
    if (this$id == null ? other$id != null :
        !this$id.equals(other$id)) return false;
    final java.lang.Object this$name = this.getName();
    final java.lang.Object other$name = other.getName();
    if (this$name == null ? other$name != null :
        !this$name.equals(other$name)) return false;
    return true;
}

@java.lang.SuppressWarnings("all")
protected boolean canEqual(final java.lang.Object other) {
    return other instanceof Artist;
}

@java.lang.Override
@java.lang.SuppressWarnings("all")
public int hashCode() {
    final int PRIME = 59;
    int result = 1;
    final java.lang.Object $id = this.getId();
    result = result * PRIME + ($id == null ? 43 : $id.hashCode());
    final java.lang.Object $name = this.getName();
    result = result * PRIME + ($name == null ? 43 : $name.hashCode());
    return result;
}
```

```java
@java.lang.Override
@java.lang.SuppressWarnings("all")
public java.lang.String toString() {
    return "Artist(id=" + this.getId() + ", name=" + this.getName() + ")";
}

@java.lang.SuppressWarnings("all")
public Artist(final Integer id, @NonNull final String name) {
    if (name == null) {
        throw new java.lang.NullPointerException(
            "name is marked @NonNull but is null"
        );
    }
    this.id = id;
    this.name = name;
}

@java.lang.SuppressWarnings("all")
public Artist(@NonNull final String name) {
    if (name == null) {
        throw new java.lang.NullPointerException(
            "name is marked @NonNull but is null"
        );
    }
    this.name = name;
}

@java.lang.SuppressWarnings("all")
public Artist() {
}
}
```

Now imagine that we add some kind of manual validation to an artist's name – such as "it must have a special character in the name." (We might be interested in having a list of artists comprised of only Ke$ha and the Artist Formerly Known as Prince, perhaps...) We'd normally write that in a method called setName(), but with the verbose implementation, the implementation has to sit alongside every other *standard* method in the class, and therefore it has a harder time standing out. It'd be easy (well, easier) to miss such a custom implementation, although there are ways to highlight it with comments, and the fact that it'd have to be longer than one line might help highlight the method, too… but with Lombok, it'd stand out like a sore thumb.[3]

Lombok isn't a mandatory tool, of course; as demonstrated, you could easily write the boilerplate methods yourself, or (more likely) have the IDE generate them. With that said, it is *very* useful, especially in a book where readers tend to have their eyes glaze over at code that isn't actually entirely relevant. For the rest of this book, you can expect to see Lombok used, because our object models are getting full-featured enough that the savings in space are significant.

8.3 Our Entity and Data Models

We're using the same entity model we described in Chapter 3 and that we've used since then. However, we want to change the **data** model slightly, to make data management more efficient.

What's the difference between an "entity model" and a "data model?" Well, in concrete terms, they're largely interchangeable. There's not a formal definition that one would use to say "this is an entity model, that is a data model." However, colloquially speaking – and as used here – an entity model describes the overall relationships between things we're working with (the entities), and a data model is a more specific description of the actual managed elements.

For example, in an **entity** model, an Artist exists (therefore it's an entity!) and it has a name. In a data model, we might include things that make working with an Artist more convenient – a generated primary key or a count of the songs for that Artist, for example – things that might be relevant for an Artist from a programming standpoint, but that aren't necessarily part of the definition of an Artist as a concept.

---

[3] I wonder if anyone's ever scanned a crowd, looking for people with sore thumbs, to see if they actually are easy to detect. When my thumb is sore, I don't wave it about making sure people know it.

Our entity model (again, Chapter 3) looks like this:

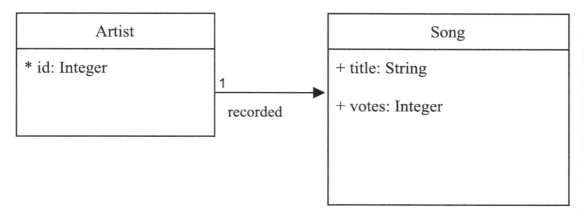

Our **data** model adds a few attributes to the entities, to create relationships and make managing the objects much more efficient:

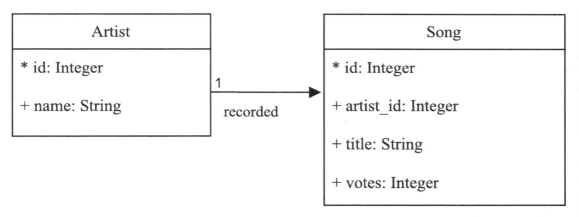

This isn't entirely descriptive – we're not including nullability or sizes into our models, but we're also not **quite** trying to build a formal entity model, either. We're mostly thinking about how we design our class structure. This is the "right way" to model data when you're proceeding from a SQL-first access model (i.e., when you anticipate using JDBC to access your data, as we are in this chapter); in our next chapter, when we look at Spring Data, we can actually design our classes first and then make sure they generate a workable database schema, rather than starting with the schema and building a workable class structure.

We've already seen the Artist.java from the Lombok section, but for the sake of completeness, let's take a look at it again.

Listing 8-6. chapter8/src/main/java/com/bsg5/chapter8/Artist.java

```
package com.bsg5.chapter8;

import lombok.AllArgsConstructor;
import lombok.Data;
import lombok.NoArgsConstructor;
import lombok.RequiredArgsConstructor;
import org.springframework.lang.NonNull;

@Data
@AllArgsConstructor
@RequiredArgsConstructor
@NoArgsConstructor
public class Artist {
    Integer id;
    @NonNull
    String name;
}
```

Now let's see what a Song looks like.

Listing 8-7. chapter8/src/main/java/com/bsg5/chapter8/Song.java

```
package com.bsg5.chapter8;

import lombok.AllArgsConstructor;
import lombok.Data;
import lombok.NoArgsConstructor;
import lombok.RequiredArgsConstructor;
import org.springframework.lang.NonNull;

@Data
@NoArgsConstructor
@AllArgsConstructor
@RequiredArgsConstructor
public class Song {
    Integer id;
    @NonNull
```

```
    Integer artistId;
    @NonNull
    String name;
    int votes;
}
```

There's nothing magical here; we're basically echoing our data model in Java source, with Lombok creating our object's methods and constructors for us. (The source file as it would be generated by delombok turns out to be 138 lines long, compared to 20 lines.)

We will want to manually create our database schema as described in Chapter 7, by setting our *platform* to h2 in application.properties and then creating a schema-h2.sql file. These files don't go in the same parts of the source tree, because the application.properties is going to apply only to our tests – we might want to use a different database in production, after all – but our schemah2.sql would be appropriate no matter what the H2 instance happens to be, whether in-memory (as in our tests) or as an external database, or whatever it might be.

H2 can run as an embedded database or as a separate database server. In addition, it can create databases on disk or in-memory, so we could have one of four different configurations.

Embedded and in-memory	Useful for testing
Embedded and on-disk	Useful for applications that run in single containers and therefore don't need to share access
External and in-memory	Useful for creating side caches, perhaps; this would be fairly rare in the real world
External and on-disk	Useful for application where multiple processes use the database, and mirrors how most other databases are used

First, the simple (and blessedly short) application.properties, which we're going to put in chapter8/src/test/resources – remember, this is for testing only, so we **want** it in the testing directory tree. (If we want a production version, we can create that in chapter8/src/main/ resources, with specific properties for production use – like an explicit JDBC URL and so forth. The version in the test directory tree would have precedence for our tests.)

The main purpose of this file is to make sure that Spring Boot knows what database platform we're using, so it will use schema-h2.sql to create our database tables.

Listing 8-8. chapter8/src/test/resources/application.properties

```
spring.datasource.platform=h2
```

Our schema-h2.sql file – which goes into our chapter8/src/main/resources directory, as it's a schema that we would want in a production application (not just for tests) – is fairly simple as well and models our entities in about as straightforward a fashion as can be done while representing our data model's intent.

Listing 8-9. chapter8/src/main/resources/schema-h2.sql

```
CREATE TABLE IF NOT EXISTS artists
(
  id   IDENTITY,
  name VARCHAR(64) NOT NULL
);
CREATE UNIQUE INDEX IF NOT EXISTS artist_name
  ON artists(name);

CREATE TABLE IF NOT EXISTS songs
(
  id        IDENTITY,
  artist_id INT,
  name      VARCHAR(64) NOT NULL,
  votes     INT DEFAULT O,
  FOREIGN KEY (artist_id) REFERENCES artists (id)
    ON UPDATE CASCADE
);
CREATE UNIQUE INDEX IF NOT EXISTS song_artist
  ON SONGS (artist_id, name);
```

The foreign key for songs deliberately cascades updates through the foreign key – so if we update an artists' record's id field, it should propagate to the songs table. We don't cascade deletes quite on purpose; imagine if we had an artist with 40 songs recorded. Deleting the artist would delete all of their song data as well. Not propagating deletions means that we'd have to **explicitly** delete the songs records associated with an artist before deleting the artist's data as well.

Lastly, it'd be nice to have some test data by default. Foreshadowing: We're going to have three different test classes in this chapter, and two of them will create their own data, but one of them won't. (ArtistControllerTest is a read-only test. As such, we need to make sure it has the data it needs in order to run properly. Thus, default data!) In anticipation of that one test, let's go ahead and take a look at our default database content, which – as it's test data and relies on no H2-specific features – is located in chapter8/src/test/resources/data.sql.

Listing 8-10. chapter8/src/test/resources/data.sql

```
INSERT INTO ARTISTS (ID, NAME)
VALUES (1, 'Threadbare Loaf');
INSERT INTO ARTISTS (ID, NAME)
VALUES (2, 'Therapy Zeppelin');
INSERT INTO ARTISTS (ID, NAME)
VALUES (3, 'Clancy In Silt');

INSERT INTO SONGS (ID, ARTIST_ID, NAME, VOTES)
VALUES (1, 1, 'Someone Stole the Flour', 4);
INSERT INTO SONGS (ID, ARTIST_ID, NAME, VOTES)
VALUES (2, 1, 'What Happened to Our First CD?', 17);
INSERT INTO SONGS (ID, ARTIST_ID, NAME, VOTES)
VALUES (3, 2, 'Medium', 4);
INSERT INTO SONGS (ID, ARTIST_ID, NAME, VOTES)
VALUES (4, 3, 'Igneous', 5);
```

The last class we want to include here is a configuration. As we're using Spring Boot, this configuration relies on sensible defaults (or defaults constructed from application. properties) – so it's nearly completely empty, with the annotations driving everything.

Listing 8-11. `chapter8/src/main/java/com/bsg5/`
`chapter8/JdbcConfiguration.java`

```
package com.bsg5.chapter8;

import org.springframework.boot.autoconfigure.SpringBootApplication;

@SpringBootApplication
public class JdbcConfiguration {
}
```

Here, we're telling Spring that it's a Spring Boot configuration, to scan this package (and packages whose names start with this one, so any class in the `com.bsg5,chapter8` package hierarchy) for Spring components and to enable Spring Web configuration.

Now we finally get to start **doing things**. All this was necessary to varying degrees, and all of it's relevant, but it's mostly been *preparatory* for actually working with data.

8.4 Accessing Data

Let's revisit our `MusicService`, as we've seen in Chapter 3 and in subsequent chapters. Our service has five primary operations:

- Retrieve songs for an artist, ordered by popularity (the most popular song is the better "hook")

- Retrieve song names for an artist (for use in autocompletion operations, which we're anticipating a more full-featured application would use)

- Retrieve a list of artist names (for use in autocompletion operations)

- Record that a song exists

- Vote for a song as a hook for a given `Artist`

The mechanism to implement these with `JdbcTemplate` is really rather easy. What we want to do is have a class – `MusicService` – that receives a `JdbcTemplate` as an autowired attribute. It can then use `JdbcTemplate.query()` and `JdbcTemplate.update()` to issue SQL against the database as needed. Let's take a look at what an implementation of `MusicService` might look like with only one method implemented.

Probably the simplest of the methods in our requirements is the one to retrieve matching artist names, such that if we pass in a "T" we get a list of strings reflecting artist names that, well, start with the letter "T." For simplicity's sake, we'll make articles like "the," "a," and "an"[4] significant – that is, "The Who" and "Who" are different band names for the purpose of matching artists. There are definitely ways of making the articles optional, and that would actually be a good idea for an enhanced version of the API, but that's outside of the scope of this chapter.

If you're interested, one way this could be accomplished is by adding another field to the `Artist` table, a field that contained the name with all of the articles stripped out. You might also "stem" the remaining words – where "stemming" means translating the word to its base, most simple form, "improbably" becomes "improb," and "threadbare loaf" becomes `threadbar loaf`. Then you'd use this artificial and internal-use-only content to do matches, perhaps in combination with the actual band name. (After all, you would want a search for "The Who" to work when typing Th and not just Wh.) This isn't even beginning to look at access patterns or machine learning for such purposes. As we said, this is better left as an exercise for future enhancement, because this exercise alone would fill a few chapters of a book.

If you're interested, there are some research papers on the topic, including

- "Algorithmic and user study of an autocompletion algorithm on a large medical vocabulary": `www.sciencedirect.com/science/article/pii/S153204641100164X`

- Apache Solr's `Suggester` implementation, which can hide a lot of details from you: `https://lucene.apache.org/solr/guide/7_7/suggester.html`

---

[4]Just in case you're interested, "a," "an," and "the" are in fact all of the articles in English. "A" and "an" are called "indefinite articles," because they refer to one of a set of objects without specifying **which** one of the set is being referred to, while "the" is called a "definite article" because it's specifying a particular object.

- Naturally, with Java's giant ecosystem, someone ported something from Python that can help quite a bit: Python's `fuzzywuzzy` library. See `https://github.com/xdrop/fuzzywuzzy` for more details.

- Lastly, a good overview that provides insight into autocomplete at Bing can be found at `https://blogs.bing.com/search-quality-insights/September-2016/more-intelligent-autocomplete`.[5]

Others can be found, although searching on Google (or Bing, or DuckDuckGo, or whatever search engine you prefer) will return a lot of user interface–oriented autocompletion mechanisms and not so much server-side information. Good hunting!

We'll get to the full implementation of `MusicRepository` soon, but let's look at an incomplete version just to get our feet wet with the API.

Listing 8-12. Part of `chapter8/src/main/java/com/bsg5/chapter8/MusicRepository.java`

```
@Repository
public class MusicRepository {
    JdbcTemplate jdbcTemplate;

    MusicRepository(JdbcTemplate template) {
        jdbcTemplate=template;
    }

    @Transactional
    public List<String> getMatchingArtistNames(String prefix) {
    String selectSQL = "SELECT name FROM artists WHERE " +
            "lower(name) like lower(?) " +
            "order by name asc";
    /*
```

---

[5]Worth mentioning: James Moore was a giant help in creating this section.

```
 * Note use of Object[] for query arguments, and
 * the use of a lambda to map from a row to a String
 */
return jdbcTemplate.query(
        selectSQL,
        new Object[]{prefix + "%"},
        (rs, rowNum) -> rs.getString("name"));
  }
}
```

These are the core observations:

- MusicRepository is marked with @Repository and is therefore a Spring bean.

- We have a JdbcTemplate reference provided by the constructor; Spring will automatically provide this for us.

- We have a single method, annotated with @Transactional, that calls JdbcTemplate.query().

There are two things about getMatchingArtistNames() that we want to think about. The first is the query() call itself – what with this chapter centering on JdbcTemplate – and the other is about transaction support.

8.4.1 JdbcTemplate.query()

There are **19** variants of query() in JdbcTemplate, and that's not even counting query methods like queryForMap, queryForObject, and queryForList, each of which has a series of overloaded signatures available. (There are more than 40 methods whose names start with query in the JdbcTemplate class.) The one used in Listing 8-12 is one of the simplest.

```
public <T> List<T> query(
  String sql,
  @Nullable Object[] args,
  RowMapper<T> rowMapper
) throws DataAccessException
```

The first argument here is a SQL query. As with JDBC, an interrogative symbol – ?, the question mark – is used as a placeholder.

The second argument is an array of Object. Each element of this array is placed into the SQL query, corresponding with the ordinal position – which means that the first ? is replaced by the first element in the Object[], the second ? is replaced by the second element in the Object[], and so forth and so on.

This version accepts a RowMapper<T> as a final argument. A RowMapper is a simple interface with one method (and returning a specific type, represented by <T>, making it a "Single Access Method" class in Java – which means it can be represented by a lambda. A RowMapper is responsible for accepting a ResultSet and a row number – an int – and mapping that row into a type of some kind; our method for querying for artist names, then, is responsible for accepting a ResultSet and returning an artist's name from that ResultSet's current row. In lambda form, it looks like:

```
(rs, rowNum) -> rs.getString("name")
```

In "traditional Java" form, it would look a little longer:

```
new RowMapper<String>() {
 @Override
    String mapRow(ResultSet rs, int rowNum) throws SQLException {
  return rs.getString("name");
 }
}
```

Either form is acceptable; they both actually compile to nearly the same code in practice, and they accomplish exactly the same thing.

This method, then, is horribly simple: it contains a SQL statement, with a parameter placeholder, that retrieves artist names from an artists table. The parameter is mangled to add a SQL wildcard character ("%") for use by the SQL LIKE operator, and the resulting data is translated from a ResultSet into a single String for each row – and as query() returns a typed List, we're able to return the resulting List<String> to the caller. (We could have used any Java type as the return type for a RowMapper; it just so happens that here we're working with simple String instances. We also don't need to worry about coercing the types, because the declarations give the compiler enough information that the compiler knows what types are being returned.)

As query() returns a List, we can then manipulate the List however we like to get specific results. Consider a method where we might look an Artist up by its id.

Listing 8-13. Part of chapter8/src/main/java/com/bsg5/chapter8/ MusicRepository.java

```
@Repository
public class MusicRepository {
    JdbcTemplate jdbcTemplate;

    MusicRepository(JdbcTemplate template) {
        jdbcTemplate=template;
    }

    @Transactional
    Artist findArtistById(Integer id) {
        return jdbcTemplate.query(
                "SELECT id, name FROM artists WHERE id=?",
                new Object[]{id},
                (rs, rowNum) ->
                        new Artist(
                                rs.getInt("id"),
                                rs.getString("name"
                                )
                        )
        )
                .stream()
                .findFirst()
                .orElse(null);
    }
}
```

If you're wondering about the lambda still, here's the "traditional form":

```
new RowMapper<Artist>() {
    @Override
    String mapRow(ResultSet rs, int rowNum) throws SQLException {
        return new Artist(
```

```
            rs.getInt("id"),
            rs.getString("name")
        );
    }
}
```

In Listing 8-13, we're doing the same thing that we saw in getMatchingArtistNames(), in structure. We have a simple SQL query with a placeholder for the id, and we pass in an object array with the id method parameter. We have a simple lambda (a one-liner, really, split apart to respect page widths for print) just as we did in getMatchingArtistNames(), except here we're mapping the ResultSet to an Artist object.

We then let Java's Stream API grab the first result of the List – which will have at most one entry. Stream.findFirst() returns an Optional<T>, so if the List<Artist> is empty, we can convert that to a null with Optional<T>.orElse(). We'll see **this** pattern in other places of the MusicRepository, too, where we search for data and take action if it isn't present.

Before we go too much farther into MusicRepository – and before we see the actual full implementation instead of snippets – let's talk about @Transactional for a bit.

8.4.2 @Transactional

If you recall Chapter 7's database interaction service, we only supported working with Artist entities, for a few reasons.

One reason was that we knew that the code was going to be thrown away (in this chapter, in the section you're reading **right now**), and adding support for Song wasn't going to add any value to the service; the Artist support was enough to communicate the points we were trying to understand.

The main reason, though, was that our code wasn't structured in a way that made supporting transactions very easy. With Spring's data access tools (like JdbcTemplate) in our toolbox, we can indicate that methods are expected to participate in a transaction very easily.

What @Transactional means is that the method annotated needs to run in a *transaction context* of some sort, which might even include "no transaction at all." A transaction context is referred to as its *propagation*. The default propagation is REQUIRED, which means that if a transaction has not yet been started, one *should* be started;

you can also have REQUIRES_NEW, which says that a new transaction will be started
for the method call even if a transaction has been started (which ... may or may not
work, depending on your datastore and configuration), and SUPPORTS, which says that
transaction semantics will be respected if a transaction has already been started, but the
method will execute nontransactionally if there is no transaction.

Propagation	Description
REQUIRED	This will participate in a transaction that's already begun or will create a transaction if none exists.
SUPPORTS	This will participate in a transaction that's already begun or will execute nontransactionally if none exists.
REQUIRES_NEW	This will suspend a transaction if one is already underway and begin a new one; the old transaction will be resumed when the new transaction completes. This may not work in all contexts.
MANDATORY	This will participate in a transaction if one currently exists and will throw an exception if a transaction does **not** already exist.
NOT_SUPPORTED	This will suspend a transaction if one is underway and will execute outside of the context of a transaction.
NEVER	This is the inverse of MANDATORY; it will throw an exception if a transaction is underway. If there's no current transaction, it will execute nontransactionally.
NESTED	This will create a new transaction **within** a currently running transaction (if one is underway). This may not work in all contexts, as the transaction manager being used needs to support nested transactions.

A @Transaction annotation can also specify that a transaction context is read-only
(with the readOnly attribute, which accepts a boolean: therefore, it would look like
@Transaction(readOnly=true) in use).

Another attribute of a transaction is isolation, which affects the visibility of actions
taken by the transaction before the transaction is committed. For example, imagine if
a transaction that takes 5 seconds to run deletes a record in the first 50 milliseconds of

the transaction; should *other* transactions be able to see the effect of the deletion before the transaction is complete? There are four specific isolation levels allowed, with an additional level of DEFAULT being provided, which means to use the underlying default isolation level for the datastore.

Isolation Level	Description
READ_UNCOMMITTED	This allows a row changed by one transaction to be read by another transaction before any changes have been committed. If the transaction fails, the second transaction might have invalid data.
READ_COMMITTED	This prevents transactions from reading data that has been changed by other transactions, until the other transactions' changes have been committed.
REPEATABLE_READ	This prevents rows from being read with changes in them (much like READ_COMMITTED) but also prevents situations where queries refetch data if it's been changed. Databases are odd, but this still makes sense when you go far enough down the rabbit hole.
SERIALIZABLE	This prevents a transaction from seeing changed data (as in REPEATABLE_READ) but also enforces that the transaction cannot see data from *any* other live transactions until *this* transaction is done; it's as if the transaction has a snapshot view of the data as it was when the transaction was begun.
NEVER	This means that if a transaction is in progress when the method is called, an exception will be thrown! (This one is fairly rare in the real world, as far as your authors can tell; they've never seen it used.)

There are other fields for the @Transactional annotation; two of them are particularly worth pointing out, even though we don't use them in this chapter.

The first is timeout. If this is provided (with something like @Transactional(timeout=5)), the transaction will end with an exception if the transaction lasts longer than the timeout value. (The default is -1, which means "no timeout.") This is valuable if you have a long-running transaction – or if you encounter a deadlock situation.

A deadlock can occur when transactions require resources that aren't available. For example, imagine if transaction "X" – tX – acquires a lock on resource A, and at the same moment, transaction "Y" – tY – acquires a lock on resource B. There's no deadlock here yet – unless in the **next** moment tX tries to acquire a lock on B, while tY tries to acquire a lock on A. Neither tX nor tY can proceed, because the resources they need are locked by the other transaction.

A transaction timeout will end the transactions after the timeout period ends, giving the program a chance to recover and proceed – and hopefully informing the programmer of the problem.

There are lots of ways to address locks like this, but they're outside of the scope of this book; you'd really need to consider the exact situation that causes the deadlock and the transactional capabilities of the specific database you're using.

With that said, a quick and simple rule of thumb is to **always** acquire resources in the same order – so tX and tY would always try to acquire resources A and B *in that order* so that tY wouldn't proceed until tX was done with both A and B. This is, as stated, a "quick and dirty" rule of thumb, and that's said very seriously; your specific problem domain may not allow such simple solutions.

The @Transactional annotation also supports a number of properties related to **rollback**. A rollback will cancel all changes created by a transaction; all locks, updates, or deletes are cancelled by a rollback. (It's a cancellation of the transaction and restores the database to its status before the transaction was begun.)

With @Transactional, you can add rollbackFor, followed by an array of classes that extend Throwable, or rollbackForClassName, followed by an array of class **names** – as strings, for example. If these exceptions are thrown by the annotated method, the transaction is rolled back as part of the method exit. There's also a noRollback and noRollbackForClassName that indicate that the transactions are **not** rolled back if the exceptions are thrown by the methods. The default is to rollback on exceptions thrown by a @Transactional method – but it's fully tuneable.

The defaults are actually quite enough for our MusicRepository. Speaking of MusicRepository, let's get back to it and actually see what the real, live implementation looks like, all 150+ lines of it.

8.4.3 The Actual MusicRepository

Here's the **actual** content of MusicRepository. There's one method we want to examine in detail: intFindArtistByName(). There are other methods that follow some of the same principles (e.g., getSong() follows nearly the same pattern that findArtistByName() uses, and voteForSong() is an essentially similar operation), but findArtistByName introduces some architecturally significant ideas into our implementation.

For completeness' sake, the content of getMatchingArtistNames() and findArtistById() is included in Listing 8-14 as well.

Listing 8-14. chapter8/src/main/java/com/bsg5/chapter8/MusicRepository. java

```
package com.bsg5.chapter8;

import org.springframework.beans.factory.annotation.Autowired;
import org.springframework.jdbc.core.JdbcTemplate;
import org.springframework.jdbc.support.GeneratedKeyHolder;
import org.springframework.jdbc.support.KeyHolder;
import org.springframework.stereotype.Repository;
import org.springframework.transaction.annotation.Transactional;

import java.sql.PreparedStatement;
import java.sql.Statement;
import java.util.List;

// tag::declaration[]
@Repository
public class MusicRepository {
    JdbcTemplate jdbcTemplate;

    MusicRepository(JdbcTemplate template) {
        jdbcTemplate=template;
    }

    // end::declaration[]
    @Autowired
    SongRowMapper songRowMapper;
```

```
    // tag::findArtistById[]
    @Transactional
    Artist findArtistById(Integer id) {
        return jdbcTemplate.query(
                "SELECT id, name FROM artists WHERE id=?",
                new Object[]{id},
                (rs, rowNum) ->
                        new Artist(
                                rs.getInt("id"),
                                rs.getString("name"
                                )
                        )
        )
                .stream()
                .findFirst()
                .orElse(null);
    }
    // end::findArtistById[]

    @Transactional
    Artist findArtistByName(String name) {
        return internalFindArtistByName(name, true);
    }

    @Transactional
    Artist findArtistByNameNoUpdate(String name) {
        return internalFindArtistByName(name, false);
    }

private Artist internalFindArtistByName(String name, boolean update) {
    String insertSQL = "INSERT into artists (name) values (?)";
    String selectSQL = "SELECT id, name FROM artists " +
            "WHERE lower(name)=lower(?)";

    return jdbcTemplate.query(
            selectSQL,
            new Object[]{name},
```

```
                (rs, rowNum) -> new Artist(
                        rs.getInt("id"),
                        rs.getString("name")
                )
    )
            .stream()
            .findFirst()
            .orElseGet(() -> {
                if (update) {
                    KeyHolder keyHolder = new GeneratedKeyHolder();
                    jdbcTemplate.update(conn -> {
                        PreparedStatement ps = conn.prepareStatement(
                                insertSQL,
                                Statement.RETURN_GENERATED_KEYS
                        );
                        ps.setString(1, name);
                        return ps;
                    }, keyHolder);
                    return new Artist(keyHolder.getKey().intValue(), name);
                } else {
                    return null;
                }
            });
    }

    @Transactional
    public List<Song> getSongsForArtist(String artistName) {
        String selectSQL = "SELECT id, artist_id, name, votes " +
                "FROM songs WHERE artist_id=? " +
                "order by votes desc, name asc";
        Artist artist = internalFindArtistByName(artistName, true);
        return jdbcTemplate.query(
                selectSQL, new Object[]{artist.getId()},
                songRowMapper);
    }
```

234

```java
@Transactional
public List<String> getMatchingSongNamesForArtist(
        String artistName,
        String prefix
) {
    String selectSQL = "SELECT name FROM songs WHERE artist_id=? " +
            "and lower(name) like lower(?) " +
            "order by name asc";
    Artist artist = internalFindArtistByName(artistName, true);
    return jdbcTemplate.query(
            selectSQL, new Object[]{artist.getId(), prefix + "%"},
            (rs, rowNum) -> rs.getString("name"));
}
// tag::getMatchingArtistNames[]
@Transactional
public List<String> getMatchingArtistNames(String prefix) {
    String selectSQL = "SELECT name FROM artists WHERE " +
            "lower(name) like lower(?) " +
            "order by name asc";
    /*
     * Note use of Object[] for query arguments, and
     * the use of a lambda to map from a row to a String
     */
    return jdbcTemplate.query(
            selectSQL,
            new Object[]{prefix + "%"},
            (rs, rowNum) -> rs.getString("name"));
}
// end::getMatchingArtistNames[]

@Transactional
public Song getSong(String artistName, String name) {
    return internalGetSong(artistName, name);
}
```

```java
private Song internalGetSong(String artistName, String name) {
    String selectSQL = "SELECT id, artist_id, name, votes FROM songs " +
            "WHERE artist_id=? " +
            "and lower(name) = lower(?)";
    String insertSQL = "INSERT INTO SONGS (artist_id, name, votes) " +
            "values(?,?,?)";
    Artist artist = internalFindArtistByName(artistName, true);
    Song song = jdbcTemplate.query(
            selectSQL,
            new Object[]{artist.getId(), name},
            songRowMapper)
            .stream()
            .findFirst()
            .orElseGet(() -> {
                KeyHolder keyHolder = new GeneratedKeyHolder();
                jdbcTemplate.update(conn -> {
                    PreparedStatement ps = conn.prepareStatement
                    (insertSQL,
                            Statement.RETURN_GENERATED_KEYS);
                    ps.setInt(1, artist.getId());
                    ps.setString(2, name);
                    ps.setInt(3, 0);
                    return ps;
                }, keyHolder);
                return new Song(keyHolder.getKey().intValue(),
                        artist.getId(),
                        name,
                        0);
            });

    return song;
}

@Transactional
public Song voteForSong(String artistName, String name) {
    String updateSQL = "UPDATE songs SET votes=? WHERE id=?";
    Song song = internalGetSong(artistName, name);
```

```
        song.setVotes(song.getVotes() + 1);
        jdbcTemplate.update(conn -> {
            PreparedStatement ps = conn.prepareStatement(updateSQL);
            ps.setInt(1, song.getVotes());
            ps.setInt(2, song.getId());
            return ps;
        });
        return song;
    }
}
```

Remember to pay no attention to the `// tag::` and `// end::` comments. This book was written with AsciiDoctor (`https://asciidoctor.org`), and these are typesetting comments to help us extract specific bits of the code as needed. The result is that we're not copying code from a source tree into the book and hoping the sample code and the book contents stay in sync; we're actually using the real code to generate the book content. There are a few exceptions, including some in this chapter (the `delombok` output, e.g., and the `RowMapper` declaration earlier), but for the most part, you're seeing the real code when you read the book, the code that is used to actually compile and run everything, so when (and if) you type it in or copy it, you're getting something that actually worked when the book was written.

The first of the things we want to examine now: `intFindArtistByName()`, an internal method with access points through two `public` methods. The first public method (`findArtistByName`) expects a `String` (the name of the artist). The second public method (`findArtistByNameNoUpdate()`) has the same argument – an artist's name – but calls the internal method such that an update is not attempted.

The private method is *not* annotated with `@Transactional` – it's a private internal method and expects to be called from a public method, one that **has** been marked as `@Transactional`. This avoids problems with exception propagation; in this class, we have enough control over exception conditions that it's *probably* not an issue, but we might as well *try* to do it right.

Internally, the first part of internalFindArtistByName() mirrors the findArtistById() method from Listing 8-13; we have a query that returns a List<Artist>, and we convert it to a stream. The .orElse() code is a little more involved, though.

This method might be used in two ways, you see: the first way implies that an Artist should be created, and the second does not. That's because when we do a search for a list of songs, we don't necessarily want to create an Artist; a search is a read-only operation, so there's no need or requirement to try to write anything – in fact, there's a desire **not** to write anything. The default "mode" of the method is to write an Artist, but we want access to a version that does not. Thus, the public version (findArtistByName()) assumes an update, and the internal version – the one that does all the work – checks to see what operations are desired.

If it's a read-only operation, we return null – our signal value for "nothing found." We could have thrown an exception, or returned an Optional, but in context, null is simpler; plus, we've already used it in other places in our code (see findArtistById() – again, Listing 8-13 – as an example).

If an update is required, then we have a few things to factor in. We need to return an Artist object, of course, and that object should be fully populated. The name is easy; we're searching for the Artist by name, so that's a logical value for the name attribute. (Does this even need to be said? ... Probably not, but we're aiming for some level of completeness here.)

However, we need to grab the id that the database assigns to the Artist, too. The way we do that is fairly simple, but there are some moving parts to consider.

1. First, we create a KeyHolder (an interface with a concrete realization of GeneratedKeyHolder). This interface has a few access methods to get keys – but the most useful (and relevant in this case) is getKey(), which returns a java.lang.Number.

2. We then use a lambda as an instance of a PreparedStatementCreator. This is a single-access method class (with the method being createPreparedStatement() and accepting a Connection); you're meant to, well, create a PreparedStatement with the proper placeholders populated. We only have one placeholder (as an Artist has only one attribute besides id) so that's ... rather simple.

3.   We pass the KeyHolder as the final argument to the
     JdbcTemplate.update() method.

Lastly, we pull out the key from the KeyHolder – with keyHolder.getKey().
intValue(), which gets an integer from the Number abstraction – and use that to build an
Artist reference.

Could we have written this to be simpler, or at least to be more straightforward?
Well... sort of. In this case, "straightforward" means "without streams or Optional," and
truthfully... it can be done, but involves a lot of temporary variables to contain local state.
The "simpler" version is actually going to have a higher cyclomatic complexity[6] than the
streaming version; the way it's written now has a design complexity of 2 and a cyclomatic
complexity of 2, and the old approach using if and checking List.size() for presence
actually has complexity scores of 3 – where lower numbers are better.

You see the same pattern in getSong(), with a private internalGetSong() method
being used to avoid nesting transactional calls made from the same class. voteForSong()
uses the internalGetSong() when it needs to, well, get a Song – the transaction
semantics are applied at the public method layer only.

In practice, you can get away (sort of) with nested transactional calls if you're careful,
but they're generally bad practice (due to how transactions are applied by Spring) and
can create some odd errors.

Testing MusicRepository

Writing MusicRepository is all well and good, but as usual, it's not worth much if it
doesn't actually work. We need a test. Luckily, we already wrote one – all the way back in
Chapter 3. What's presented here is a modification of MusicServiceTests from Chapter 3
(Listing 3-17), without the superclass structure.

---

[6]Cyclomatic complexity is, well, way out of scope for this book, but now that we've mentioned
it, it's a way of calculating the number of independent paths through a method, by looking at
the control flow. Basically, every nested difference in control flow adds to the complexity of a
method. The streamed version of findArtistByName(String, boolean) looks complex because
it's got some nested method calls and it's a less familiar set of operations for many programmers,
but it's actually simpler because there are fewer branches in the code; thus it gets a lower real
complexity score. With that said, the goal of programming is to get something done, as opposed
to a mandate to use streams or whatever – so you should feel free to do what makes sense to you
and what you are able to make work.

Chapter 3 created `MusicServiceTests` as an abstract superclass for a series of tests, so we could issue the same tests against multiple implementations of `MusicService` by altering configuration mechanisms. We don't have that concern in this chapter, so this test is slightly simpler in organization. The actual code to do the tests is the same, even though every method is slightly different because we've added things like @BeforeMethod to our toolbox since Chapter 3.

Listing 8-15. chapter8/src/test/java/com/bsg5/
chapter8/MusicRepositoryTest.java

```
package com.bsg5.chapter8;

import org.springframework.beans.factory.annotation.Autowired;
import org.springframework.boot.test.context.SpringBootTest;
import org.springframework.jdbc.core.JdbcTemplate;
import org.springframework.test.context.testng.
AbstractTestNGSpringContextTests;
import org.testng.annotations.BeforeMethod;
import org.testng.annotations.Test;

import java.util.List;
import java.util.function.Consumer;

import static org.testng.Assert.assertEquals;

@SpringBootTest(webEnvironment = SpringBootTest.WebEnvironment.RANDOM_PORT)
public class MusicRepositoryTest extends AbstractTestNGSpringContextTests {
    @Autowired
    MusicRepository musicRepository;

    @Autowired
    JdbcTemplate jdbcTemplate;

    private Object[][] model = new Object[][]{
            {"Threadbare Loaf", "Someone Stole the Flour", 4},
            {"Threadbare Loaf", "What Happened To Our First CD?", 17},
```

```java
        {"Therapy Zeppelin", "Medium", 4},
        {"Clancy in Silt", "Igneous", 5}
};

void iterateOverModel(Consumer<Object[]> consumer) {
    for (Object[] data : model) {
        consumer.accept(data);
    }
}

void populateData() {
    iterateOverModel(data -> {
        for (int i = 0; i < (Integer) data[2]; i++) {
            musicRepository.voteForSong((String) data[0], (String)
            data[1]);
        }
    });
}

@BeforeMethod
void clearDatabase() {
    jdbcTemplate.update("DELETE FROM songs");
    jdbcTemplate.update("DELETE FROM artists");
    populateData();
}

@Test
void testSongVoting() {
    iterateOverModel(data ->
            assertEquals(
                    musicRepository.getSong((String) data[0],
                            (String) data[1]).getVotes(),
                    ((Integer) data[2]).intValue()
            ));
}
```

```
    @Test
    void testSongsForArtist() {
        List<Song> songs = musicRepository.getSongsForArtist
        ("Threadbare Loaf");
        assertEquals(songs.size(), 2);
        assertEquals(songs.get(0).getName(), "What Happened To Our First CD?");
        assertEquals(songs.get(0).getVotes(), 17);
        assertEquals(songs.get(1).getName(), "Someone Stole the Flour");
        assertEquals(songs.get(1).getVotes(), 4);
    }

    @Test
    void testMatchingArtistNames() {
        List<String> names = musicRepository.getMatchingArtistNames("Th");
        assertEquals(names.size(), 2);
        assertEquals(names.get(0), "Therapy Zeppelin");
        assertEquals(names.get(1), "Threadbare Loaf");
    }

    @Test
    void testMatchingSongNamesForArtist() {
        List<String> names = musicRepository.getMatchingSongNamesForArtist(
                "Threadbare Loaf", "W"
        );
        assertEquals(names.size(), 1);
        assertEquals(names.get(0), "What Happened To Our First CD?");
    }
}
```

There's a few things of note.

First, we have a method annotated with @BeforeMethod. TestNG (and other testing frameworks) has mechanisms to run specific methods before and after different stages in a given test; in this case, we want to run clearDatabase() (which clears the database and then populates it with known data) before executing any and every method marked with @Test. We could also run methods **after** each test, with @AfterMethod, and we have other annotations available as well, like @BeforeClass and @BeforeTest, each of which have their own significant behaviors. See `https://testng.org/doc/documentation-main.html#annotations` for more details. JUnit certainly has its own analogs to this behavior with `@BeforeEach` and `@BeforeAll`.

Second, note the use of `@SpringBootTest (webEnvironment = SpringBootTest.WebEnvironment.RANDOM_PORT)` for the class-level annotation. In the context of **this** test, the port makes little sense – but we're going to use it later in this chapter, so bear with it for now. We're using this annotation here because of the configuration itself (and it's copied from the other tests from the rest of the chapter, actually, so it becomes part of standard practice for this section of the book); it's simple enough that we simply marked this as a web-enabled configuration, and therefore in order to get the full initialization to run properly, we need to mark this as a test that is also web-enabled. We could have avoided this by using multiple configurations, all tied together in a sort of "top-level" configuration class, but that'd serve little purpose other than preventing the need for one annotation and consuming more trees when the book is printed.

It'd be nice to reuse the test from Chapter 3, but it's fundamentally difficult to do as written – because the base class for Chapter 3 tests is in the `src/tests` directory, and therefore it isn't exported for use by other projects. We could have created a `testsupport` project that **did** export classes for use in testing, but that would have introduced a lot of complexity for such an early chapter. We will see this technique applied in Chapter 9, when we want to reuse tests for two completely separate persistence layers.

8.5 Adding the REST Endpoints

We now have a `MusicService` implementation that uses a database to store data with `JdbcTemplate` – so our interactions with the database are reasonably safe, easy to maintain, and clear to anyone moderately familiar with SQL. It's time for us to tie all of it together into an actual web application to show all of the pieces working together.[7]

---

[7]This chapter will finish what we started in Chapter 7. Our prior chapter added a web interface for parts of a music service, but didn't include all of our requirements because it wasn't the right place to bring up transactions. After this section, you could write a rich client to interact with the services and have a functioning application.

8.5.1 The **ArtistController**

Let's start small, by recreating our ArtistController from Chapter 7, except better this time. (We can't reuse the code because the underlying services have changed.) This is effectively the same code as in Chapter 7, except it adds a decode() method as mentioned briefly in Chapter 6 for completeness (we want to be able to handle band names with spaces, question marks, and other odd characters) and autowires the MusicService via the constructor. We'll also need an ArtistNotFoundException just as in Chapter 7.

Listing 8-16. chapter8/src/main/java/com/bsg5/chapter8/ ArtistController.java

```java
package com.bsg5.chapter8;

import org.springframework.http.MediaType;
import org.springframework.web.bind.annotation.*;
import org.springframework.web.util.UriUtils;

import java.nio.charset.Charset;
import java.util.List;

@RestController
public class ArtistController {
    private MusicRepository service;

    ArtistController(MusicRepository service) {
        this.service = service;
    }

    String decode(Object data) {
        return UriUtils.decode(data.toString(), Charset.defaultCharset());
    }

    @GetMapping(value = "/artists/{id}",
        produces = MediaType.APPLICATION_JSON_VALUE)
    Artist findArtistById(@PathVariable int id) {
        Artist artist = service.findArtistById(id);
```

```
    if (artist != null) {
        return artist;
    } else {
        throw new ArtistNotFoundException();
    }
}

/*
 * if no artist name is provided, the exception path is
 * always chosen and an IllegalArgumentException is thrown.
 */
@GetMapping(value = {"/artists/search/{name}", "/artist/search/"},
    produces = MediaType.APPLICATION_JSON_VALUE)
Artist findArtistByName(
    @PathVariable(required = false) String name
) {
    if (name != null) {
        Artist artist = service.findArtistByNameNoUpdate(decode(name));
        if (artist != null) {
            return artist;
        } else {
            throw new ArtistNotFoundException();
        }
    } else {
        throw new IllegalArgumentException("No artist name submitted");
    }
}

@PostMapping(value="/artists",
    produces = MediaType.APPLICATION_JSON_VALUE)
Artist saveArtist(@RequestBody Artist artist) {
    return service.findArtistByName(artist.getName());
}

@GetMapping(value={"/artists/match/{name}", "/artists/match/"},
    produces = MediaType.APPLICATION_JSON_VALUE)
```

```
    List<String> findArtistByMatchingName(
        @PathVariable(required = false)
            String name
    ) {
        return service.getMatchingArtistNames(name != null ?
        decode(name) : "");
    }
}
```

We can see in findArtistByName() the use of "traditional" (i.e., non-streamed) straightforward code to work with the result of findArtistByName(). We could have written this with streams; this next example includes a method to convert the null from MusicService.findArtistByName() into an Optional<Artist>. Let's take a look and then work out what it all means.

We're still doing REST badly. When we create an Artist – or a Song, as we'll see – we should be returning a Location header in the response that includes an endpoint that will return a newly created object.

Why not?

Well… one reason is that the web interface here isn't really meant to be all that complete – the web layer of Spring is very thorough, and we're barely skimming the surface of what it can do; we're mostly showing code that **can** work, as opposed to code that works fantastically well. This chapter's long enough as it is.

Listing 8-17. A streamed version of findArtistByName

```
/*
 * this method serves to migrate the MusicService' findArtistByName()
 * to something that accepts and returns an Optional
 */
Optional<Artist> findArtistByName(Optional<String> name, boolean update) {
  return Optional.of(service.findArtistByName(
    decode(
      name.orElseThrow(
```

```
      () -> new IllegalArgumentException("No artist name supplied")
    )
  )
));
}

@GetMapping({"/artist/search/{name}", "/artist/search/"})
Artist findArtistByName(
  @PathVariable(required = false) Optional<String> name
) {
  Optional<Artist> artistOptional = findArtistByName(name, false);
  return artistOptional.orElseThrow(
    ArtistNotFoundException::new
  );
}
```

The class-local findArtistByName() here exists for two reasons: one is to convert the result of MusicService.findArtistByName() into an Optional<Artist>. Obviously, if the service returned an Optional itself instead of returning null for "no artist found," we wouldn't need the conversion. The other reason is to make sure we call decode() if a valid-looking name is passed in, and to throw an exception otherwise.

Do we **need** this functionality? Actually, no. We could always simply not map "/artists/search/" in the controller. However, this would mean that calling /artists/search/ – with no artist name – would return an HTTP "not found" error instead of an "invalid invocation" error (a 404 instead of a 400, in HTTP error code parlance). You could solve **that** by adding a specific mapping that returned the correct error code.

Which way is best? Well… the one that works. There's not really a "best" here, although arguments can be made for every aspect of the code. You should use the approach you find most sensible.

The cyclomatic complexity of the "simple" version – the one in the actual sample code – is 3 (it has multiple branches and execution paths). The cyclomatic complexity of the streamed code – all of it, both methods – is **1**. In terms of code metrics, the streamed versions are actually **simpler** than the more straightforward code. That doesn't mean that the streamed versions are better – and we're not using them, since the API of MusicService doesn't return an Optional<Artist> anyway. This example is just to illustrate the (ahem) options available to programmers.

And now the exception class, which has an annotation to tell Spring to convert it to an HTTP error code just as in Chapter 7.

Listing 8-18. `chapter8/src/main/java/com/bsg5/chapter8/`
`ArtistNotFoundException.java`

```
package com.bsg5.chapter8;

import org.springframework.http.HttpStatus;
import org.springframework.web.bind.annotation.ResponseStatus;

@ResponseStatus(code = HttpStatus.NOT_FOUND, reason = "Artist not found")
public class ArtistNotFoundException extends RuntimeException{

  /**
   *
   */
  private static final long serialVersionUID = 7057185664051689118L;
}
```

Now, we have a workable interface for working with `Artist` entities over HTTP. We can't do anything with `Song` entities yet, but let's get the simple things running first. (We can't do anything with a `Song` if we can't do anything with an `Artist`, after all.)

Of course we can't have an `ArtistController` without something to actually test it, so let's take a look at `ArtistControllerTest` – again, a near analog to what we saw in Chapter 7, although it's slightly different to accommodate the slight difference in configuration approaches. We're not actually touching the `MusicService` directly here – everything is through the controller, using the form of actual HTTP requests; it's possible (and likely) there are error conditions not being tested, but in general if these tests all pass, our ability to work with `Artist` records is guaranteed.

Listing 8-19. `chapter8/src/test/java/com/bsg5/`
`chapter8/ArtistControllerTest.java`

```
package com.bsg5.chapter8;

import org.springframework.beans.factory.annotation.Autowired;
import org.springframework.boot.test.context.SpringBootTest;
import org.springframework.boot.test.web.client.TestRestTemplate;
```

```java
import org.springframework.boot.web.server.LocalServerPort;
import org.springframework.core.ParameterizedTypeReference;
import org.springframework.http.HttpMethod;
import org.springframework.http.HttpStatus;
import org.springframework.http.ResponseEntity;
import org.springframework.test.context.testng.
AbstractTestNGSpringContextTests;
import org.springframework.web.util.UriUtils;
import org.testng.annotations.DataProvider;
import org.testng.annotations.Test;

import java.nio.charset.Charset;
import java.util.List;

import static org.testng.Assert.*;
import static org.testng.Assert.assertEquals;

@SpringBootTest(webEnvironment = SpringBootTest.WebEnvironment.RANDOM_PORT)
public class ArtistControllerTest extends AbstractTestNGSpringContextTests
{
    @LocalServerPort
    private int port;
    @Autowired
    private TestRestTemplate restTemplate;

    String encode(Object data) {
        return UriUtils.encode(data.toString(),
            Charset.defaultCharset());
    }

    @DataProvider
    Object[][] artistData() {
        return new Object[][]{
            new Object[]{1, "Threadbare Loaf"},
            new Object[]{2, "Therapy Zeppelin"},
            new Object[]{3, "Clancy in Silt"},
```

```
            new Object[]{-1, null},
            new Object[]{-1, "Not A Band"}

    };
}

@Test(dataProvider = "artistData")
public void testGetArtist(int id, String name) {
    String url = "http://localhost:" + port + "/artists/" + id;
    ResponseEntity<Artist> response =
        restTemplate.getForEntity(url, Artist.class);
    if (id != -1) {
        assertEquals(response.getStatusCode(), HttpStatus.OK);
        Artist artist = response.getBody();
        Artist data = new Artist(id, name);

        assertEquals(artist.getId(), data.getId());
        // note: the corrected service returns the *proper* name
        assertEquals(
            artist.getName().toLowerCase(),
            data.getName().toLowerCase()
        );
    } else {
        assertEquals(response.getStatusCode(), HttpStatus.NOT_FOUND);
    }
}

@Test(dataProvider = "artistData")
public void testSearchForArtist(int id, String name) {
    String url = "http://localhost:" + port + "/artists/search/" +
        (name != null ? encode(name) : "");
    ResponseEntity<Artist> response =
        restTemplate.getForEntity(url, Artist.class);
    if (name != null) {
        if (id == -1) {
            assertEquals(response.getStatusCode(),
                HttpStatus.NOT_FOUND);
```

```java
        } else {
            assertEquals(response.getStatusCode(), HttpStatus.OK);
            Artist artist = response.getBody();
            Artist data = new Artist(id, name);

            assertEquals(artist.getId(), data.getId());
            // note: the corrected service returns the *proper* name
            assertEquals(
                artist.getName().toLowerCase(),
                data.getName().toLowerCase()
            );
        }
    } else {
        assertEquals(
            response.getStatusCode(),
            HttpStatus.BAD_REQUEST
        );
    }
}

@Test
public void testSaveExistingArtist() {
    String url = "http://localhost:" + port + "/artists";
    Artist newArtist = restTemplate.getForObject(url + "/1",
    Artist.class);

    ResponseEntity<Artist> response =
        restTemplate.postForEntity(url, newArtist, Artist.class);
    assertEquals(response.getStatusCode(), HttpStatus.OK);
    Artist artist = response.getBody();
    assertNotNull(artist);

    int id = artist.getId();
    assertEquals(id, newArtist.getId().intValue());
    assertEquals(artist.getName(), newArtist.getName());
```

```
        response = restTemplate.getForEntity(url + "/" + id, Artist.class);
        assertEquals(response.getStatusCode(), HttpStatus.OK);

        Artist foundArtist = response.getBody();
        assertNotNull(foundArtist);
        assertEquals(artist, foundArtist);
    }

    @DataProvider
    public Object[][] artistSearches() {
        return new Object[][]{
            new Object[]{"", 3},
            new Object[]{"T", 2},
            new Object[]{"Th", 2},
            new Object[]{"Thr", 1},
            new Object[]{"C", 1},
            new Object[]{"Z", 0}
        };
    }

    @Test(dataProvider = "artistSearches")
    public void testSearches(String name, int count) {
        ParameterizedTypeReference<List<Artist>> type =
            new ParameterizedTypeReference<>() {
            };
        String url = "/artists/match/" + encode(name);
        ResponseEntity<List<Artist>> response = restTemplate.exchange(
            url,
            HttpMethod.GET,
            null,
            type
        );
        assertEquals(response.getStatusCode(), HttpStatus.OK);
        List<Artist> artists = response.getBody();
        assertNotNull(artists);
        assertEquals(artists.size(), count);
    }
```

```java
// We need this to run AFTER testSearches completes, because
// testSearches adds to the artist list and therefore we
// might get one more artist than we're expecting out of
// some searches.
@Test(dependsOnMethods = "testSearches")
public void testSaveArtist() {
    String url = "http://localhost:" + port + "/artists";
    Artist newArtist = new Artist(0, "The Broken Keyboards");

    ResponseEntity<Artist> response = restTemplate.postForEntity(
        url,
        newArtist,
        Artist.class
    );
    assertEquals(response.getStatusCode(), HttpStatus.OK);

    Artist artist = response.getBody();
    assertNotNull(artist);
    int id = artist.getId();
    assertNotEquals(id, 0);
    assertEquals(artist.getName(), newArtist.getName());

    response = restTemplate.getForEntity(url + "/" + id, Artist.class);
    assertEquals(response.getStatusCode(), HttpStatus.OK);

    Artist foundArtist = response.getBody();
    assertNotNull(foundArtist);
    assertEquals(artist, foundArtist);
}
}
```

8.5.2 The SongController

Now for new code – let's add a SongController. This is a fairly simple controller, as you can see – nearly everything is delegated to the MusicService. The same approaches that we discussed for ArtistController apply here as well.

Listing 8-20. chapter8/src/main/java/com/bsg5/chapter8/SongController.java

```java
package com.bsg5.chapter8;

import org.springframework.http.MediaType;
import org.springframework.web.bind.annotation.GetMapping;
import org.springframework.web.bind.annotation.PathVariable;
import org.springframework.web.bind.annotation.RestController;
import org.springframework.web.util.UriUtils;
import java.nio.charset.Charset;
import java.util.List;

@RestController
public class SongController {
    private MusicRepository service;

    SongController(MusicRepository service) {
        this.service = service;
    }

    String decode(Object data) {
        return UriUtils.decode(data.toString(), Charset.defaultCharset());
    }

    @GetMapping(value="/artists/{name}/vote/{title}",
        produces = MediaType.APPLICATION_JSON_VALUE)
    Song voteForSong(@PathVariable String name, @PathVariable String title) {
        return service.voteForSong(decode(name), decode(title));
    }

    @GetMapping(value="/artists/{name}/song/{title}",
        produces = MediaType.APPLICATION_JSON_VALUE)
    Song getSong(@PathVariable String name, @PathVariable String title) {
        return service.getSong(decode(name), decode(title));
    }
```

```
@GetMapping(value="/artists/{name}/songs",
    produces = MediaType.APPLICATION_JSON_VALUE)
List<Song> getSongsForArtist(@PathVariable String name) {
    return service.getSongsForArtist(decode(name));
}

@GetMapping(value={"/artists/{name}/match/{title}",
    "/artists/{name}/match/"},
    produces = MediaType.APPLICATION_JSON_VALUE)
List<String> findSongsForArtist(@PathVariable String name,
                                @PathVariable(required = false)
                                    String title) {
    return service.getMatchingSongNamesForArtist(decode(name),
        title != null ? decode(title) : "");
}
}
```

At last, we come to what is arguably the most important test in the project – the SongControllerTest. Our other tests are important for incremental development and test-specific things. This test, however, covers nearly everything our project does in one class. (It doesn't **quite** cover everything, because we didn't want to repeat some of the simpler tests in ArtistControllerTest.)

Listing 8-21. chapter8/src/test/java/com/bsg5/ chapter8/SongControllerTest.java

```
package com.bsg5.chapter8;

import org.springframework.beans.factory.annotation.Autowired;
import org.springframework.boot.test.context.SpringBootTest;
import org.springframework.boot.test.web.client.TestRestTemplate;
import org.springframework.boot.web.server.LocalServerPort;
import org.springframework.core.ParameterizedTypeReference;
import org.springframework.http.HttpMethod;
import org.springframework.http.HttpStatus;
import org.springframework.http.ResponseEntity;
import org.springframework.jdbc.core.JdbcTemplate;
import org.springframework.test.context.testng.AbstractTestNGSpringContextTests;
```

```
import org.springframework.web.util.UriUtils;
import org.testng.annotations.BeforeMethod;
import org.testng.annotations.Test;

import java.nio.charset.Charset;
import java.util.List;
import java.util.function.Consumer;

import static org.testng.Assert.assertEquals;
import static org.testng.Assert.assertNotNull;

@SpringBootTest(webEnvironment = SpringBootTest.WebEnvironment.RANDOM_PORT)
public class SongControllerTest extends AbstractTestNGSpringContextTests {
    @LocalServerPort
    private int port;
    @Autowired
    private TestRestTemplate restTemplate;
    @Autowired
    JdbcTemplate jdbcTemplate;

    private Object[][] model = new Object[][]{
            {"Threadbare Loaf", "Someone Stole the Flour", 4},
            {"Threadbare Loaf", "What Happened To Our First CD?", 17},
            {"Therapy Zeppelin", "Medium", 4},
            {"Clancy in Silt", "Igneous", 5}
    };

    @BeforeMethod
    void clearDatabase() {
        jdbcTemplate.update("DELETE FROM songs");
        jdbcTemplate.update("DELETE FROM artists");
        populateData();
    }

    void iterateOverModel(Consumer<Object[]> consumer) {
        for (Object[] data : model) {
            consumer.accept(data);
        }
    }
```

```
String encode(Object data) {
    return UriUtils.encode(data.toString(), Charset.defaultCharset());
}

void populateData() {
    iterateOverModel(data -> {
        for (int i = 0; i < (Integer) data[2]; i++) {
            String url = "http://localhost:"
                + port
                + "/artists/"
                + encode(data[0])
                + "/vote/"
                + encode(data[1]);

            ResponseEntity<Song> response =
                restTemplate.getForEntity(url, Song.class);
            assertEquals(response.getStatusCode(), HttpStatus.OK);
        }
    });
}

@Test
void testSongVoting() {
    iterateOverModel(data -> {
        String url = "http://localhost:"
            + port
            + "/artists/"
            + encode(data[0])
            + "/song/"
            + encode(data[1]);

        ResponseEntity<Song> response =
            restTemplate.getForEntity(url, Song.class);
        assertEquals(response.getStatusCode(), HttpStatus.OK);
        Song song = response.getBody();
        assertNotNull(song);
```

```java
            assertEquals(song.getName(), data[1]);
            assertEquals(song.getVotes(), ((Integer) data[2]).intValue());
        });
    }

    @Test
    void testSongsForArtist() {
        ParameterizedTypeReference<List<Song>> type =
            new ParameterizedTypeReference<>() {
        };
        String url = "http://localhost:"
            + port
            + "/artists/"
            + encode("Threadbare Loaf")
            + "/songs";
        ResponseEntity<List<Song>> response = restTemplate.exchange(
                url,
                HttpMethod.GET,
                null,
                type
        );
        assertEquals(response.getStatusCode(), HttpStatus.OK);
        List<Song> songs =response.getBody();

        assertEquals(songs.size(), 2);
        assertEquals(songs.get(0).getName(), "What Happened To Our
        First CD?");
        assertEquals(songs.get(0).getVotes(), 17);
        assertEquals(songs.get(1).getName(), "Someone Stole the Flour");
        assertEquals(songs.get(1).getVotes(), 4);
    }

    @Test
    void testMatchingSongNamesForArtist() {
        ParameterizedTypeReference<List<String>> type =
            new ParameterizedTypeReference<>() {
        };
```

```
String url = "http://localhost:"
    + port
    + "/artists/"
    + encode("Threadbare Loaf")
    + "/match/" +
    encode("W");
ResponseEntity<List<String>> response = restTemplate.exchange(
        url,
        HttpMethod.GET,
        null,
        type
);

List<String> names = response.getBody();
assertEquals(names.size(), 1);
assertEquals(names.get(0), "What Happened To Our First CD?");
    }
}
```

From a coding standpoint, it's not particularly complex, but it is fairly comprehensive.

8.6 Next Steps

This chapter has been a bit of a journey through transaction support, `JdbcTemplate` usage, and testing of integrated services. Thankfully, the core concepts are fairly easy to summarize: using Spring's data access mechanism gives you trivial access to transaction support, and the Spring interfaces are really easy to use despite presenting a wide array of options. One limitation, though, is that we're still manually writing SQL for use with a relational database.

In our next chapter, we are going to take a look at another data abstraction from Spring, called "Spring Data." With Spring Data, we can write interfaces to access nearly **any** database, whether relational or not, and we will see how to make our queries programmatically verifiable.

Persistence with Spring and Spring Data

In Chapter 8 we finally stopped looking at configuration and presentation mechanisms, and we looked at accessing a relational database with `JdbcTemplate`. In this chapter, we're going to look at accessing data again – with a Spring project called "Spring Data," which can provide a mostly data-agnostic view of data access.

Spring Data unifies data access for Spring, providing common access to not only different databases but different APIs – like JPA (the Java Persistence API) and our old friend JDBC, but different **types** of databases like MongoDB, Neo4J, and others.

9.1 Introduction

We've tended to progress from the simplest use of technology to more advanced, but this chapter will invert things slightly, starting with JPA; JDBC and SQL are base-level technologies (and are used under the hood of JPA), but the problem with JDBC is that it is, well, JDBC – and it relies heavily on a live data structure, something you'd see in a running database with a fully functional, realized schema. That means that there are aspects of rigid data access that may or may not work, depending on the database, because it is the "system of record," the canonical description of what the data looks like. When we compile our application, we don't know if the database even exists, or what the schema looks like, which makes automatic tooling for that database rather difficult.

JPA, however, allows us to describe what the application should see as a data model. We can use a JPA data model and change the underlying structure all we like (as long as we also tell JPA what the underlying structure is), but we can also know at compile time what the program sees as the data model. That means that when we first compile our application, regardless of whether the database exists or not, we can know how to expect

© Joseph B. Ottinger and Andrew Lombardi 2019
J. B. Ottinger and A. Lombardi, *Beginning Spring 5*, https://doi.org/10.1007/978-1-4842-4486-9_9

to access our data (because it's described in code) – which means we can have a high degree of assurance that our application will access the data correctly, if perhaps not efficiently.[1]

Why don't we know if the data access is efficient or not? The answer is simple: we might design our object model in such a way that the database uses unindexed data, or more tables than it needs, for example, such that queries require table scans and so forth. JPA isn't a magic bullet that gives you an excellent schema no matter how you describe the data; it'll generally help you create a **functioning** schema, but you still have to understand how relational databases work to really fine-tune the data model. It sure would be nice to have magic performance sauce, though.

We're going to cover a few different storage mechanisms behind the Spring Data abstraction layer, but this chapter will hearken back to Chapters 3 and 8 and their usage of tests. Once we have the services working, it's a trivial matter to add REST endpoints in front of the services (as we saw in Chapters 7 and 8), so we're not going to distract ourselves here by adding a web-enabled front end in this chapter.

9.2 General Architecture

Spring Data extends the concept of a `Repository<T,ID>`, a generalized access layer for a given datastore and entity. We've already seen the @Repository annotation, but here we'll see an interface (also called `Repository<T,ID>`, where T is the type being stored and ID is a primary key type, extended with `CrudRepository<T,ID>>` and `PagingAndSort ingRepository<T,ID>`) that Spring will implement **for** you (for the most part) via proxies.

Proxies> in Java aren't really in scope for this book, unfortunately. With that said, though, here's a very cursory overview of one method: you can define an object (called a `Proxy`) that intercepts method calls, and arbitrarily execute code in a handler object. Since the proxy has access to the method signatures of the calls and the instance being called, the handler can execute code before or after the actual method bodies – or it can avoid calling the actual method bodies in the first place.

---

[1]Remember when we mentioned "suffering-oriented programming" back in Chapter 2?

With classes that implement `Repository<T,ID>`, the interface is used to manufacture method bodies out of (nearly) whole cloth, and the effect is that we define a simple interface and Spring magically implements the interface for us. There's obviously no magic – it's just a `Proxy` – but it makes using Spring Data a lot easier than it might have otherwise been.

It's worth noting that there are multiple mechanisms for proxies in Spring. The default is to use Java's innate proxy mechanisms, but under certain circumstances, Spring will use a library called CGLIB and build a different kind of proxy with it instead.

You will define the entity with Java and then create an interface (or set of interfaces) to describe how to manipulate that entity in the data storage system. The `Repository<T,ID>` interface is just a marker, in and of itself; it has no methods, but indicates to Spring that implementations work with databases somehow.

What's the use of `Repository<T,ID>` if it has no methods?

Well, sometimes you want to limit access to methods through the use of fine-grained interfaces. For example, one might have a `Controller` that has no ability to save entities; if we wanted to, we could define a `Repository<T,ID>` that only defined methods to read data, while the actual instance had methods to save or update entities. The `Controller` might receive a copy of the read-only interface from Spring, and therefore the **compiler** can enforce the requirement that it never save entities.

The `CrudRepository<T,ID>` interface, which extends `Repository<T,ID>`, defines operations for reading, writing, updating, removing, and **even** querying the database – and Spring Data applies some magic such that you can even specify queries **in the interface** without you having to know how to actually query the database itself. In Chapter 7 we saw methods like `findAllArtistsByName()`, which selected all artists whose names matched a wildcard, without being case-sensitive; with Spring Data, we define a method **signature** in the repository and get nearly the same functionality. (We'd want to build the wildcard externally, although there **are** ways to do it with the interface itself.)

Listing 9-1. Spring Data's equivalent to `findAllArtistsByName` from Chapter 7

```
public interface ArtistRepository extends Repository<Artist, Integer> {
    List<Artist> findLikeNameIgnoreCase(String name);
}
```

Building a `Repository<T,ID>` involves three source files. For a given repository, you will have

1. A Spring configuration (which can, of course, serve for multiple repositories)

2. An entity type (an object that represents data), with a primary key of some sort

3. An interface that implements `Repository<T,ID>` (or `CrudRepository<T,ID>`, or `PagingAndSortingRepository` `<T,ID>`, in practice), with the entity type and its primary key type

There are also variations of interface creation, to allow for different levels of method access. We'll show some of these as we go through the chapter.

9.2.1 An Important Note About Requirements

This chapter will demonstrate accessing two database systems: an embedded H2 database (just as in Chapters 7 and 8) and a MongoDB database. We're going to use a project that allows us to embed MongoDB, so you don't have to have MongoDB running (or installed).

9.3 Creating Our Project Structure

Chapter 9 is actually made up of four subprojects. They are

- `chapter9common`, which contains base classes and interfaces used by the other Chapter 9 projects

- `chapter9test`, which contains tests that our Spring Data implementations should be able to pass

- chapter9jpa, which contains an implementation and configuration for JPA

- chapter9mongodb, which contains an implementation and configuration for MongoDB

The chapter9test module has its test classes in src/main/java, which means the classes are available to projects that import chapter9test – and we'll be using them as dependencies for the testing phase.

Now let's start creating our project structure – as there are four separate projects, there's a lot here, but it's rather repetitive.

Listing 9-2. Creating the directory structure with POSIX

```
mkdir -p chapter9common/src/main/java
mkdir -p chapter9common/src/main/resources
mkdir -p chapter9common/src/test/java
mkdir -p chapter9common/src/test/resources
mkdir -p chapter9test/src/main/java
mkdir -p chapter9test/src/main/resources
mkdir -p chapter9test/src/test/java
mkdir -p chapter9test/src/test/resources
mkdir -p chapter9jpa/src/main/java
mkdir -p chapter9jpa/src/main/resources
mkdir -p chapter9jpa/src/test/java
mkdir -p chapter9jpa/src/test/resources
mkdir -p chapter9mongodb/src/main/java
mkdir -p chapter9mongodb/src/main/resources
mkdir -p chapter9mongodb/src/test/java
mkdir -p chapter9mongodb/src/test/resources
```

There's an alternative to this, of course, and since we're programmers, it's actually nicer and easier, using the bash shell and a touch of scripting. (It's also the way the project was actually created when writing this chapter. Just don't tell the editor!)

Listing 9-3. Creating the directory structure with POSIX

```
for i in common test jpa mongodb; do
  for j in main test; do
    for k in java resources; do
      mkdir -p chapter9$i/src/$j/$k;
    done;
  done;
done
```

We need to walk through our chapter9common and chapter9test projects before actually getting into code we can actually execute, because these projects serve as the basis for our chapter9jpa and chapter9mongodb projects. (They also contain more code than the jpa and mongodb projects do. The chapter9jpa and chapter9mongodb projects' source code is mostly made up of classes that extend or implement classes from chapter9common or chapter9test, with very little actual *source code.*)

9.3.1 The Common Code

The chapter9common project contains five interfaces, one abstract class, and one class that will end up being a Spring component. They are

- BaseEntity – A generic interface that defines accessors and mutators for a generic identifier

- BaseArtist – An interface that defines access to a name field for an artist and extends BaseEntity

- BaseSong – An interface that defines access to an implementation of BaseArtist, a song's name, and the number of votes for a song as well as extending BaseEntity

- BaseArtistRepository – An interface which defines how we will access entities that extend BaseArtist

- BaseSongRepository – An interface which defines how we will access entities that extend BaseSong

- `BaseMusicService` – An abstract class that orchestrates the various repository methods

- `WildcardConverter` – A class that provides a mechanism for constructing wildcards for services

Here's a class diagram, in UML, that purports to show the relationship between the various classes. When we implement concrete versions of this structure in `chapter9jpa` and `chapter9mongodb`, we'll basically be finalizing versions of the base classes.

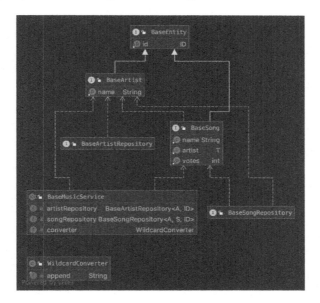

Most of these are really pretty simple. Because they're generic, though, their class declarations tend to be rather long; the reason is that different databases might treat primary keys differently; therefore we need to have a way to define primary keys on a case-by-case basis.

We're using "database" in the general sense of "application that stores data," not in the "relational database" sense.

For example, for relational databases, primary keys are often best generated as integers of some sort, but with document databases like MongoDB, the primary keys are generated as UUIDs represented as `String` instances. We could coerce the types to be common (therefore using UUIDs everywhere, or integers), but that feels like we're pouring optimizations down the drain for no good reason (unless, of course, you consider a simpler interface a "good reason," which you very well might).

First, let's take a look at the build script for chapter9common. It has some variations on some of our prior build scripts.

Listing 9-4. chapter9common/build.gradle

```
plugins {
    id 'org.springframework.boot' version '2.1.4.RELEASE' apply false
}

apply plugin: 'io.spring.dependency-management'

dependencyManagement {
    imports {
        mavenBom org.springframework.boot.gradle
            .plugin.SpringBootPlugin.BOM_COORDINATES
    }
}

dependencies {
    compile "org.springframework.data:spring-data-commons"
    compile "org.springframework:spring-tx"
    compile "org.springframework:spring-beans"
}
```

We actually do some magic in this build to get the dependency resolution to work without marking this as an actual Spring Boot project itself; we include the Spring Boot plugin, but then add apply false. This means that the io.spring.dependency-management is available to the project, and we can apply it without the rest of Spring Boot being kicked into motion.

However, the dependency management requires information about the versions to import; thus, we also add a dependencyManagement block and forcibly include the versions from the Spring Boot plugin.

It's a little backward, in that we're importing a plugin, disabling it, and then reenabling specific aspects of it, but it's caused by Spring Boot's design in and of itself; Spring Boot emphasizes simple projects rather than nested projects (like the projects in this chapter) so we're having to use mechanisms to give us access to the bits of Spring

Boot that we want, and nothing more, as chapter9common is not actually a Spring Boot project; it's an artifact that **uses** Spring Boot.

This is slightly dependent on the version of Gradle in use. With newer versions of Gradle, you can use an enforcedPlatform to do this; it's a little cleaner to use. If you're on the current version of Gradle, you can alter these projects to be cleaner (and use the new scopes, too); see https://docs.gradle.org/current/ userguide/ managing_transitive_dependencies.html#sec:bom_ import for more detail.

So let's take a look at our entity interfaces, to start with; they're simple (except for the generic declarations, which are only going to get worse as we progress through the chapter9common project).

First, the BaseEntity interface, which accepts an ID type.

Listing 9-5. chapter9common/src/main/java/com/bsg5/chapter9/common/ BaseEntity.java

```
package com.bsg5.chapter9.common;

public interface BaseEntity<ID> {
    ID getId();

    void setId(ID id);
}
```

This is simple enough; it's an interface, so it contains no state itself (no properties), but it does indicate that any class that implements BaseEntity has access to an Id property of some kind, passed to the compiler as a generic type, <ID>.

Let's take a look at BaseArtist, next, as it uses BaseEntity and adds access to a property of its own.

Listing 9-6. `chapter9common/src/main/java/com/bsg5/chapter9/common/` `BaseArtist.java`

```
package com.bsg5.chapter9.common;

public interface BaseArtist<ID>
    extends BaseEntity<ID> {

    /**
     * Get the artist name
     */
    String getName();

    void setName(String name);
}
```

It has a generic parameter, just as `BaseEntity` does, but only uses it to defer **to** `BaseEntity`.

`BaseSong` is a little more complicated, because it needs to provide access to something that implements `BaseArtist`. It has **two** generic parameters: one is a type that implements `BaseArtist`, and the other is the type for the identifier for `BaseEntity`.

Listing 9-7. `chapter9common/src/main/java/com/bsg5/chapter9/common/` `BaseSong.java`

```
package com.bsg5.chapter9.common;

public interface BaseSong<
    T extends BaseArtist<ID>,
    ID
    > extends BaseEntity<ID> {
    T getArtist();

    void setArtist(T artist);

    /**
     * Get the song name
     */
```

```java
    String getName();

    void setName(String name);

    int getVotes();

    void setVotes(int votes);
}
```

Now we start getting into the fun stuff; we're going to look at `BaseArtistRepository`, which actually uses Spring Data to provide functionality, and after that we'll look at `BaseSongRepository`, `BaseMusicService`, and `WildcardConverter`. Once we understand `BaseArtistRepository`, the other classes will be fairly simple to walk through.

Listing 9-8. chapter9common/src/main/java/com/bsg5/chapter9/common/
BaseArtistRepository.java

```java
package com.bsg5.chapter9.common;

import java.util.List;
import java.util.Optional;

import org.springframework.data.repository.CrudRepository;

public interface BaseArtistRepository<
    T extends BaseArtist<ID>,
    ID
    > extends CrudRepository<T, ID> {
    List<T> findAllByNameIsLikeIgnoreCaseOrderByName(String name);

    Optional<T> findByNameIgnoreCase(String name);
}
```

On its surface, this interface seems fairly simple. It has two generic parameters; one is something that implements `BaseArtist`, and the other is the primary key type. It also implements an interface, `CrudRepository`, which is our bridge to a lot of functionality.

`CrudRepository` exposes a number of useful and standard methods for, well, CRUD – "create," "read," "update," and "delete" – operations. The `ArtistRepository`'s declaration means that this is an implementation of `CrudRepository` that works with types that extend `BaseArtist`, with a primary key type represented by ID. The `CrudRepository` interface itself exposes the following methods.

Method Signature	Description
`<S extends T>` `S save(S entity)`	This saves an entity and returns a type assignable to the entity type. (If passed an `Artist`, what you will get back will be equivalent to an `Artist`.) It may also mutate the entity passed as an argument if the save operation assigns visible values (i.e., if saving the entity generates a primary key). It might not be the same type because some persistence mechanisms (like Hibernate) return a proxy that is assignable to the type instead of a simple type itself.

`<S extends T> Iterable<S>`
`saveAll(Iterable<S>`
`entities)`
	This will save a collection of entities; you can pass it any collection that the JVM can iterate through. This can emulate a batch operation in some limited circumstances, although transactional operations at a service level might be better.

`Optional<T>` `findById(ID id)`	This will do a primary key lookup for the entity type based on the primary key passed to it. If it is not found, it will return `Optional.empty()`.
`boolean existsById(ID id)`	This will indicate if the database has an entity of the correct type with the passed-in `id`.
`Iterable<T> findAll()`	This will return an `Iterable` of the entity type.

`Iterable<T>`
`findAllById(Iterable<ID>`
`ids)`
	This will return an `Iterable` for every existing entity that has a matching `id` in the collection of primary keys.

`long count()`	This will give you the count of all entities of the correct type in the repository. (This is a surprise, we're sure.)
`void deleteById(ID id)`	This will delete an entity from the datastore if one exists with this `id`.
`void delete(T entity)`	This will delete an entity from the datastore if the entity matches one that exists.
`void deleteAll(Iterable<?` `extends T> entities)`	This will delete all matching entities from the datastore.
`void deleteAll()`	This will delete all existing entities of this type from the datastore.

PagingAndSortingRepository() adds two methods to CrudRepository to aid with pagination (and sorting!) as well as serving as a marker for other methods to be available. The methods are findAll(Sort), where Sort represents options for sorting, and findAll(Pageable pageable), where pageable represents pagination and sorting options. They're both fairly simple methods, but they're not part of this chapter's scope.

However, BaseArtistRepository also defines two other methods:

```
List<T> findAllByNameIsLikeIgnoreCaseOrderByName(String name);
```

```
Optional<T> findByNameIgnoreCase(String name);
```

These methods are implemented by Spring Data via a dynamic proxy, and their functionality is derived from their names, in a fairly specific grammar. The grammar can be thought of like this:

- A query type, such as

    - find, which can return a collection or a single entity; you can get a collection by having a return type of List, for example; you can also return a java.util.Stream of the entity type if the underlying data persistence mechanism supports it.

    - read, which operates in the same way as find.

    - query, which operates in the same way as find.

    - get, which operates in the same way as find. get, read, query, and find are all equivalent in application and meaning; they're just present to allow programmers to use whatever query semantics they choose.

    - count, which returns a count of entities matching the query.

- A modifier, such as

    - Top, First, or Bottom followed by an optional number (1 is the default, so Top1 and Top are the same).

    - Distinct to apply distinctiveness to the results; this would apply to queries based on attributes other than the id or other unique fields.

- An optional entity type (which is not necessary but might add human-readability to the method name). You might say findArtistByName or findByName – which you prefer is up to you.

- By, which indicates the beginning of the criteria for the query

- A list of criteria, comprised of…

  - An attribute of the entity, such as Name (for Artist.name). Traversals are acceptable, so if you were to have, say, a Person entity with a reference to an Address which itself contained a city, it's acceptable to say findByAddressCity to use the city name as part of the query criteria.

  - IgnoreCase will cause the query to be case-insensitive, with the actual implementation depending on the datastore – JPA will call UPPER() on the attributes, for example.

  - Operators, the availability of which depends on the specific datastore implementation. Examples include

    - Between

    - LessThan

    - GreaterThan

    - Like

- Optional ordering, comprised of

  - OrderBy

  - An attribute name, like Name for an Artist or Song

  - An optional direction of either Asc or Desc

- A separator of And between the first and all subsequent criteria

This is not the **actual** grammar, obviously – for that we'd end up with four or five pages of Backus-Naur diagrams, which are designed to illustrate formal grammars – but hopefully it makes the naming system more clear.

If we have an `ArtistRepository<Artist, Integer>` (and we will!), if we want to find an `Artist` – here denoted by `<T>`, since T extends `BaseArtist` – by name without worrying about exact case matches, our query name would be expressed as `findByNameIgnoreCase(String name)`. It might return an `Optional<Artist>` or an `Artist` reference; if it's `Artist`, it will return `null` if the name doesn't exist in the database (i.e., the criteria failed). If it's `Optional<Artist>`, then a failure to match the criteria will return `Optional.empty()` – a form useful primarily for work with streams.

Worth noting: While Spring Data's query generator is amazingly powerful, it tends to yield rather complicated method names, and validation of the query name is a little… lacking. This places the burden for getting it right on you, the programmer. However, there's a library called "Querydsl" (`www.querydsl.com/`) that can fix this somewhat, by providing typesafe queries for Spring Data.

With Querydsl, you'd use an annotation processor to generate a "metamodel" – much like JPA's criteria modeling, actually – and use that model to generate queries that can be validated by the compiler itself. You'd use the metamodel's methods and attributes to build programmatic criteria for the query, instead of typing in names. This means you'd also (hopefully) have method names that were much easier to type.

However, Querydsl integration is still somewhat in flux. If you're using Maven and a particular project organization, it's (probably) fine, but Gradle integration is still in progress. For the purposes of **this** book, Querydsl is something to watch, but it's not ready.

Let's take a quick look at `BaseSongRepository`. This interface is substantively the same as `BaseArtistRepository`, although the declaration is longer because it has to have a reference to something that extends `BaseArtist` (because the `BaseSong` declaration needs it, too). This is also why we use `A extends BaseArtist<ID>` in the declaration; the `Repository` itself doesn't use A, but needs A declared to understand how a `BaseSong<A, ID>` is constructed. (There are other ways we could have constructed this, but this involved less nesting of types.)

Listing 9-9. chapter9common/src/main/java/com/bsg5/chapter9/common/
BaseSongRepository.java

```java
package com.bsg5.chapter9.common;

import org.springframework.data.repository.CrudRepository;

import java.util.List;
import java.util.Optional;

public interface BaseSongRepository<
    A extends BaseArtist<ID>,
    S extends BaseSong<A, ID>,
    ID
    > extends CrudRepository<S, ID> {
    Optional<S> findByArtistIdAndNameIgnoreCase(
            ID artistId, String name
    );

    List<S> findByArtistIdOrderByVotesDesc(ID artistId);

    List<S> findByArtistIdAndNameLikeIgnoreCaseOrderByNameDesc(
            ID artistId, String name
    );
}
```

Next, let's take a quick look at our `WildcardConverter`, which mainly provides a single method, called `convertToWildCard(String)`. It's very simple, of course. The reason this class exists is because some databases use special characters to match wildcards; SQL uses %, for example, while Neo4J uses a regular expression (like ".*"). Other databases might use different characters or, as we'll see with MongoDB, nothing at all. With this class, we can get our Spring configuration to build our `WildcardConverter` appropriately for our database, and our `BaseMusicService` doesn't have to change at all.

276

Listing 9-10. chapter9common/src/main/java/com/bsg5/chapter9/common/
WildcardConverter.java

```java
package com.bsg5.chapter9.common;

public class WildcardConverter {
    private final String append;

    public WildcardConverter(String append) {
        this.append = append;
    }

    public String convertToWildCard(String data) {
        return data + append;
    }
}
```

It's time for us to look at BaseMusicService, which uses classes that implement BaseSongRepository and BaseArtistRepository. This is an abstract class. Classes that extend BaseMusicService will need to do four things:

- Have the correct class signature

- Delegate to this class' constructor

- Implement createArtist(String), which creates an instance of something that implements BaseArtist

- Implement createSong(Artist, String), which creates an instance of something that implements BaseSong

Apart from that – and we'll see how this class is used shortly, we promise! – this class implements every functional requirement of our music service from Chapters 3 and 8, along with providing two extra methods to access a Song and an Artist directly, by their id. (This is a useful feature for REST services, as we'll see in limited fashion in Chapter 10.) It actually looks more daunting than it actually is. We know the code's verbose – it's a factor of this class being one of the most important ones in the entire chapter.

Listing 9-11. chapter9common/src/main/java/com/b0sg5/chapter9/common/ BaseMusicService.java

```java
package com.bsg5.chapter9.common;

import org.springframework.transaction.annotation.Transactional;

import java.util.List;
import java.util.stream.Collectors;

public abstract class BaseMusicService<
    A extends BaseArtist<ID>,
    S extends BaseSong<A, ID>,
    ID
    > {
    private BaseArtistRepository<A, ID> artistRepository;
    private BaseSongRepository<A, S, ID> songRepository;
    private WildcardConverter converter;

    protected BaseMusicService(
        BaseArtistRepository<A, ID> artistRepository,
        BaseSongRepository<A, S, ID> songRepository,
        WildcardConverter converter
    ) {
        this.artistRepository = artistRepository;
        this.songRepository = songRepository;
        this.converter = converter;
    }

    protected abstract A createArtist(String name);

    protected abstract S createSong(A artist, String name);

    @Transactional
    public void voteForSong(String artistName, String songTitle) {
        S song = getSong(artistName, songTitle);
        song.setVotes(song.getVotes() + 1);
        songRepository.save(song);
    }
```

```
@Transactional
public S getSong(String artistName, String songTitle) {
    A artist = getArtist(artistName);
    return songRepository
        .findByArtistIdAndNameIgnoreCase(artist.getId(), songTitle)
        .orElseGet(() -> {
            S entity = createSong(artist, songTitle);
            songRepository.save(entity);
            return entity;
        });
}

@Transactional
public A getArtist(String artistName) {
    return artistRepository
        .findByNameIgnoreCase(artistName)
        .orElseGet(() -> {
            A entity = createArtist(artistName);
            artistRepository.save(entity);
            return entity;
        });
}

@Transactional
public List<S> getSongsForArtist(String artistName) {
    A artist = getArtist(artistName);
    return songRepository.findByArtistIdOrderByVotesDesc(artist.
    getId());
}

@Transactional(readOnly = true)
public List<String> getMatchingArtistNames(String artistName) {
    return artistRepository
        .findAllByNameIsLikeIgnoreCaseOrderByName(
            converter.convertToWildCard(artistName))
        .stream()
        .map(A::getName)
```

```java
            .collect(Collectors.toList());
    }

    @Transactional
    public A getArtistById(ID id) {
        return artistRepository.findById(id).orElse(null);
    }

    @Transactional
    public S getSongById(ID id) {
        return songRepository.findById(id).orElse(null);
    }

    @Transactional(readOnly = true)
    public List<String> getMatchingSongNamesForArtist(
        String artistName,
        String songTitle
    ) {
        A artist = getArtist(artistName);
        return songRepository
            .findByArtistIdAndNameLikeIgnoreCaseOrderByNameDesc(artist.
            getId(),
                converter.convertToWildCard(songTitle))
            .stream()
            .map(S::getName)
            .collect(Collectors.toList());
    }
}
```

Now we've seen a set of classes that can be used to build an application. It's time for us to create the second of this chapter's four projects: chapter9test, which will contain three abstract classes that represent test suites. As with BaseMusicService, they're not extremely short (but they're also not extremely long!) – and the result will be that the "test code" in our JPA and MongoDB projects will be impressively short (mostly consisting of class declarations, in fact).

9.3.2 The **chapter9test** Project

The chapter9test project, like chapter9common, is not a "real" Spring Boot project; it's an artifact that a Spring Boot project would use. It's a little unique in that it's meant to be imported into other modules' **test** scopes, so it exports everything via src/main/java.

The build.gradle for chapter9test is very similar to the build.gradle for chapter9common.

Listing 9-12. chapter9test/build.gradle

```
plugins {
    id 'org.springframework.boot' version "2.1.4.RELEASE" apply false
}

apply plugin: 'io.spring.dependency-management'

dependencyManagement {
    imports {
        mavenBom org.springframework.boot.gradle
            .plugin.SpringBootPlugin.BOM_COORDINATES
    }
}

dependencies {
    compile "org.springframework.boot:spring-boot-starter-test"
    compile "org.testng:testng:$testNgVersion"
    compile project(":chapter9common")
}
```

Note that it has a compile dependency on TestNG and spring-boot-starter-test. When we import this project into chapter9jpa and chapter9mongodb, we'll do it at testCompile scope, so the TestNG and spring-boot-starter-test dependencies will be at test scope for downstream dependencies, too. (We're not polluting our classpaths.)

There are three sets of tests in chapter9test: BaseArtistRepositoryTests, BaseSongRepositoryTests, and BaseMusicServiceTests. Every one of them is fairly simple; the goal is to exercise the target of the tests, but with Spring injecting implementations of the services.

Thus, when we **use** these tests, we'll have a Spring configuration that references the necessary services, and these classes will use whatever is provided. As with chapter9common, this makes for some odd declarations, but it's nothing too complicated – just verbose.

Let's take a look at our first test, BaseArtistRepositoryTests.

Listing 9-13. chapter9test/src/main/java/com/bsg5/chapter9/test/ BaseArtistRepositoryTests.java

```
package com.bsg5.chapter9.test;

import com.bsg5.chapter9.common.BaseArtist;
import com.bsg5.chapter9.common.BaseArtistRepository;
import com.bsg5.chapter9.common.WildcardConverter;
import org.springframework.beans.factory.annotation.Autowired;
import org.springframework.test.context.testng.
AbstractTestNGSpringContextTests;
import org.testng.annotations.BeforeMethod;
import org.testng.annotations.Test;

import java.util.List;
import java.util.Optional;

import static org.testng.Assert.assertEquals;
import static org.testng.Assert.assertTrue;

public abstract class BaseArtistRepositoryTests<
    A extends BaseArtist<ID>,
    ID
    > extends AbstractTestNGSpringContextTests {
    @Autowired
    BaseArtistRepository<A, ID> artistRepository;

    // to allow access to createWildcard...
    @Autowired
    WildcardConverter converter;

    protected abstract A createArtist(String name);
```

```
@BeforeMethod
public void clearDatabase() {
    artistRepository.deleteAll();
}

@Test
public void testOperations() {
    // see if the database is empty
    assertEquals(artistRepository.count(), 0);

    A firstEntity = createArtist("Threadbare Loaf");
    A secondEntity = createArtist("Therapy Zeppelin");

    // save the first artist only.
    artistRepository.save(firstEntity);

    Optional<A> artist = artistRepository.findById(firstEntity.getId());
    assertTrue(artist.isPresent());
    assertEquals(artist.get(), firstEntity);

    List<A> query =
        artistRepository.findAllByNameIsLikeIgnoreCaseOrderByName(
            converter.convertToWildCard("th")
        );
    assertEquals(query.size(), 1l);
    assertEquals(query.get(0), firstEntity);

    artistRepository.save(secondEntity);
    query = artistRepository.findAllByNameIsLikeIgnoreCaseOrderByName(
        converter.convertToWildCard("th")
    );
    assertEquals(query.size(), 2);
}
}
```

Everything here is fairly straightforward for a base class; implementations will need to provide a way to create an artist instance somehow (via createArtist()) – but as we'll see in a few pages, a concrete instance of BaseArtistRepositoryTests is mostly boilerplate. The class itself fits in three lines.

Note that in Chapter 3 we used a different approach; instead of putting tests in a superclass, we had child classes delegate to a superclass. Chapter 3's approach is probably "safer" in a lot of ways, especially as your tests grow in complexity and features. We opted for this approach in **this** chapter mostly because we didn't want to repeat more code than we absolutely needed to. The chapter's long enough and got enough code in it as it is without adding another set of identical lines in every concrete test class.

BaseSongRepositoryTests is longer, but that's because BaseSongRepository does more work; it has to interact with artists, after all. It uses @BeforeMethod to reset the database (whichever database it is!) before testing the BaseSongRepository instance.

Listing 9-14. chapter9test/src/main/java/com/bsg5/chapter9/test/ BaseSongRepositoryTests.java

```
package com.bsg5.chapter9.test;

import static org.testng.Assert.assertEquals;
import static org.testng.Assert.assertNotNull;

import java.util.List;
import java.util.Optional;

import org.springframework.beans.factory.annotation.Autowired;
import org.springframework.test.context.testng.
AbstractTestNGSpringContextTests;
import org.testng.annotations.BeforeMethod;
import org.testng.annotations.Test;

import com.bsg5.chapter9.common.BaseArtist;
import com.bsg5.chapter9.common.BaseArtistRepository;
import com.bsg5.chapter9.common.BaseSong;
import com.bsg5.chapter9.common.BaseSongRepository;
import com.bsg5.chapter9.common.WildcardConverter;
```

```java
public abstract class BaseSongRepositoryTests<
    A extends BaseArtist<ID>,
    S extends BaseSong<A, ID>,
    ID>
    extends AbstractTestNGSpringContextTests {
    @Autowired
    BaseArtistRepository<A, ID> artistRepository;
    @Autowired
    BaseSongRepository<A, S, ID> songRepository;
    @Autowired
    WildcardConverter converter;

    protected abstract A createArtist(String name);

    protected abstract S createSong(A artist, String name);

    @BeforeMethod
    public void clearDatabase() {
        songRepository.deleteAll();
        artistRepository.deleteAll();
        buildModel();
    }

    private Object[][] model = new Object[][]{
        {"Threadbare Loaf", "Someone Stole the Flour", 4},
        {"Threadbare Loaf", "What Happened To Our First CD?", 17},
        {"Therapy Zeppelin", "Mfbrbl Is Not A Word", 0},
        {"Therapy Zeppelin", "Medium", 4},
        {"Clancy in Silt", "Igneous", 5}
    };

    private void buildModel() {
        for (Object[] data : model) {
            String artistName = (String) data[0];
            String songTitle = (String) data[1];
            Integer votes = (Integer) data[2];
```

```
            Optional<A> artistQuery = artistRepository
                .findByNameIgnoreCase(artistName);
            A artist = artistQuery.orElseGet(() -> {
                A entity = createArtist(artistName);
                artistRepository.save(entity);
                return entity;
            });
            Optional<S> songQuery = songRepository
                .findByArtistIdAndNameIgnoreCase(artist.getId(),
                    songTitle);
            if (songQuery.isEmpty()) {
                S song = createSong(artist, songTitle);
                song.setVotes(votes);
                songRepository.save(song);
            }
        }
    }
}

@Test
public void testOperations() {
    A artist = artistRepository
        .findByNameIgnoreCase("therapy zeppelin")
        .orElseThrow();
    List<S> songs = songRepository
        .findByArtistIdAndNameLikeIgnoreCaseOrderByNameDesc(
            artist.getId(),
            converter.convertToWildCard("m")
        );
    assertEquals(songs.size(), 2);

    songs = songRepository
        .findByArtistIdOrderByVotesDesc(artist.getId());
    assertEquals(songs.size(), 2);

    // we know the votes assigned by default,
    // and they should be in descending order.
```

```
        // "Medium" has four votes...
        assertEquals(songs.get(0).getName(), "Medium");
        assertEquals(songs.get(0).getVotes(), 4);
        // "Mfbrbl" is liked by nobody. I mean, REALLY.
        assertEquals(songs.get(1).getVotes(), 0);
    }
}
```

Lastly, we have the longest of our test classes, BaseMusicServiceTests. This one is conceptually the same as BaseSongRepositoryTests, except it works with BaseMusicService instead; the mechanisms it uses are pretty much exactly the same as what we see in BaseSongRepositoryTests.

There's one thing to note, though: the abstract ID getNonexistentId() method. The base class has no idea what a valid ID looks like, so classes that use this will need to implement this method, hopefully with an identifier that won't naturally occur, such that the tests that use this method – testFindArtistById() and testFindSongById() – will successfully check for an object that doesn't exist.

Listing 9-15. chapter9test/src/main/java/com/bsg5/chapter9/test/
BaseMusicServiceTests.java

```
package com.bsg5.chapter9.test;

import com.bsg5.chapter9.common.*;
import org.springframework.beans.factory.annotation.Autowired;
import org.springframework.test.context.testng.
AbstractTestNGSpringContextTests;
import org.testng.annotations.BeforeMethod;
import org.testng.annotations.Test;

import java.util.List;
import java.util.function.Consumer;

import static org.testng.Assert.*;

public abstract class BaseMusicServiceTests<
    A extends BaseArtist<ID>,
    S extends BaseSong<A, ID>,
    ID
```

```java
> extends AbstractTestNGSpringContextTests {
@Autowired
BaseMusicService<A, S, ID> musicService;
@Autowired
BaseArtistRepository<A, ID> artistRepository;
@Autowired
BaseSongRepository<A, S, ID> songRepository;

private Object[][] model = new Object[][]{
    {"Threadbare Loaf", "Someone Stole the Flour", 4},
    {"Threadbare Loaf", "What Happened To Our First CD?", 17},
    {"Therapy Zeppelin", "Medium", 4},
    {"Clancy in Silt", "Igneous", 5}
};

@BeforeMethod
public void clearDatabase() {
    songRepository.deleteAll();
    artistRepository.deleteAll();
    populateService();
}

protected abstract ID getNonexistentId();

void iterateOverModel(Consumer<Object[]> consumer) {
    for (Object[] data : model) {
        consumer.accept(data);
    }
}

void populateService() {
    iterateOverModel(data -> {
        for (int i = 0; i < (Integer) data[2]; i++) {
            musicService.voteForSong((String) data[0], (String)
            data[1]);
        }
    });
}
```

```java
@Test
void testSongVoting() {
    iterateOverModel(data ->
        assertEquals(
            musicService.getSong((String) data[0],
                (String) data[1]).getVotes(),
            ((Integer) data[2]).intValue()
        ));
}

@Test
void testSongsForArtist() {
    List<S> songs =
        musicService.getSongsForArtist("Threadbare Loaf");
     assertEquals(songs.size(),
        2);
    assertEquals(songs.get(0).getName(),
        "What Happened To Our First CD?");
    assertEquals(songs.get(0).getVotes(),
        17);
    assertEquals(songs.get(1).getName(),
        "Someone Stole the Flour");
    assertEquals(songs.get(1).getVotes(),
        4);
}

@Test
void testMatchingArtistNames() {
    List<String> names = musicService.getMatchingArtistNames("Th");
    assertEquals(names.size(), 2);
    assertEquals(names.get(0), "Therapy Zeppelin");
    assertEquals(names.get(1), "Threadbare Loaf");
}
```

```java
    @Test
    void testFindArtistById() {
        A artist = musicService.getArtist("Threadbare Loaf");
        assertNotNull(artist);
        A searched = musicService.getArtistById(artist.getId());
        assertNotNull(searched);
        assertEquals(artist.getName(), searched.getName());
        searched = musicService.getArtistById(getNonexistentId());
        assertNull(searched);
    }

    @Test
    void testFindSongById() {
        S song = musicService.getSong("Therapy Zeppelin",
            "Medium");
        assertNotNull(song);
        S searched = musicService.getSongById(song.getId());
        assertNotNull(searched);
        assertEquals(song.getName(), searched.getName());
        searched = musicService.getSongById(getNonexistentId());
        assertNull(searched);
    }

    @Test
    void testMatchingSongNamesForArtist() {
        List<String> names =
            musicService.getMatchingSongNamesForArtist(
                "Threadbare Loaf", "W"
            );
        assertEquals(names.size(),
            1);
        assertEquals(names.get(0),
            "What Happened To Our First CD?");
    }
}
```

It's time we actually got to **using** Spring Data instead of preparing to use it.

9.3.3 **The chapter9jpa Project**

JPA – the Java Persistence API – is a specification that provides idiomatic object/relational mapping (or "ORM") for Java. In other words, it's designed to map data from a database table (or sets of tables), where data is stored in rows and columns, and a Java object model.

We saw some of that in Chapter 8, except we were doing the conversion manually (and only when querying the database).

There are a number of JPA implementations. Hibernate (https://hibernate.org) is *probably* the most influential object-relational mapper for Java, just as Spring is *probably* the most influential Dependency Injection library for Java. Alternatives to Hibernate include OpenJPA (https://openjpa.apache.org/), EclipseLink (www.eclipse.org/eclipselink/), and DataNucleus (www.datanucleus.org/) – among others – but in this chapter we're going to use what Spring Data provides for us, which is Hibernate.

Let's take a quick look at our build.gradle. There are a few things to note:

- It includes a test-time dependency on chapter9test.

- It has the same limited plugin configuration and dependency management that chapter9common and chapter9test have. This is because we're going to use chapter9jpa as a dependency in Chapter 10.

- It uses Lombok (as described in Chapter 8) and specifies Lombok as an annotation processor in the same manner that Chapter 8 did.

- It has a dependency on spring-boot-starter-data-jpa and on h2 as a sample database.

- It imports jackson-annotations because we want to use an annotation in one of the entity classes – which we'll see (and explain) when we look at the Artist implementation.

Listing 9-16. chapter9jpa/build.gradle

```
plugins {
    id 'org.springframework.boot' version "2.1.4.RELEASE" apply false
}

apply plugin: 'io.spring.dependency-management'
```

```
dependencyManagement {
    imports {
        mavenBom org.springframework.boot.gradle
            .plugin.SpringBootPlugin.BOM_COORDINATES
    }
}

dependencies {
    compile "com.h2database:h2:1.4.199"
    compile "org.springframework.boot:spring-boot-starter-data-jpa"
    compile project(":chapter9common")

    compile "com.fasterxml.jackson.core:jackson-
    annotations:$jacksonVersion"
    compileOnly "org.projectlombok:lombok:1.+"
    annotationProcessor "org.projectlombok:lombok"

    testCompile project(":chapter9test")
}
```

The hard work for us is actually already done, in chapter9common. What this project needs to do is verbose (because it's in Java, and Java idiomatically puts classes in their own source files, which means a lot of repetitive boilerplate), but it's still surprisingly simple:

- Implement all of the base classes

- Provide a Spring configuration

Let's get to it. We have to implement BaseArtist, BaseSong, BaseArtistRepository, BaseSongRepository, and BaseMusicService; thankfully, all of them are very short, but we still have to have them. Then we'll have to build a configuration, and then we'll need to extend our test classes, too.

First, the Artist class. This is a JPA entity, and we're going to use Lombok to fill it out; note that it extends BaseArtist and uses Integer as the identifier type. It also uses regular JPA annotations to define relationships between artists and songs.

You'll note the use of @JsonIgnore as an annotation on the songs reference; this is required in this case by our rather simple object structure, in which an Artist has a reference to a set of Song objects, and each of those Song objects has a reference back to the Artist. This has implications when serializing object structures – and since this module is used in Chapter 10, we have to account for serialization issues or else we'll see stack overflows.

Listing 9-17. chapter9jpa/src/main/java/com/bsg5/chapter9/jpa/Artist. java

```java
package com.bsg5.chapter9.jpa;

import com.bsg5.chapter9.common.BaseArtist;
import com.fasterxml.jackson.annotation.JsonIgnore;
import lombok.Data;
import lombok.EqualsAndHashCode;
import lombok.NoArgsConstructor;
import lombok.RequiredArgsConstructor;
import org.springframework.lang.NonNull;

import javax.persistence.*;
import java.util.ArrayList;
import java.util.List;

@Entity
@Data
@NoArgsConstructor
@RequiredArgsConstructor
@EqualsAndHashCode(exclude = "songs")
public class Artist implements BaseArtist<Integer> {
    @Id
    @GeneratedValue(strategy = GenerationType.AUTO)
    Integer id;
    @NonNull
    String name;
    @OneToMany(
        cascade = CascadeType.ALL,
        mappedBy = "artist",
        fetch = FetchType.EAGER
    )
```

```
    @OrderBy("votes DESC")
    @JsonIgnore
    List<Song> songs = new ArrayList<>();
}
```

We can't use this without a reference to Song.

Listing 9-18. chapter9jpa/src/main/java/com/bsg5/chapter9/jpa/Song.java

```
package com.bsg5.chapter9.jpa;

import com.bsg5.chapter9.common.BaseSong;
import lombok.AllArgsConstructor;
import lombok.Data;
import lombok.NoArgsConstructor;
import lombok.RequiredArgsConstructor;
import org.springframework.lang.NonNull;

import javax.persistence.*;

@Entity
@Data
@NoArgsConstructor
@RequiredArgsConstructor
@AllArgsConstructor
@Table(indexes = {
    @Index(
        name = "artist_song",
        columnList = "artist_id,name",
        unique = true
    )
})
public class Song implements BaseSong<Artist, Integer> {
    @Id
    @GeneratedValue(strategy = GenerationType.AUTO)
    Integer id;
    @ManyToOne
    @NonNull
```

```
    Artist artist;
    @NonNull
    String name;
    int votes;
}
```

Again, this is a fairly standard (and probably naïve) implementation of a JPA entity.

The ArtistRepository is actually incredibly simple: it's just an interface that uses concrete types for BaseArtistRepository. That's it. The only information added here is in the interface definition.

Listing 9-19. chapter9jpa/src/main/java/com/bsg5/chapter9/jpa/ ArtistRepository.java

```
package com.bsg5.chapter9.jpa;

import com.bsg5.chapter9.common.BaseArtistRepository;

public interface ArtistRepository
    extends BaseArtistRepository<Artist, Integer> {
}
```

The SongRepository is done in the exact same manner: it exists solely to add type information to BaseSongRepository.

Listing 9-20. chapter9jpa/src/main/java/com/bsg5/chapter9/jpa/ SongRepository.java

```
package com.bsg5.chapter9.jpa;

import com.bsg5.chapter9.common.BaseSongRepository;

public interface SongRepository
    extends BaseSongRepository<Artist, Song, Integer> {
}
```

Lastly, we have MusicService – and here we have something a little more complicated, but not very much so. We need to implement two methods to create instances of Artist and Song, and we also want to delegate to BaseMusicService' constructor.

It's not marked as a @Component, however, because we're going to specifically construct it in the Spring configuration. (The type resolution, caused by all of the generics being thrown about, makes explicit configuration far easier to use.)

Listing 9-21. chapter9jpa/src/main/java/com/bsg5/chapter9/jpa/ MusicService.java

```
package com.bsg5.chapter9.jpa;

import com.bsg5.chapter9.common.BaseMusicService;
import com.bsg5.chapter9.common.WildcardConverter;
import org.springframework.stereotype.Component;

public class MusicService extends BaseMusicService<Artist, Song, Integer> {
    MusicService(
        ArtistRepository artistRepository,
        SongRepository songRepository,
        WildcardConverter converter
    ) {
        super(artistRepository, songRepository, converter);
    }

    @Override
    protected Artist createArtist(String name) {
        return new Artist(name);
    }

    @Override
    protected Song createSong(Artist artist, String name) {
        return new Song(artist, name);
    }
}
```

The only thing left, then, is a Spring configuration. We'll do this with a class called JpaConfiguration.

Listing 9-22. `chapter9jpa/src/main/java/com/bsg5/chapter9/jpa/`
`JpaConfiguration.java`

```java
package com.bsg5.chapter9.jpa;

import com.bsg5.chapter9.common.WildcardConverter;
import org.springframework.boot.SpringBootConfiguration;
import org.springframework.boot.autoconfigure.domain.EntityScan;
import org.springframework.context.annotation.Bean;
import org.springframework.data.jpa.repository.config.
EnableJpaRepositories;

@SpringBootConfiguration
@EnableJpaRepositories
@EntityScan
public class JpaConfiguration {
    @Bean
    WildcardConverter converter() {
        return new WildcardConverter("%");
    }

    @Bean
    MusicService musicService(
        ArtistRepository artistRepository,
        SongRepository songRepository,
        WildcardConverter converter
    ) {
        return new MusicService(artistRepository, songRepository, converter);
    }
}
```

Here, we leverage Spring Boot to do most of the work, with @SpringBootConfiguration. This will scan the current package (and any packages whose names start with com. bsg5.chapter9.jpa) for Spring components – which will catch our MusicService and ArtistRepository and SongRepository interfaces; with @EnableJpaRepositories we're informing Spring of what kind of services to implement (and where to look for classes that have the @Repository annotation).

We also use the @EntityScan annotation to force scanning for entities (classes marked with @Entity) in the current package (and any "subpackages" – i.e., packages whose names start with this package's name). We won't need this to run our tests – the test annotations will do this for us – but in "real code" we'll want it.

We also create our JPA-compatible WildcardConverter as a component.

Note that we're not doing anything to create any resources for JPA; no datasources, no EntityManager references, nothing. Spring Boot is doing that for us, through the spring-boot-starter-data-jpa dependency. By default we'll have an in-memory version of whatever database is in our classpath (H2, in this project); if we wanted to (and we do), we can use application.properties and set a JDBC URL with spring.datasource.url=jdbc:h2:file:chapter9jpa, or whatever value makes sense. As an example, see Listing 9-23.

Listing 9-23. chapter9jpa/src/main/resources/application.properties

```
spring.datasource.url=jdbc:h2:./chapter9jpa;DB_CLOSE_DELAY=-1;
spring.datasource.username=sa
spring.datasource.password=

spring.jpa.hibernate.ddl-auto=update
```

Our tests for chapter9jpa look a lot like the rest of the code. We have three tests, each extending one of the classes from the chapter9test project, adding type information specific to chapter9jpa and, occasionally, implementing a method or two to help the tests instantiate classes of the right type.

Here's the first test, ArtistRepositoryTests.

Listing 9-24. chapter9jpa/src/test/java/com/bsg5/chapter9/jpa/ArtistRepositoryTests.java

```
package com.bsg5.chapter9.jpa;

import com.bsg5.chapter9.test.BaseArtistRepositoryTests;
import org.springframework.boot.test.autoconfigure.orm.jpa.DataJpaTest;
```

```
@DataJpaTest
public class ArtistRepositoryTests
    extends BaseArtistRepositoryTests<Artist, Integer> {
    protected Artist createArtist(String name) {
        return new Artist(name);
    }
}
```

Note the use of @DataJpaTest.

SongRepositoryTests is effectively the same.

Listing 9-25. chapter9jpa/src/test/java/com/bsg5/chapter9/jpa/
SongRepositoryTests.java

```
package com.bsg5.chapter9.jpa;

import org.springframework.boot.test.autoconfigure.orm.jpa.DataJpaTest;

import com.bsg5.chapter9.test.BaseSongRepositoryTests;

@DataJpaTest
public class SongRepositoryTests
    extends BaseSongRepositoryTests<Artist, Song, Integer> {
    @Override
    protected Artist createArtist(String name) {
        return new Artist(name);
    }

    @Override
    protected Song createSong(Artist artist, String name) {
        return new Song(artist, name);
    }
}
```

And lastly, let's see MusicServiceTests, which is similar to the prior two tests in that it mostly serves to provide concrete types to the generic superclass, along with implementing getNonexistentId(), with an absurdly high identifier.

Listing 9-26. chapter9jpa/src/test/java/com/bsg5/chapter9/jpa/
MusicServiceTests.java

```
package com.bsg5.chapter9.jpa;

import org.springframework.boot.test.autoconfigure.orm.jpa.DataJpaTest;

import com.bsg5.chapter9.test.BaseMusicServiceTests;

@DataJpaTest
public class MusicServiceTests
    extends BaseMusicServiceTests<Artist, Song, Integer> {
    @Override
    protected Integer getNonexistentId() {
        return 1928491;
    }
}
```

As you can see, the chapter9jpa project really doesn't add much. It provides concrete entities (Artist and Song), and the configuration provides a WildcardConverter; MusicService, too, provides an easy way to build our entity instances, but that's about it. The rest of the project's code is providing concrete types for various interfaces.

Could we have built our base classes differently, in particular to make it so we didn't have to provide methods like createArtist() and createSong()? The answer, of course, is "yes," and in multiple ways. We could have derived the concrete class references in BaseMusicService, for example (the references aren't available for BaseMusicService but would have been for child classes, and we could have exploited that).

We could also have passed in concrete references (i.e., Artist.class) to BaseMusicService's constructor and used those references to build new objects, as well.

In the end, which approach you choose really depends on which approach you *prefer*. Here, one of the simplest approaches possible was chosen – abstract methods that, given data, pass back valid instances. It's simple, and hard to screw up.

It violates DRY – "don't repeat yourself" – especially when you consider that the signature of each of the copied methods looks exactly the same. In this case, the choice was made deliberately to write the methods over again in the interest of space and simplicity; if we abstracted everything out, we'd have another whole set of classes to go through.

If we wanted to, we could write a configuration that ran a Spring Boot application as we saw in Chapter 8; all that would be left would be the creation of a functional user interface, and we'd have a working music application, using a relational database for data storage.

Now let's see how much work we have to do to use a **different** data provider – MongoDB.

9.3.4 The chapter9mongodb Project

MongoDB (`https://mongodb.com`) is an open source database that represents data as collections of documents in binary JSON. As such, it uses a dynamic, flexible schema. It's loosely grouped among "NoSQL databases," those data management systems that don't SQL to manipulate data. It's also a good example of what makes NoSQL both good and bad: incredible speed and scalability, occasionally obscure querying and modeling, and a typical provider-specific approach to transactions.[2]

Thankfully, Spring Data makes using MongoDB fairly trivial, and it matches the pattern we saw in the JPA example, with the use of the Spring Data MongoDB module.

9.3.5 Getting MongoDB

We're going to use a library that allows us to **embed** MongoDB for our tests, so you don't have to have MongoDB installed. Of course, you might actually *want* to have MongoDB installed locally, rather than relying on an embedded installation; if you build an application using MongoDB, an external dependency isn't unexpected, after all. Here's

---

[2]This explanation of what MongoDB is was edited from `https://searchdatamanagement.techtarget.com/definition/MongoDB`, which is actually a good reference. This book isn't trying to sell you on MongoDB (or anything else, beyond Spring, of course), so we're covering products only as much as we need to.

how you can install MongoDB should you so choose; note that the tests will still use an embedded version, but it's easy to run MongoDB if that's what you want to do.

On OSX, it's as simple as running `brew install mongo`.

On Ubuntu, MongoDB can be installed with `apt-get install mongodb`.

On Windows, you can install MongoDB by going to its download page (www.mongodb.com/download-center/community) and grabbing the proper MSI file.

You'd start MongoDB trivially by finding an empty directory and running it.

Listing 9-27. Starting MongoDB

```
mkdir /var/tmp/musicdata
mongod --noauth -dbpath /var/tmp/musicdata
```

Consult the instructions on `https://mongodb.com` for your specific operating system if this doesn't work properly for you. Note also that this starts MongoDB without authentication; this is **solely** useful for running tests and other such operations of little long-term value.

9.3.6 The Code for the `chapter9mongodb` Project

Our `build.gradle` looks very similar to our `chapter9jpa build.gradle`. Instead of `spring-boot-starter-data-jpa`, it uses `spring-boot-starter-data-mongodb`, and it also includes one more test dependency, `de.flapdoodle.embed:de.flapdoodle.embed.mongo:2.2.0`. This dependency is going to allow our tests to actually download and start an embedded MongoDB instance so we don't have to make sure MongoDB is running before executing any of our tests.

Listing 9-28. chapter9mongodb/build.gradle

```
plugins {
    id 'org.springframework.boot' version '2.1.4.RELEASE'
}

apply plugin: 'io.spring.dependency-management'

dependencies {
```

```
compile("org.springframework.boot:spring-boot-starter-data-mongodb")
compile project(':chapter9common')

compileOnly 'org.projectlombok:lombok:1.+'
annotationProcessor 'org.projectlombok:lombok:1.+'

testCompile 'de.flapdoodle.embed:de.flapdoodle.embed.mongo:2.2.0'
testCompile project(':chapter9test')
}
```

The entities for the chapter9mongodb project are actually the core substantive difference between this and the chapter9jpa project. The other classes will look pretty much exactly the same, with the primary differences being in package declarations (since the chapter9mongodb project uses com.bsg5.chapter9.mongodb instead of com.bsg5.chapter9.jpa).

However, even in our entities the differences are minor; in Artist, for example, instead of using @Entity, we use @Document, for example, and the primary key is a String instead of an Integer.

Listing 9-29. chapter9mongodb/src/main/java/com/bsg5/chapter9/mongodb/Artist.java

```
package com.bsg5.chapter9.mongodb;

import com.bsg5.chapter9.common.BaseArtist;
import lombok.Data;
import lombok.NoArgsConstructor;
import lombok.RequiredArgsConstructor;
import org.springframework.data.annotation.Id;
import org.springframework.data.mongodb.core.mapping.Document;
import org.springframework.lang.NonNull;

@Document
@Data
@NoArgsConstructor
@RequiredArgsConstructor
public class Artist implements BaseArtist<String> {
    @Id
```

```
    String id;
    @NonNull
    String name;
}
```

The Song is also nearly identical. There are differences, of course; we see the use of @CompoundIndexes to declare a unique index between the artist and the name of the song. (In this, it's a close analog to how a relational database implements compound indexes. The ":1" in the index structure refers to sort order, which isn't relevant for our application but still needs to be specified.) We also refer to an Artist as a @DBRef, which is a way of telling Spring to store a reference to a valid Artist document in the field. The result is that we still use the object in the exact same way as we would have with JPA – after all, we're using the exact same interfaces – but we're helping Spring Data determine what the object model should look like.

Listing 9-30. chapter9mongodb/src/main/java/com/bsg5/chapter9/ mongodb/Song.java

```
package com.bsg5.chapter9.mongodb;

import com.bsg5.chapter9.common.BaseSong;
import lombok.Data;
import lombok.NoArgsConstructor; import lombok.RequiredArgsConstructor;
import org.springframework.data.annotation.Id;
import org.springframework.data.mongodb.core.index.CompoundIndex;
import org.springframework.data.mongodb.core.index.CompoundIndexes;
import org.springframework.data.mongodb.core.mapping.DBRef;
import org.springframework.data.mongodb.core.mapping.Document;
import org.springframework.lang.NonNull;

@Document
@Data
@NoArgsConstructor
@RequiredArgsConstructor
@CompoundIndexes(
        @CompoundIndex(unique = true, def = "{'artist':1, 'name':1}")
)
```

```java
public class Song implements BaseSong<Artist, String> {
    @Id
    String id;
    @NonNull
    @DBRef
    Artist artist;
    @NonNull
    String name;
    int votes;
}
```

Now we get to the truly repetitive bits of the chapter: we're going to see ArtistRepository, SongRepository, and MusicService for the chapter9mongodb project, and except for the package, all three will look nearly exactly like the versions from chapter9jpa.

First, the ArtistRepository.

Listing 9-31. chapter9mongodb/src/main/java/com/bsg5/chapter9/mongodb/ArtistRepository.java

```java
package com.bsg5.chapter9.mongodb;

import com.bsg5.chapter9.common.BaseArtistRepository;

public interface ArtistRepository
    extends BaseArtistRepository<Artist, String> {
}
```

Next, the SongRepository.

Listing 9-32. chapter9mongodb/src/main/java/com/bsg5/chapter9/mongodb/SongRepository.java

```java
package com.bsg5.chapter9.mongodb;

import com.bsg5.chapter9.common.BaseSongRepository;
import org.springframework.stereotype.Repository;
```

```
public interface SongRepository
    extends BaseSongRepository<Artist, Song, String> {
}
```

Next, the MusicService.

Listing 9-33. chapter9mongodb/src/main/java/com/bsg5/chapter9/mongodb/
MusicService.java

```java
package com.bsg5.chapter9.mongodb;

import com.bsg5.chapter9.common.BaseMusicService;
import com.bsg5.chapter9.common.WildcardConverter;
import org.springframework.stereotype.Component;

@Component
public class MusicService extends BaseMusicService<Artist, Song, String> {
    MusicService(
        ArtistRepository artistRepository,
        SongRepository songRepository,
        WildcardConverter converter
    ) {
        super(artistRepository, songRepository, converter);
    }

    @Override
    protected Artist createArtist(String name) {
        return new Artist(name);
    }

    @Override
    protected Song createSong(Artist artist, String name) {
        return new Song(artist, name);
    }
}
```

Before we get to the tests – which will, by the way, look very familiar, just like our other classes so far – we should look at the `MongoConfiguration`. It, too, will be very familiar, with a few differences: we use `@EnableMongoRepositories` instead of `@EnableJpaRepositories`.

Just as we saw in the `chapter9jpa` project, we initialize a `WildcardConverter` – but here, the wildcard is applied by MongoDB, and not with a special character.

Listing 9-34. chapter9mongodb/src/main/java/com/bsg5/chapter9/mongodb/MongoConfiguration.java

```java
package com.bsg5.chapter9.mongodb;

import com.bsg5.chapter9.common.WildcardConverter;
import org.springframework.boot.SpringBootConfiguration;
import org.springframework.boot.autoconfigure.domain.EntityScan;
import org.springframework.context.annotation.Bean;
import org.springframework.data.mongodb.repository.config.
EnableMongoRepositories;

@SpringBootConfiguration
@EnableMongoRepositories
@EntityScan
public class MongoConfiguration {
    @Bean
    WildcardConverter converter() {
        return new WildcardConverter("");
    }

    @Bean
    MusicService musicService(
        ArtistRepository artistRepository,
        SongRepository songRepository,
        WildcardConverter converter
    ) {
        return new MusicService(artistRepository, songRepository, converter);
    }
}
```

We could have declared this as a @Bean in a configuration, rather than having it picked up as a @Component, of course. We'd have done so in a test-only configuration class (remember, this is a class located in src/test/java so it will only be in the classpath for the tests). This way, though, we have a single configuration that we could reuse for a running application without modification or duplication.

It's time to see our tests. However, here we have a new class to consider: MongodDBRunner. This class is a simple Spring bean (marked with @Component), and it uses the de.flapdoodle.embed.mongo dependency to create a valid (and running) MongoDB instance. The instance will shut down when the Spring context shuts down. Since it's located in the com.bsg5.chapter9.util package – and we're scanning for components – when this component is loaded, a local copy of MongoDB will be downloaded and run for the duration of the tests. The MongoDB code will be cached for future invocations, so it won't have to be downloaded over and over again.

Here's the code.

Listing 9-35. chapter9mongodb/src/test/java/com/bsg5/chapter9/util/ MongoDBRunner.java

```java
package com.bsg5.chapter9.util;

import de.flapdoodle.embed.mongo.MongodExecutable;
import de.flapdoodle.embed.mongo.MongodProcess;
import de.flapdoodle.embed.mongo.MongodStarter;
import de.flapdoodle.embed.mongo.config.IMongodConfig;
import de.flapdoodle.embed.mongo.config.MongodConfigBuilder;
import de.flapdoodle.embed.mongo.config.Net;
import de.flapdoodle.embed.mongo.distribution.Version;
import de.flapdoodle.embed.process.runtime.Network;
import org.springframework.stereotype.Component;

import java.io.IOException;

@Component
public class MongoDBRunner {
    private MongodStarter starter = MongodStarter.getDefaultInstance();

    public MongoDBRunner() {
        try {
```

```java
        String bindIp = "localhost";
        int port = 12345;

        IMongodConfig mongodConfig = new MongodConfigBuilder()
                .version(Version.Main.PRODUCTION)
                .net(new Net(bindIp, port, Network.localhostIsIPv6()))
                .build();
        MongodExecutable mongodExecutable = starter.
        prepare(mongodConfig);
        MongodProcess mongod = mongodExecutable.start();
    } catch(IOException e) {
        throw new RuntimeException(e);
    }
  }
}
```

After that, it's all downhill and mercifully short, to boot. First, the ArtistRepositoryTests class.

Listing 9-36. chapter9mongodb/src/test/java/com/bsg5/chapter9/mongodb/ArtistRepositoryTests.java

```java
package com.bsg5.chapter9.mongodb;

import com.bsg5.chapter9.test.BaseArtistRepositoryTests;
import org.springframework.boot.test.autoconfigure.data.mongo.
DataMongoTest;

@DataMongoTest
public class ArtistRepositoryTests
    extends BaseArtistRepositoryTests<Artist, String> {
    protected Artist createArtist(String name) {
        return new Artist(name);
    }
}
```

Here, we see the use of @DataMongoTest instead of DataJpaTest.

Next, the SongRepositoryTests class.

Listing 9-37. chapter9mongodb/src/test/java/com/bsg5/chapter9/mongodb/
SongRepositoryTests.java

```
package com.bsg5.chapter9.mongodb;

import com.bsg5.chapter9.test.BaseSongRepositoryTests;
import org.springframework.boot.test.autoconfigure.data.mongo.
DataMongoTest;

@DataMongoTest
public class SongRepositoryTests
    extends BaseSongRepositoryTests<Artist, Song, String> {
    @Override
    protected Artist createArtist(String name) {
        return new Artist(name);
    }

    @Override
    protected Song createSong(Artist artist, String name) {
        return new Song(artist, name);
    }
}
```

And now the MusicServiceTests class, which is as simple as we've come to expect, with the getNonexistentId() method returning a random UUID (which should fulfill the requirements of nonexistence).

Listing 9-38. chapter9mongodb/src/test/java/com/bsg5/chapter9/mongodb/
MusicServiceTests.java

```
package com.bsg5.chapter9.mongodb;

import com.bsg5.chapter9.test.BaseMusicServiceTests;
import org.springframework.boot.test.autoconfigure.data.mongo.
DataMongoTest;

import java.util.UUID;
```

```
@DataMongoTest
public class MusicServiceTests
    extends BaseMusicServiceTests<Artist, Song, String> {
    @Override
    protected String getNonexistentId() {
        return UUID.randomUUID().toString();
    }
}
```

9.4 Tying Up Loose Ends

So far, we've seen how Spring Data makes accessing data storage much easier than it might otherwise be, allowing us to access both relational database and a MongoDB database with two sets of classes that are far more similar than different – even though the underlying data models are **incredibly** different. You can see the same sort of benefit from accessing nearly any database that has support in Spring Data.

It's worth noting that the interfaces we've seen in this chapter could actually slide fairly easily into the web front end shown in Chapter 8. We've maintained transactionality and actually gained simplicity and flexibility; with JPA, we get support for most (if not all) relational databases, and changing the code for MongoDB is trivial. We could migrate to other databases like Cassandra or Neo4J with just as little effort.

9.5 Next Steps

In Chapter 10, we shift away from data management and into Spring Security, which provides authentication and authorization support for Spring applications – with a particular focus on managing access via the Web.

Spring Security

Security is critical in any application with access to live information – even public information.[1] Security means controlling access to features and information; unless Annie is specifically granted access to Frank's information, Frank's data should be **safe** and, from Annie's perspective, invisible. Naturally, Spring has a powerful and capable security project – called, of all things, Spring Security – that allows you to control nearly every aspect of application security.

In this chapter, we're going to develop two modules – `chapter10` and `chapter10custom` – and we're going to use one of the simple web applications we built in Chapter 9, the `chapter9jpa` project, and layer on a simple interface to authenticate and control authorization to our resources.

10.1 Introduction

The Spring Security subproject was originally a separate project started in 2003 named Acegi Security System.[2] After developing separately from Spring itself for 3 years, it was officially adopted in 2007 by Spring and renamed Spring Security. Today, the subproject is the standard for authentication and access control for Spring. It provides enough boilerplate to allow you to use it without any customization and is extensible enough to allow any specific implementation details your particular authentication and authorization requirements might need.

---

[1]Even public information needs to be controlled – see how sources like Wikipedia have to constantly combat users including their own biases as sources of truth.

[2]Fun thing discovered while researching the origin of Spring Security: "Acegi" is a made-up word using the first, third, fifth, seventh, and ninth letters of the Latin alphabet. Your authors do not know why people think computer programmers are weird.

© Joseph B. Ottinger and Andrew Lombardi 2019
J. B. Ottinger and A. Lombardi, *Beginning Spring 5*, https://doi.org/10.1007/978-1-4842-4486-9_10

Like many other Spring projects (including Spring Data, as shown in Chapter 8), the Spring Security subproject is further subdivided into many other subprojects based on features. At its most basic level, the three Spring Security libraries you'll generally want to include by default are `spring-security-core`, `spring-security-config`, and `spring-security-web`.

Here we'll talk about several of the most prominent modules and the requirement they can help you achieve.

Library	Description
`spring-security-core`	The core library is required for all applications using Spring Security. It includes access control and authentication classes and interfaces and can be used for standalone or remote needs.
`spring-security-config`	This is a core library as well – providing, of all things, configuration via Java or XML.
`spring-security-web`	This library includes the necessary filters and web security infrastructure for using Spring Security in your web applications.
`spring-security-test`	This provides support for testing a Spring Security application. It maps easiest with JUnit but we'll be able to do the same trickery with TestNG.
`spring-security-acl`	This provides access control to specific operations on specific Java object instances in your application. With this, you can say that a specific user has the ability to execute specific methods on specific object instances, for example, although you can certainly rely on access control that isn't quite **that** specific. (Usually, people rely on role access and not specific user access… but you have the ability to choose what features you require.)
`spring-security-ldap`	This library provides access to LDAP, the "Lightweight Directory Access Protocol," for authentication and provisioning.

There are plenty of other libraries to mention like OAuth (which has its own artifact group, `org.springframework.security.oauth`, with many artifacts to provide specific features) and JOSE.[3] Support also exists for CAS (a single sign-on system; CAS stands for "Central Authentication Service") and OpenID (a broad Internet authentication specification) and, well, `insert your security apparatus here`, whether in an official capacity or through one of the many open source integrations out there. There are libraries that focus on just the authentication aspect and those that integrate the different ideas surrounding authorization.

Authentication and Authorization

When we speak about authentication, we're trying to correctly assert that the thing hitting our resources is what, or who, it claims to be. When we speak about this in regard to web-based authentication, we're generally talking about a host of different methods, with the simplest being HTTP BASIC access, all the way to more involved mechanisms like OpenID or CAS.

Authorization is a set of one or many rules that determine who, once authenticated, is allowed to do what. For example, if Jennifer authenticates as an ADMIN, then she may have Create/Read/Update/Delete access to all entities in the system, whereas John may have USER access and only be able to view and update items associated with their account.

Let's take a look at how we can start configuring a web application and then a REST API using Spring Security.

10.2 Configuration

In this section we'll discuss a lot of the configurable options available to us with Spring Security. We're going to keep the module structure simple so we can focus on how to get up and running quickly.

First, we need to create our directory structure, starting in the overall project directory.

---

[3]JOSE stands for Javascript Object Signing and Encryption. See `https://tools.ietf.org/html/rfc7165`, for example.

Listing 10-1. Creating the directory structure with POSIX

```
mkdir -p chapter10/src/main/java/com/bsg5/chapter10
mkdir -p chapter10/src/webapp/WEB-INF/templates
mkdir -p chapter10/src/test/java/com/bsg5/chapter10
```

We will need to set up our Gradle configuration file – build.gradle – as in previous chapters.[4] We'll be adding some dependencies for Spring Security – namely, spring-security-core, spring-security-config, and spring-security-web. The rest has been copied from previous chapters to give us the ability to run a Tomcat instance with a simple Gradle target.

Listing 10-2. chapter10/build.gradle

```
plugins {
    id 'war'
    id 'java'
    id 'org.gretty' version '2.2.0'
}

dependencies {
    compileOnly 'javax.servlet:javax.servlet-api:4.0.1'

    compile "org.springframework:spring-core:$springFrameworkVersion"
    compile "org.springframework:spring-context:$springFrameworkVersion"
    compile "org.springframework:spring-web:$springFrameworkVersion"
    compile "org.springframework:spring-webmvc:$springFrameworkVersion"
    compile group: "org.springframework.security",
        name: "spring-security-core",
        version: "$springFrameworkVersion"
    compile group: "org.springframework.security",
        name: "spring-security-config",
        version: "$springFrameworkVersion"
```

---

[4]Also note that it uses the properties of the top-level build.gradle from Chapter 2, so the Java version and Spring versions are inherited.

```
    compile group: "org.springframework.security",
        name: "spring-security-web",
        version: "$springFrameworkVersion"

    compile "org.jtwig:jtwig-web:5.87.0.RELEASE"
    compile "org.jtwig:jtwig-spring:5.87.0.RELEASE"
    compile "com.fasterxml.jackson.core:jackson-databind:$jacksonVersion"

    testCompile "org.springframework:spring-test:$springFrameworkVersion"
    testCompile "org.testng:testng:$testNgVersion"
    testCompile 'org.hamcrest:hamcrest-all:1.3'

    compile project(":chapter3")
}
```

For simplicity's sake, we're going to focus on Java-only configuration; XML configuration is certainly doable, but it's rather verbose.

Without further ado[5] let's see what steps we'll need to secure our first web application.

The first thing we'll do is make sure that Spring Security is registered for every URL in our application. Spring Security needs to register itself within the war for its servlet filter or the springSecurityFilterChain which is the name Spring Security uses for the FilterChainProxy namespace.

Spring Security works over the Web by using the servlet filter mechanism to intercept HTTP calls, matching the calls' contents to the security mappings. It does the same thing for method calls, except with a dynamic proxy instead of a servlet filter. Therefore, we need to make sure the security filter is registered with the servlet container, or the classloaders, for Security to work its magic.

To do this, we'll create a class named GatewaySecurityWebApplicationInitializer which just extends AbstractSecurityWebApplicationInitializer and Spring Security will do the rest. Let's look at it now.

---

[5]Your authors aren't sure exactly how much "ado" we've had so far, or how to measure "ado" or in what unit, but by golly, we're done with the "ado."

Listing 10-3. chapter10/src/main/java/com/bsg5/chapter10/
GatewaySecurityWebApplicationInitializer.java

```
package com.bsg5.chapter10;

import org.springframework.security.web.context.
AbstractSecurityWebApplicationInitializer;

public class GatewaySecurityWebApplicationInitializer extends
AbstractSecurityWebApplicationInitializer

}
```

Now that Spring Security is ready to filter any route going to our application, let's finish configuring Spring MVC and point it to our security-based config. Let's have another look at our initializer class, and we'll look at how it changes for our Spring Security changes.

Listing 10-4. chapter10/src/main/java/com/bsg5/chapter10/
GatewayAppInitializer.java

```
package com.bsg5.chapter10;

import org.springframework.web.servlet.support.
AbstractAnnotationConfigDispatcherServletInitializer;

public class GatewayAppInitializer extends
AbstractAnnotationConfigDispatcherServletInitializer
    @Override
    protected Class<?>[] getRootConfigClasses() {
        return new Class[]{GatewaySecurityConfig.class};
    }

    @Override
    protected Class<?>[] getServletConfigClasses() {
        return new Class[]{GatewayAppWebConfig.class};
    }
```

```
    @Override
    protected String[] getServletMappings() {
        return new String[]{"/"};
    }
}
```

Our initializer which does a lot of the work that our web.xml used to do is set up mostly the same as before. We have some web-based configurations we identify with the getServletConfigClasses method just like before. The other common thread that we've seen before is getServletMappings – and we're looking to process all things in this instance from the root so we pass back a /. The new entry is for our non-web-related config (which Spring Security falls under) so we return that config from our getRootConfigClasses method.

Listing 10-5. chapter10/src/main/java/com/bsg5/chapter10/ GatewayAppWebConfig.java

```
package com.bsg5.chapter10;

import org.jtwig.spring.JtwigViewResolver;
import org.springframework.context.annotation.Bean;
import org.springframework.context.annotation.ComponentScan;
import org.springframework.context.annotation.Configuration;
import org.springframework.web.servlet.ViewResolver;
import org.springframework.web.servlet.config.annotation.EnableWebMvc;
import org.springframework.web.servlet.config.annotation.
ViewResolverRegistry;
import org.springframework.web.servlet.config.annotation.WebMvcConfigurer;

@Configuration
@EnableWebMvc
@ComponentScan(basePackages = {"com.bsg5.chapter10", "com.bsg5.chapter3.mem03"})
public class GatewayAppWebConfig implements WebMvcConfigurer {

    @Override
    public void configureViewResolvers(ViewResolverRegistry registry) {
        registry.viewResolver(jtwigViewResolver());
    }
```

```
    @Bean
    public ViewResolver jtwigViewResolver() {
        JtwigViewResolver viewResolver = new JtwigViewResolver();
        viewResolver.setPrefix("web:/WEB-INF/templates/");
        viewResolver.setSuffix(".jtwig.html");
        return viewResolver;
    }

}
```

Listing 10-5 should look familiar since we started doing this with Spring MVC in Chapter 6. We're ensuring that Spring MVC is enabled with the annotation @EnableWebMvc, doing a @ComponentScan of the relevant packages we'll need for this project, and configuring the Jtwig view resolvers with the configureViewResolvers and jtwigViewResolver methods. Let's move on to the more relevant to this chapter piece which is the security config.

Listing 10-6. chapter10/src/main/java/com/bsg5/ chapter10/GatewaySecurityConfig.java

```
package com.bsg5.chapter10;

import org.springframework.context.annotation.Bean;
import org.springframework.security.config.annotation.web.builders.
HttpSecurity;
import org.springframework.security.config.annotation.web.configuration.
EnableWebSecurity;
import org.springframework.security.config.annotation.web.configuration.
WebSecurityConfigurerAdapter;
import org.springframework.security.core.authority.SimpleGrantedAuthority;
import org.springframework.security.core.userdetails.User;
import org.springframework.security.core.userdetails.UserDetails;
import org.springframework.security.core.userdetails.UserDetailsService;
import org.springframework.security.crypto.bcrypt.BCryptPasswordEncoder;
import org.springframework.security.crypto.password.PasswordEncoder;
import org.springframework.security.provisioning.
InMemoryUserDetailsManager;
```

```
import java.util.Collections;

@EnableWebSecurity
public class GatewaySecurityConfig extends WebSecurityConfigurerAdapter {

    @Override
    @Bean
    public UserDetailsService userDetailsService() {
        InMemoryUserDetailsManager manager = new InMemoryUserDetails
        Manager();

        UserDetails adminUser = User
            .withUsername("admin")
            .password(encoder().encode("admin123"))
            .authorities("FULL_PRIVILEGES")
            .roles("ADMIN")
            .build();

        manager.createUser(adminUser);

        return manager;
    }

    @Bean
    public PasswordEncoder encoder() {
        return new BCryptPasswordEncoder();
    }

    @Override
    protected void configure(HttpSecurity http) throws Exception {
        http.authorizeRequests()
            .antMatchers("/home").permitAll()
            .antMatchers("/dashboard").authenticated()
            .and()
            .formLogin();
    }
}
```

Let's take this in sections. First we'll talk through the class definition.

Listing 10-7. chapter10/src/main/java/com/bsg5/chapter10/
GatewaySecurityConfig.java

```
@EnableWebSecurity
public class GatewaySecurityConfig extends WebSecurityConfigurerAdapter {
```

The annotation @EnableWebSecurity will let Spring Security know to use this class for configuration. Our extended abstract base class WebSecurityConfigurerAdapter is a convenience class which has sensible defaults already defined. We're going to override a few simple methods in our first example, namely, userDetailsService and configure.

Listing 10-8. chapter10/src/main/java/com/bsg5/chapter10/
GatewaySecurityConfig.java

```
@Override
@Bean
public UserDetailsService userDetailsService() {
    InMemoryUserDetailsManager manager = new InMemoryUserDetailsManager();

    UserDetails adminUser = User
        .withUsername("admin")
        .password(encoder().encode("admin123"))
        .authorities("FULL_PRIVILEGES")
        .roles("ADMIN")
        .build();

    manager.createUser(adminUser);

    return manager;
}
```

Our example is meant to be simple and get you started so we'll use the convenient InMemoryUserDetailsManager[6] to achieve that. We can create our UserDetails object using the User object's builder pattern.

---

[6]InMemoryUserDetailsManager is provided as a developer-friendly way to "manage users" so that developers can focus on the actual security mechanisms without having to worry about having to configure how to track users. It's in-memory only, so it isn't useful outside of the context of testing or early development.

Some things to note as we progress, we're storing the password encoded and identifying that by making our encoder available in the encoder method which just so happens to use BCrypt. Each user needs to have a GrantedAuthority and Role attached to it, and while it may not seem so, the particular String used here is arbitrary. (There are best practices for what values to use. See the Note following this paragraph for more.)

We will use our manager object to create a user and return that manager as part of our UserDetailsService.

The class we used earlier being in-memory is only good for proof of concept uses, not for anything production level. What's important is that whatever implementation is chosen implements UserDetailsService at a minimum. If you are implementing your lookup via a database, you can look into JdbcUserDetailsManager which will work for UserDetails and Group management.

GrantedAuthority and Roles

It may be confusing at first to see two different distinctions for a user, one being GrantedAuthority and the other being Role. A GrantedAuthority is a privilege which is finer grained than a role, something like READ_AUTHORITY or WRITE_ AUTHORITY, and is purely arbitrary and up to you how to name or handle. Spring Security offers a method for this to check the authority hasAuthority. On the other end, we have Role which can be a more coarse-grained definition of what a user is within your system. A Role can be used with the hasRole method and is usually represented like ADMIN or USER or SUPERUSER – again it is arbitrary and up to you.

Listing 10-9. chapter10/src/main/java/com/bsg5/chapter10/ GatewaySecurityConfig.java

```java
@Override
protected void configure(HttpSecurity http) throws Exception {
    http.authorizeRequests()
        .antMatchers("/home").permitAll()
        .antMatchers("/dashboard").authenticated()
        .and()
        .formLogin();
}
```

There are going to always be several ways of performing some functions with Spring, and Spring Security is no exception. The HttpSecurity object follows a builder pattern, and if we choose to do the configuration in this class, we can override configure which passes in an HttpSecurity object for us to use. The other configuration method commonly used is with XML which we won't be covering as we're opting for class-based configuration, and annotation-based on the method level which will be discussed later in the chapter.

The HttpSecurity uses the builder pattern that we can use to configure things, so we're going to show the most important options in a table. Not all of the following methods are members of HttpSecurity, but all of them can run .build() because they extend from HttpSecurityBuilder.

Method	Description
and	Useful for method chaining as it returns the SecurityBuilder object
authorizeRequests	Restricts access based upon HttpServletRequest
antMatchers	Matchers that allow you to permit or restrict used in conjunction with the authorizeRequests call
formLogin	Ensures we're using a form-based login
httpBasic	Utilizes the simple HTTP Basic authentication method
hasRole	Ensures that for the configured matched route, it has a specific role
permitAll	URLs matched before this method are allowed by anyone
loginPage	Specifies URL to send users if login required; if using WebSecurityConfigurerAdapter, a default login page is generated if not specified
cors	Adds a corsFilter to the matched requests, can use a corsFilter named bean, or a corsConfigurationSource can be specified
rememberMe	Allows you to configure remember me authentication even if HttpSession is empty

For several of the preceding methods, and the even more available in the HttpSecurity object, there may be other builder methods which won't return HttpSecurity; the and method will return HttpSecurity so that you have access to chain other SecurityBuilder implementations together.

In the next section, we'll talk about defining custom login and logout routes. For now, we'll take full advantage of the default behavior in Spring Security and the power that affords for rapid prototyping of your application. Later you will see what the default Spring Security login page looks like.

Listing 10-10. The configure() method

```
protected void configure(HttpSecurity http) throws Exception {
    http
        .antMatcher("/")
        .authorizeRequests()
        .anyRequest().hasRole("ADMIN")
        .and()
        .httpBasic();
}
```

The preceding code will ensure any request to this page is met with a BASIC auth challenge using .httpBasic() and needing a role for the authenticated user of ADMIN. If you remember from the previous section, here's how we defined everything to get this page:

Spring Security is going to handle any of the messaging and display options if we don't define anything custom, so if the user enters invalid credentials, they'll receive an appropriate error message:

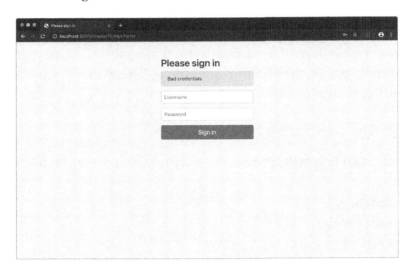

In our configuration earlier, we're defining the route at the root needing to have ADMIN-based privileges in order to continue. It makes sense for us to define a simple page to show the user upon successful login. For now we're using a very simple controller.

Listing 10-11. chapter10/src/main/java/com/bsg5/chapter10/ HomeController.java

```java
package com.bsg5.chapter10;

import org.springframework.stereotype.Controller;
import org.springframework.web.bind.annotation.GetMapping;

@Controller
public class HomeController {

    @GetMapping("/home")
    public String home() {
        return "home";
    }

}
```

Our template which we've defined will use the Jtwig resolver as defined in our `WebMvcConfigurer`.

Listing 10-12. `chapter10/src/main/webapp/WEB-INF/templates/home.jtwig.html`

```
<!DOCTYPE html>
<html>
<head>
    <title>Home Page</title>
</head>
<body>
<a href="dashboard">Admin Dashboard</a>
</body>
</html>
```

After a successful login, Spring Security will handle the functionality necessary to authenticate and further authorize the user to view the home page:

10.2.1 Customizing Your Security

In order to show a few more customizable features of Spring Security, we'll be creating another top-level project for `chapter10custom`. To create the directory structure, follow a similar path.

Listing 10-13. Creating the chapter10custom directory structure with POSIX

```
mkdir -p chapter10custom/src/main/java/com/bsg5/chapter10
mkdir -p chapter10custom/src/webapp/WEB-INF/templates
mkdir -p chapter10custom/src/test/java/com/bsg5/chapter10
```

Probably the easiest thing is to copy the `build.gradle` and the following classes from the `chapter10` project to our new project `GatewaySecurityWebApplicationInitializer.java`, `GatewayAppWebConfig`, `GatewayAppInitializer`, and the rest we'll edit and show later. If you'd like to do this from the command line from the `src` directory, you can do the following.

Listing 10-14. Copying over unchanged Java code

```
cp chapter10/src/main/java/com/bsg5/chapter10/
GatewaySecurityWebApplicationInitializer.ja
    /chapter10custom/src/main/java/com/bsg5/chapter10/GatewaySecurity
    WebApplicationInitializer.
cp chapter10/src/main/java/com/bsg5/chapter10/GatewayAppWebConfig.java \
    chapter10custom/src/main/java/com/bsg5/chapter10/GatewayAppWebConfig.java
cp chapter10/src/main/java/com/bsg5/chapter10/GatewayAppInitializer.java \
    chapter10custom/src/main/java/com/bsg5/chapter10/GatewayAppInitializer.java
cp chapter10/build.gradle chapter10custom/build.gradle
```

Defining your own custom login/logout routes within Spring Security is probably the first thing to do once you've gotten a handle on things. We can do this with an update to our config – and to make things easier, we'll be pulling from a class that we'll modify to support custom login/logout.

Listing 10-15. `chapter10custom/src/main/java/com/bsg5/` `chapter10/GatewaySecurityConfig.java`

```
package com.bsg5.chapter10;

import org.springframework.context.annotation.Bean;
import org.springframework.security.config.annotation.method.configuration.
EnableGlobalMethodSecurity;
import org.springframework.security.config.annotation.web.builders.
HttpSecurity;
```

```
import org.springframework.security.config.annotation.web.configuration.
EnableWebSecurity;
import org.springframework.security.config.annotation.web.configuration.
WebSecurityConfigurerAdapter;
import org.springframework.security.core.userdetails.User;
import org.springframework.security.core.userdetails.UserDetails;
import org.springframework.security.core.userdetails.UserDetailsService;
import org.springframework.security.crypto.bcrypt.BCryptPasswordEncoder;
import org.springframework.security.crypto.password.PasswordEncoder;
import org.springframework.security.provisioning.
InMemoryUserDetailsManager;
import org.springframework.security.web.util.matcher.AntPathRequestMatcher;

@EnableWebSecurity
@EnableGlobalMethodSecurity(
    securedEnabled = true,
    jsr250Enabled = true,
    prePostEnabled = true)
public class GatewaySecurityConfig extends WebSecurityConfigurerAdapter {

    @Bean
    public UserDetailsService userDetailsService() {
        InMemoryUserDetailsManager manager = new InMemoryUserDetailsManager();
        UserDetails adminUser = User
            .withUsername("admin")
            .password(encoder().encode("admin123"))
            .authorities("FULL_PRIVILEGES")
            .roles("ADMIN")
            .build();
        UserDetails regularUser = User
            .withUsername("user")
            .password(encoder().encode("user123"))
            .authorities("READ_ACCESS")
            .roles("USER")
            .build();
```

```
        manager.createUser(adminUser);
        manager.createUser(regularUser);

        return manager;
    }

    @Bean
    public PasswordEncoder encoder() {
        return new BCryptPasswordEncoder();
    }

    @Override
    protected void configure(HttpSecurity http) throws Exception {
        http.authorizeRequests()
            .antMatchers("/home", "/login").permitAll()
            .antMatchers("/dashboard").authenticated()
            .and()
            .formLogin()
            .loginPage("/login")
            .defaultSuccessUrl("/dashboard")
            .and()
            .logout()
            .logoutRequestMatcher(new AntPathRequestMatcher("/logout"));
    }
}
```

The configure() method is the only change here, and we've basically added /login to the permitAll chain and defined our own custom loginPage which will use /login and a defaultSuccessUrl which will forward the user to /dashboard. In the config you'll see some attributes for EnableGlobalMethodSecurity which we'll cover in the next section on Securing Service Methods. It is not common to enable all of these at once, you'll likely use securedEnabled or the jsr250Enabled if you want to use the standard. The most flexible option is to use prePostEnabled which will allow you to use Method Security Expressions and is further defined in the docs: https://docs.spring.io/spring-security/site/docs/5.0.x/reference/html5/#method-security-expressions.

That along with a new HomeController as defined here.

Listing 10-16. chapter10custom/src/main/java/com/bsg5/chapter10/
HomeController.java

```
package com.bsg5.chapter10;

import org.springframework.stereotype.Controller;
import org.springframework.web.bind.annotation.GetMapping;

@Controller
public class HomeController {

    @GetMapping("/home")
    public String home() {
        return "home";
    }

    @GetMapping("/login")
    public String login() {
        return "login";
    }

}
```

Our new template being the login template.

Listing 10-17. chapter10custom/src/main/webapp/WEB-INF/templates/login.
jtwig.html

```
<!DOCTYPE html>
<html>
<head>
    <title>Login Page</title>
</head>
<body>

<form action="login" method="POST">
    <p>
        <label for="username">Username</label>
        <input type="text" id="username" name="username" />
    </p>
```

```
    <p>
        <label for="password">Password</label>
        <input type="password" id="password" name="password" />
    </p>
    <button type="submit">Login</button>
</form>
</body>
</html>
```

As you can see, we're pointing our template to POST to log in with username and password as parameters. This will yield the following page when you attempt to access a protected resource (one marked with authenticated and in this case it's /dashboard):

10.3 Securing a REST Application

In the last section, we were pretty sure we were done creating new subprojects, but security always has other plans. We'll create our last top-level project and name it chapter10jpa. This section will pull in the subproject chapter9jpa and see how to integrate Spring Security with our work from Chapter 9. Here's how we'll create the directory structure.

Listing 10-18. Creating the chapter10jpa directory structure with POSIX

```
mkdir -p chapter10jpa/src/main/java/com/bsg5/chapter10
mkdir -p chapter10jpa/src/webapp/WEB-INF/templates
mkdir -p chapter10jpa/src/test/java/com/bsg5/chapter10
```

One other great thing about pulling in the code from Chapter 9 is it uses Spring Boot which we haven't dealt with in this chapter yet. As we've seen in other chapters that leveraged Spring Boot, Boot makes a lot of this stuff very easy.

First things first, let's build our new Gradle configuration file – build.gradle – and as always note that the top-level build.gradle is used for some inherited properties. We'll pull in the necessary dependencies for Spring Boot including a new one spring-boot-starter-security which will do a lot of the leg work for us and the chapter9common and chapter9jpa subprojects which give us access to MusicService and the dependencies.

Listing 10-19. chapter10jpa/build.gradle

```
plugins {
    id 'org.springframework.boot' version '2.1.5.RELEASE'
}

apply plugin: 'io.spring.dependency-management'
apply plugin: 'org.springframework.boot'

dependencies {
    compile("org.springframework.boot:spring-boot-starter-web")
    compile project(':chapter9jpa')
}
```

To use Spring Boot, we will need to define a @SpringBootApplication class which we'll do later in our MainApplication. We are making use of @Bean classes in the Chapter 9 codebase so our scanBasePackages will include com.bsg5.chapter9.jpa along with our package in Chapter 10 com.bsg5.chapter10.

Listing 10-20. chapter10jpa/src/main/java/com/bsg5/chapter10/
MainApplication.java

```
package com.bsg5.chapter10;

import org.springframework.boot.SpringApplication;
import org.springframework.boot.autoconfigure.SpringBootApplication;
```

```
@SpringBootApplication(scanBasePackages = {
    "com.bsg5.chapter9.jpa",
    "com.bsg5.chapter10"
})
public class MainApplication {
    public static void main(String[] args) {
        SpringApplication.run(MainApplication.class, args);
    }
}
```

With this one class, we now have a Spring Boot application and can run it using the following Gradle command: gradle :chapter10jpa:bootRun. Once it starts up, you'll have a working Tomcat instance ready for action. We haven't actually defined any endpoints yet though, so you'll be met with a lot of 404 (not found) errors. Let's fix that and create a @RestController for accessing and creating Song entries in our data source. We will define two endpoints just to keep things simple, one will retrieve (GET) a resource by identifier and the other will create (POST) a new resource.

Listing 10-21. chapter10jpa/src/main/java/com/bsg5/chapter10/SongController.java

```
package com.bsg5.chapter10;

import com.bsg5.chapter9.jpa.MusicService;
import com.bsg5.chapter9.jpa.Song;
import org.springframework.http.MediaType;
import org.springframework.web.bind.annotation.GetMapping;
import org.springframework.web.bind.annotation.PathVariable;
import org.springframework.web.bind.annotation.PostMapping;
import org.springframework.web.bind.annotation.RequestBody;
import org.springframework.web.bind.annotation.RestController;

    private MusicService service;

    SongController(MusicService service) {
        this.service = service;
    }
```

```
@GetMapping(value = "/songs/{id}",
    produces = MediaType.APPLICATION_JSON_VALUE)
    Song song = service.getSongById(id);

    if (song != null) {
        return song;
    } else {
        throw new SongNotFoundException();
    }
}

@PostMapping(value="/songs",
    consumes = MediaType.APPLICATION_JSON_VALUE,
    produces = MediaType.APPLICATION_JSON_VALUE)
    Song songLookup  = service.getSong(song.getArtist().getName(),
    song.getName());

    if(songLookup != null) {
        return songLookup;
    } else {
        throw new SongNotFoundException();
    }
}
}
```

We are defining two methods here; the first is getSongById which takes a
@PathVariable of id which we'll use the MusicService to look up in the database. If it
doesn't exist, we're going to throw a SongNotFoundException which is the same code we
saw in Chapter 9 for ArtistNotFoundException.

The second method is for creating a new Song. It's going to consume a JSON object
which we'll create a sample you can use to submit later and will produce/return the
newly created object in the response. You can use the following curl command to see
this in action for the save.

Listing 10-22. Curl request to save song

```
curl --header "Content-Type: application/json" \
  --request POST \
```

```
--data '{"name":"Someone Stole The Flour","artist":{"name": "Threadbare Loaf"}}' \
http://localhost:8080/songs
```

After creating this new song entry, we can use a simple curl again to request our entry.

Listing 10-23. Curl to get song

```
curl --header "Content-Type: application/json" http://localhost:8080/songs/2
```

Now that we have a very simple REST controller in place, let's see what it would look like with Spring Security integrated. The only thing we really have to do to secure the app and start requiring authentication is to add the following build.gradle dependency to the project after spring-boot-starter-web.

Listing 10-24. Adding spring-boot-starter-security

```
compile("org.springframework.boot:spring-boot-starter-security")
```

This will set up some magic defaults adding security to all URLs starting from /*, using BASIC authentication as the default, and having a default username with user.

You may be asking yourself: "That's great but what about the password?" When you run the app with gradle :chapter10jpa:bootRun, you will see something similar in the output.

Listing 10-25. Generated password from Spring Boot

```
Using generated security password: df1a58e9-7ac2-4d01-9e6e-41e36c06ddb9
```

If you were to try and hit the GET endpoint without authentication details, you'd see something like this from Spring Boot.

Listing 10-26. Curl response without authentication

```
{"timestamp":"2019-06-27T16:22:16.070+0000","status":401,"error":"Unauthorized",
"message":"
```

So instead let's authenticate and get our Threadbare Loaf entry with our credentials. If you remember from earlier, that means the username of user and whatever was listed in the generated security password section. In the following example, we'll just use the one I've already listed earlier for consistency.

Listing 10-27. Curl with authentication

```
curl \
  -u user:df1a58e9-7ac2-4d01-9e6e-41e36c06ddb9 \
  --header "Content-Type: application/json" \
  http://localhost:8080/songs/2
{"id":2,"artist":{"id":1,"name":"Threadbare Loaf"},"name":"Someone Stole
The Flour","votes":
```

So simple and easy to do, and you get it nearly for free here. This is obviously not going to work for a production application and the single user is only for test purposes. Let's take a look at a new config that we can create which allows us to create our own users and roles and override the Spring Boot defaults.

Listing 10-28. chapter10jpa/src/main/java/com/bsg5/ chapter10/GatewaySecurityConfig.java

```java
package com.bsg5.chapter10;

import org.springframework.context.annotation.Configuration;
import org.springframework.security.config.annotation.authentication.
builders.AuthenticationManagerBuilder;
import org.springframework.security.config.annotation.web.builders.
HttpSecurity;
import org.springframework.security.config.annotation.web.configuration.
WebSecurityConfigurerAdapter;
import org.springframework.security.crypto.password.NoOpPasswordEncoder;

@Configuration
public class GatewaySecurityConfig extends WebSecurityConfigurerAdapter {

    @Override
    protected void configure(AuthenticationManagerBuilder auth) throws
    Exception {
        auth.inMemoryAuthentication()
            .passwordEncoder(NoOpPasswordEncoder.getInstance())
            .withUser("user").password("user123")
            .roles("USER").and()
```

```
            .withUser("admin").password("admin123")
            .roles("USER", "ADMIN");
    }

    @Override
    protected void configure(HttpSecurity http) throws Exception {
        http
            .httpBasic()
            .and()
            .authorizeRequests()
            .antMatchers("/songs/**")
            .hasRole("USER")
            .antMatchers("/**")
            .hasRole("ADMIN")
            .and()
            .csrf().disable()
            .headers().frameOptions().disable();
    }

}
```

A good portion of the preceding code should be very familiar to you already.

Our `configure()` method does a similar thing to the previous `userDetailsService` override which we used in previous examples. We're setting up two users using the `NoOpPasswordEncoder` using the credentials of `user:user123` for the USER role and `admin:admin123` for a role with both USER and ADMIN privileges.

Our second overridden `configure` method we've seen previously but are using a few new methods on `HttpSecurity`. Due to the usage of REST here, we don't need to use CSRF – which is used to prevent cross-site request forgery with JavaScript – and we'll disable the special frame headers that are added by default. Other than those things, we're securing `/songs/**` with role USER and can now use the simpler credentials already defined. When you've got this new class added, terminate the existing `bootRun` and rerun it with `gradle :chapter10jpa:bootRun`. We can copy the existing curl command in Listing 10-27 and replace the credentials with `user:user123` and should see a similar result.

Now you have seen how simple it is to set up security with Spring Boot and REST endpoints.

10.4 New in Spring Security 5

The latest version of Spring Security comes with several new and exciting features as well. In the short sections later, we'll go into a little more detail but they include a new OAuth 2.0 Login class, security support in your Reactive programs, and a new DelegatingPasswordEncoder.

10.4.1 OAuth 2.0 Login

Spring Security 5 has introduced a convenience for configuring OAuth 2.0[7] external authorization servers via the OAuth2LoginConfigurer class. We'll talk briefly about how we can use this class at a very bare bones level which makes configuration for OAuth 2.0 even easier. In order to use the new spring-security-oauth2-client, you'll need to include the following in gradle:

```
compile group: 'org.springframework.security', name: 'spring-security-
oauth2-client', version:
```

Naturally, Spring Boot makes all of this much easier. Here, we're going to show how to set up Google and Facebook logins with Spring Boot. In order to use OAuth 2.0 with either, you'll need to obtain client credentials for each. By default Spring Boot will configure the redirect URI in the following format /login/oauth2/code/{registrationId} so keep that in mind when entering that into the forms for Google and/or Facebook.

Next, in our application.properties file, we'll need to put in the relevant client id and secret that you received from Google and Facebook:

```
spring.security.oauth2.client.registration.google.client-id=<your client id>
spring.security.oauth2.client.registration.google.client-secret=<your
client secret>
```

```
spring.security.oauth2.client.registration.facebook.client-id=<your client id>
spring.security.oauth2.client.registration.facebook.client-secret=<your
client secret>
```

---

[7]OAuth is an open standard for authorizing access to a web site or application without supplying passwords and is commonly used by Google, Facebook, Twitter, and many more.

When these properties show up in your Spring Boot application, it will initialize the
OAuth2ClientAutoConfiguration class and all the supporting beans.

The basic config that we can get setup for authenticating with the OAuth2 Client is
listed as follows:

```
@Configuration
public class OAuthSecurityConfig extends WebSecurityConfigurerAdapter {

    @Override
    protected void configure(HttpSecurity http) throws Exception {
        http.authorizeRequests()
            .anyRequest().authenticated()
            .and()
            .oauth2Login();
    }
}
```

With the preceding configuration whenever we're attempting to access a protected
URL, the application will redirect to an autogenerated Spring Boot login page with
buttons for Google and Facebook available for login. Methods available from the
oauth2Login() method are varied but some that are pretty useful to configure and not
accept the defaults:

- loginPage("/my_login") – Allows you to configure an endpoint to
  serve the login screen rather than the Spring Boot default

- defaultSuccessUrl() – The redirect to use upon success

- failureUrl() – The redirect to use should the login fail (i.e., the user
  uses invalid credentials)

- successHandler() – Custom logic handler for a
  successful user authentication which must implement
  AuthenticationSuccessHandler that generally would be a redirect
  or forward to a success page

- failureHandler() – Custom logic handler for authentication failure
  which implements AuthenticationFailureHandler that usually
  redirects to the authentication page to try again

There are certainly more options which you can view more of within the documentation. See https://spring.io/projects/spring-security-oauth.

10.4.2 Reactive Support

The Spring framework with version 5 has brought the Reactive Stack as a first class citizen with its libraries. We'll touch on a bit of the reactive support in Spring 5 in the next chapter (which discusses a bit more of the reactive programming paradigm with Reactor and RxJava). We'll just shamelessly copy the example available in the docs.

Listing 10-29. Using Spring Security with WebFlow

```
@Bean
WebFilter springSecurityFilterChain(ReactiveAuthenticationManager manager) {
  HttpSecurity http = http();
  http.authenticationManager(manager);
  http.httpBasic();

  AuthorizeExchangeBuilder authorize = http.authorizeExchange();
  authorize.antMatchers("/admin/**").hasRole("ADMIN");
  authorize.antMatchers("/users/{user}/**").access(this::currentUser
  MatchesPath);
  authorize.anyExchange().authenticated();
  return http.build();
}
```

In Listing 10-29 you'll see that just as in other cases that were nonreactive, we're setting up any specific mappings using the springSecurityFilterChain. You'll add the preceding code into your config for Spring Security just like you would for the Servlet stack. A full example of how to secure a Reactive WebFlux application is out of scope for this small section, so we'll just link off to the sample provided in the Spring Security project on GitHub available at https://github.com/spring-projects/spring-security/tree/5.1.x/samples/boot/hellowebflux.

10.4.3 DelegatingPasswordEncoder

If you've ever had to migrate to a new encoding method for passwords due to requirements changing or because you finally realized that MD5 is not secure, Spring Security 5 brings you flexibility and power of supporting multiple password encoders using a prefix. The password will be stored with a key such as {bcrypt} and then the encoded password.

If you're okay with using the defaults available in the PasswordEncoderFactories, you can grab an instance like so.

Listing 10-30. Getting default Spring Security DelegatingPasswordEncoder

```
PasswordEncoder passwordEncoder =
    PasswordEncoderFactories.createDelegatingPasswordEncoder();
```

By default it will encode with bcrypt and decode with prefix any of the following keys: ldap, MD4, MD5, noop, pbkdf2, scrypt, SHA-1, SHA-256, sha256. If you have an existing set of passwords in the database and they are not prefixed with the preceding method, you'll have to perform updates to the password data, or you can choose to use a custom DelegatingPasswordEncoder where you can specify the decodings you want to support and the encoding you'll use for any new passwords and can set a default for any passwords that don't have an encoding prefix prior to the password data. Let's take a look at Listing 10-31 to see how this works.

Listing 10-31. chapter10/src/main/java/com/bsg5/chapter10/
CustomDefaultPasswordEncoderFactories.java

```
@SuppressWarnings("deprecation")
static PasswordEncoder createDelegatingPasswordEncoder() {
    String idForEncode = "bcrypt";

    PasswordEncoder defaultEncoder = NoOpPasswordEncoder.getInstance();
    Map<String, PasswordEncoder> encoders = new HashMap<>();
    encoders.put("bcrypt", new BCryptPasswordEncoder());
    encoders.put("noop", defaultEncoder);
    encoders.put("SHA-256", new MessageDigestPasswordEncoder("SHA-256"));

    DelegatingPasswordEncoder delegatingPasswordEncoder =
        new DelegatingPasswordEncoder(idForEncode, encoders);
    delegatingPasswordEncoder.setDefaultPasswordEncoderForMatches
    (defaultEncoder);
```

```
    return delegatingPasswordEncoder;
}
```

As you can see from the preceding snippet, we're encoding all passwords with
bcrypt. We have defined a custom set of methods for decryption including bcrypt,
SHA-256, and plaintext (coded as noop). We've chosen to restrict our list to these three
rather than the default Spring PasswordEncoderFactories which includes ldap, MD4,
MD5, noop, pbkdf2, scrypt, SHA-1, SHA-256, and sha256. To use it we can inject
the @Bean into our code that uses the PasswordEncoder like so.

Listing 10-32. Injected @Bean for PasswordEncoder

```
@Bean
public PasswordEncoder passwordEncoder() {
    return DefaultPasswordEncoderFactories.createDelegatingPasswordEncoder();
}
```

Now we have a PasswordEncoder that is flexible enough to accept historic encodings
and is set up to allow for changes in the future to how passwords are stored based on the
ever-changing landscape of best practices for password storage. We've only scratched
the very surface of the power that exists in Spring Security. The subproject has support
for the simple like HTTP BASIC, Digest, and Form-based authentication to the more
complex like OpenID, JOSSO, and SSO using Central Authentication Service (CAS). It
has integrations which allow you to pull data from LDAP, Kerberos, and even Windows
NTLM. It offers functionality that you would expect for a security framework to provide
and with configurability at its core to modify to your heart's content.

The most important thing about the preceding text is if you're using anything standard or
best practice in the industry, Spring Security likely has you covered. If not, it is fully pluggable
and customizable to work with your particular custom authentication implementations.

10.5 Next Steps

In our 11th and final chapter, we'll look at some of the other projects that make up the
Spring ecosystem – not many of them, because there are many, **many** fully functioning
and useful projects that provide features to Spring, but these are some of the ones that
have caught our eyes recently.

CHAPTER 11

Next Steps

By now, we've read about Spring and Dependency Injection, along with topics like web services (particularly REST services), transaction, persistence, and security. These are likely to be the "most important" parts of the Spring ecosystem, generally speaking, but we've barely scratched the surface of the Spring ecosystem itself, much less projects that use Spring without being part of the Spring project.

In this chapter, we'd like to look at some of the things programmers will possibly run into in the real world. It's very far from complete; a book covering everything would take up multiple volumes and, in the end, be incomplete: new projects and features are developed all the time.

Note that this chapter has no code to speak of. This chapter isn't trying to demonstrate features, even with limited scope; here, we're merely pointing out some interesting projects in the wider Spring ecosystem. As such, they tend to be things the authors noticed as being interesting or relevant in some way, and that we thought might spark readers' interest as they develop their own projects.

11.1 Spring WebMVC.fn

In Chapters 6, 7, and 10, we looked at using WebMVC, Spring's project for creating HTTP endpoints. WebMVC isn't your only option for creating endpoints, even in Spring, but one new project, called "WebMVC.fn," can make creating a web front end even **easier**.

An example showing WebMVC.fn can be found at `https://github.com/spring-tips/webmvc-fn` – it's still under development, but it provides a "Domain-Specific Language" for creating controllers. You'd declare a `Component` of some kind with methods that return `ServerResponse` objects – much like we do today with WebMVC.

© Joseph B. Ottinger and Andrew Lombardi 2019
J. B. Ottinger and A. Lombardi, *Beginning Spring 5*, https://doi.org/10.1007/978-1-4842-4486-9_11

A Domain-Specific Language – or DSL – is a language or subset of grammar specialized for a specific application domain.

Languages like Java are very generalized, but code written in Java can target specific domains quite easily; you can, for example, create an abstraction of a Door that understands how to open or close itself.

However, you're still expressing the actions in Java. Opening and closing doors is a fundamentally simple process to model, but consider simulating electronic signals as an example; it's easy to write Java code to express concrete electronics concepts, but to an engineer, the Java code would have all kinds of extra information that the engineer wouldn't need and might not understand.

A DSL, on the other hand, is usually designed to fit the problem space it describes very tightly, and an engineer would ideally be able to read an "electronics DSL" without having to deal with very much of the underlying programming language being used.

Popular examples of DSLs for the JVM include Gradle (which uses a DSL for building projects, as we've seen through the entire book), JavaFX, and Processing (see https://processing.org/). There are, of course, many, many more – including WebMVC.fn itself. But you knew that, because we started off by describing WebMVC.fn as a DSL!

Instead of mapping the endpoints in the Component, though, you'd create **another** bean, of type RouterFunction<ServerResponse>, which has a convenient fluent API for creating endpoints for handling GET requests, POST requests, filtering, and so forth.

Listing 11-1 shows the WebMVC.fn sample project.

Listing 11-1. WebMVC.fn route configuration example

```
@Bean
RouterFunction<ServerResponse> routes(PersonHandler ph) {
  var root = "";
  return route()
    .GET(root + "/people", ph::handleGetAllPeople)
    .GET(root + "/people/{id}", ph::handleGetPersonById)
```

```
    .POST(root + "/people", ph::handlePostPerson)
    .filter((serverRequest, handlerFunction) -> {
      try {
        log.info("entering HandlerFilterFunction");
        return handlerFunction.handle(serverRequest);
      }
      finally {
        log.info("exiting HandlerFilterFunction");
      }
    })
    .build();
}
```

It takes a little bit of getting used to, in part because Java isn't quite as flexible for creating domain-specific languages as programming languages like Scala, Kotlin, or Groovy, so the DSL isn't quite as clean as it might be – it's going to have Java-isms like lambdas, method references, and concrete type declarations, as you can see from Listing 11-1.

However, WebMVC.fn does allow you to centralize the endpoint configuration. If you have 17 different classes that are serving as `Controller` objects today, WebMVC.fn would allow you to change them back to ordinary `Component` classes – and have one location for configuration of all of the endpoints, instead of forcing a programmer to chase down which of those 17 classes actually provides a specific endpoint.

Is this a worthy goal? Honestly, yes (or, well, "maybe"); a good design will allow you to easily map between an endpoint and a specific `Controller`, but having the `Controller` objects handle their own endpoint construction means that they have a wider visibility to the grand design and deployment of the application than perhaps they should.

It's a minor design decision, in the end (after all, WebMVC works now, and you can manually register endpoints just as WebMVC.fn does, just with more code and in idiomatic Java), but it's still a neat idea. You can still accomplish similar things without WebMVC.fn (by registering the endpoints in a central location, but without WebMVC. fn's DSL), but the DSL makes it far more convenient than it otherwise might be.

As usual, Spring provides flexibility such that you can design your application in nearly any fashion you would like.

11.2 Spring Reactive

Reactive programming is easily summarized as "programming with asynchronous data streams."[1]

We've seen example code where streams were preferred to traditional loops and other such iterative mechanisms (in particular, in Chapters 3, 8, and 9) – the primary difference between traditional streams and reactive streams is that reactive code tends to have asynchronous datasources, so there's typically not an explicit end to the stream.

In a traditional streaming model, there's a data collection phase – where you're getting a list of `Artist` or `Song` instances – and when you have all of those instances, **then** you can process them. Retrieving the instances is a **blocking operation** and represents a place in your code that cannot progress until the blocking operation completes.

On the other hand, reactive programming is asynchronous, as we stated: we might indicate that we want to get a list of instances, and **when they are available**, do something with them. We don't block execution of the code while waiting for the instances to come back from a data source; we set up something to handle the instances when they arrive, and exit.

In practice, this tends to yield some incredible performance gains, because a database call (for example) might mean a 10-millisecond pause for a given thread; with reactive programming, there is no pause at all. The thread can be used to do other things instead.

The cost, of course, is that you have to write your code to use reactive models. We've been leaning that direction throughout the book, with the emphasis on lambdas and streams, but for many Java programmers, this is still a somewhat new approach – even though it was introduced with Java 8, in 2014.

With Spring 5, Spring provides a `spring-webflux` module that serves as nearly a drop-in replacement for WebMVC. Spring Web Reactive adapts the concepts in WebMVC and migrates them to a reactive model, including the option to specify inputs and outputs that don't necessarily **have** to block on input or output; you could use this to provide a series of data points as they become available (like stock ticker prices) – both as input **and** output – simply by changing the types from `Artist`, for example, to `Flux<Artist>`.

---

[1]"Reactive programming is programming with asynchronous data streams" is taken from `https://gist.github.com/staltz/868e7e9bc2a7b8c1f754`, which summarizes reactive programming quite well, despite some adult language that may not be perfectly appropriate for some minors.

If this sounds complex on first read, don't worry – it isn't very simple. However, if you can write code to use WebMVC, it's fairly easy to migrate to Spring Web Reactive and add features and performance gains as you understand how to leverage the reactive model.

There's even a `spring-boot-starter-webflux` to allow easy usage with Spring Boot – and if you're going to work with Spring Reactive, this is probably the way you should go.

11.3 Message Queues and Spring

A message queue is a form of asynchronous service-to-service communication.[2] In a queue architecture, there are three basic components:

- A host application like RabbitMQ (`www.rabbitmq.com`) or ActiveMQ (`https://activemq.apache.org/`)

- A producer (something that sends messages to the host application)

- A consumer (something that retrieves messages from the host application)

Note that a given service can be both a producer and a consumer, and that this is actually quite common; also, a producer isn't limited to one type of production, nor is it limited to one type of consumption.

There are two primary message models in queueing systems: publish/subscribe (or "pub/sub") and point-to-point (or "PtP").

The two models are different in how messages are delivered:

- In a pub/sub model, a message is delivered immediately to every available consumer. This message stream is often referred to as being a "topic" (and this is indeed how the Java Message Service refers to pub/sub queues).

- In a PtP model, a message is distributed to one and only one consumer, no matter how many consumers might be listening on a given message stream; the message stream is also called a "queue"

---

[2]This definition is shamelessly taken verbatim from `https://aws.amazon.com/message-queue/` – we wanted to write our own purely original definition but this one kept being better than everything we came up with.

to differentiate it from a topic. How the messages are assigned to consumers is up to the queue itself – but usually messages are distributed in a "round robin" algorithm, meaning that messages are **usually** evenly distributed among available listeners.

A chat room is a good example of a topic; a message from one person goes to every other person who happens to be in the room when the message is sent.

An asynchronous logging service is a good example of a queue; a producer generates a log message and sends it to the message service, where one of multiple possible listeners retrieves the message and decides what to do with it.

As referred to earlier, Java has a standard specification for working with message queues, called the Java Message Service (or "JMS"). JMS is like JDBC: the specification covers how the API is used, but not how the API works. You'd use a JMS library for each given message queue host; ActiveMQ has one, and RabbitMQ has one of its own. (For RabbitMQ, see `www.rabbitmq.com/jms-client.html` for how to access RabbitMQ over JMS.)

Spring also has a module for working with JMS, `spring-amqp`; in particular, it provides the `JmsTemplate` class as well as providing annotations like `@JmsListener` to allow components to retrieve messages from a queue or topic with fairly little effort (see `https://spring.io/guides/gs/messaging-jms/` for more details). You still have to configure the host connection, but after that, using a queue or topic is a matter of using the `JmsTemplate.send()` method (although the `JmsTemplate` class is actually **extraordinarily** flexible, and it's quite possible you'd never use `send()` by itself, as there are other methods that are likely to fit an exact scenario more completely).

RabbitMQ actually deserves some special treatment here.

Most messaging providers use version 1.0 of the Advanced Message Queueing Protocol, or AMQP (`www.amqp.org`). RabbitMQ, however, by default uses AMQP 0.9, and the JMS client for RabbitMQ is designed to work with RabbitMQ's message service.

You have options, though: you can always install AMQP 1.0 as a plugin for RabbitMQ, or you can use AMQP 0.9 directly from Spring, using a `RabbitTemplate` as provided by the `spring-rabbit` dependency, which would be a rough equivalent to the `JmsTemplate` as provided by the `spring-amqp` module.

Why would you use a message queue? They're ideal for massively scaled and transactional asynchronous operations; consider bank transactions as an example. Normally, when you create charges against your bank account, the bank stores a set of operations (withdrawals and deposits) and posts them at a specific time; since message queues can be transactional, failures can be reprocessed until they're successfully handled. In addition to making a complex architecture fairly simple to work with (as processes have simple inputs and outputs), the transactional nature of consumption in PtP scenarios makes the code **safe**.[3]

11.4 GraphQL

In Chapter 6 we mentioned REpresentational State Transfer, or REST, which is a common and popular way to work with data models over HTTP. REST is usually pretty simple; the hardest thing about REST is creating endpoints that make sense from an external API's perspective. (Another thorny problem is how to handle versioning of endpoints, for when things change and yet you still need to support the "old way.")

For example, do we access Song instances through their Artist reference or by title? It makes more sense to use song titles, because a given song title might be used by multiple artists... but how, then, do you refer to songs created by a specific artist? We have answers that satisfy us for the sake of this book, of course, but in more complex models, questions like these can be less easy to answer.

Also, REST endpoints tend to be fairly coarse; if you request a Song, you're typically going to get every attribute of that Song, whether the request needs it or not. You can obviously tune the output of a REST request such that it does not contain every attribute (as we do when we create the autocompletion services), but usually creating a projection[4] involves creating extra object classes to represent the projection, and that ends up being a lot of work for most projects (even though projections can be far more

---

[3]For topics, "safe" means slightly different things. If there are no listeners for a pub/sub topic, the messages sent to the topic tend to vanish: imagine saying something in an empty room and you'll have an example of what would happen. There's nobody to listen, so whatever you said will be lost. With a queue, however, it's more like a bulletin board; put a message on a bulletin board, and a consumer will pick up the message when they come by.

[4]A "projection," if you aren't aware, is a custom collection of fields, normally in the context of a database query of some kind. If you were to request a name from one source and an account balance from a **different** source, that'd be called a "projection." Yes, this is awfully stuffy.

efficient than returning large objects). It's simpler just to return giant objects, even though that can impact processing speed and network transfer time.

Is returning "giant objects" a bad thing? Well… as usual, it depends. If the objects can be represented in serialized form in relatively little space, it probably doesn't matter, especially if it can be represented in a few thousand bytes.

A network packet – or segment, actually – is usually sized around 1500 bytes, roughly 1400 of which are usable by applications; the remainder makes up headers and other metadata for the packet. If the serialized form of an object fits into one or two network packets, it's **probably** not a big deal to not worry about the extra data being transmitted.

Of course, if you're handling millions of such requests and your data takes up **two** network packets and you only need to transfer **some** of that data… maybe it'd be cost-effective to trim the results down such that they're slimmer.

Or, of course, one could look into libraries like GraphQL.

GraphQL (`https://graphql.org/`) is a query language and library designed to work with APIs such that clients can actually define what attributes are requested and can also specify that a **graph** of the data is to be returned.

In our music gateway example, we might have two endpoints to get an `Artist` and every `Song` for that artist, if we wanted all of the related data. With GraphQL, we could build a request that requested both sets of data (the `Artist` and related `Song` objects), possibly only including specific attributes from both object types instead of **everything**.

Since it's done with a **query language**, the API designer doesn't even have to anticipate ahead of time what fields should be included or what the resulting graph should look like. (The consumer of the API, of course, has to be aware of what is being returned; the **consumer** has to be aware of the data, but that's why the consumer specifies the nature of the data in the first place.)

The programmer simply defines what fields and objects **might** be available and then uses the GraphQL library to handle the request's inputs and outputs.

Since the query language is actually separated from the object model, it's trivial to add features to the endpoints without having to change client code; the clients would request the data they need, and the presence of **additional** data in the API wouldn't matter.

Does this mean, then, that programmers should toss out their musty and archaic REST endpoints in favor of GraphQL?

Probably not. GraphQL is, like many other things, a useful tool; it implies that clients have a certain responsibility in knowing what data is to be requested, and that's not always the case. In fact, one developer known by the authors has run into multiple environments where GraphQL was used as "magic sauce" – only to rip it out and see benefits across the projects. That doesn't mean that GraphQL is **bad** – it only means that GraphQL is a tool and, like most other tools, needs to be used in the appropriate environment and conditions. Under those conditions, GraphQL can be **very** useful; when those conditions aren't present, it's like the proverbial bicycle to a fish.

The Java library for GraphQL can be found at `https://github.com/graphql-java/graphql-java`; there's also a Spring Boot starter for GraphQL, at `www.graphql-java-kickstart.com/spring-boot/`.

11.5 Rivescript

It's been a goal of programmers for at **least** 70 years to have computers able to converse intelligently with humans; Alan Turing developed the "Turing Test" in 1950 as a measure of how well computers could exhibit intelligent behavior, long before computers were powerful enough to even try convincing conversation.

The first well-known (to your authors!) "conversation program" was ELIZA (see `https://en.wikipedia.org/wiki/ELIZA`), written by Joseph Weizenbaum a full **16 years later**, and it did so by recognizing key phrases and words and echoing them back to participants. (Some consider ELIZA to have passed the Turing Test, but this tends to rely on a naïve human as a participant; ELIZA's pretty predictable, even over the course of a single conversation.)

There have been other conversational programs – ALICE (`www.chatbots.org/chatbot/a.l.i.c.e/`) comes to mind. ALICE uses a language for creating conversations, called AIML (see `www.pandorabots.com/docs/aiml-reference/` for more). We'll look at some AIML in a bit, for comparison purposes.

ALICE and ELIZA are interesting historically, but are they **useful**? The Magic 8-ball says yes; it turns out that the requirements for having a conversation, even scripted, are incredibly useful from a customer service perspective, regardless of industry.

For example, consider reporting a power outage; a program can easily navigate a conversation about power outages, because most people report power outages in similar ways (e.g., "My power is out! I live at…").

When you have a pattern of conversation, you can write a script to navigate that conversation and extract relevant information, something that a program can use just as well as telemarketers can.

Telemarketers typically use literal scripts for their sales calls. They open with a predetermined greeting and follow a script based on responses. In this, telemarketers are basically acting as mechanical turks: they're humans doing exactly what a computer would do, just with different inputs and outputs… although it should be noted that there are in fact ways for computers to understand the spoken word as well as **generate** speech, so a computer can indeed replace a human being in the telemarketing industry, given enough investment in the scripting and interfaces for speech.

That means that you could create a workable script to take pizza orders, or respond to inquiries about order statuses, or even respond to problem reports as with the earlier power outages example.

The solution space for chatbots, as programs that converse with humans are called, involves two core areas: one is the communication medium, and the other is the conversation itself.

The medium might be Internet Relay Chat, or Twitter, or Slack, or Facebook, or even SMS or a live telephone call; really, if you can imagine a way for a computer to receive or send information, you can set a program to use it. It would then be a matter of handling speech recognition or language recognition.

The conversation is a little trickier, because programmers have to anticipate the variety and flexibility of input.

Imagine a greeting: one of your authors might say "Hey, y'all!" instead of "Hello," because he's from Florida, while the other author might say "Greetings, person" because he's from California and he's slightly odd.

Are these both greetings? After all, they're not "Hello." What's more, if they **are** greetings – and they are – what's the appropriate response? To one, the appropriate response might be "What up, yo?" while "Hi there, person!" might be appropriate for another; scripts have to consider whether to maintain context and tone in their interactions. (If I'm ordering a pizza, "What up, yo?" might be okay, but if I'm complaining about a broken water main, I don't want to have my angry salutation to get a flippant "How's it going?" as a response.)

AIML is actually quite powerful, but there are alternatives, some of which might fit a flexible chatbot implementation even better. One is called "RiveScript" (`www.rivescript.com`).

Both AIML and RiveScript have a format based around call and response; you write an expression that matches an input (such as "hello") and then produce a response ("hi there"). AIML uses XML or CSV to create a script, with the XML being much longer but also much clearer.

Listing 11-2. AIML script to say "hello" back to a user

```
<?xml version = "1.0" encoding = "UTF-8"?>
<aiml version="1.0.1" encoding = "UTF-8"?>
  <category>
    <pattern>HELLO</pattern>
    <template>Hi there!</template>
  </category>
</aiml>
```

RiveScript, on the other hand, uses a more freeform input format.

Listing 11-3. RiveScript salutations

```
!version=2.0

+ hello
- hi there!
```

RiveScript also has support for context (it can sample words from input), randomization of output, and calling subroutines to generate output based on input; as such, it's actually incredibly powerful. The scripting language is quite clear compared to AIML's XML or CSV formats (the CSV equivalent for the salutation looks like `0,HELLO,,,Hi there!,salutation.aiml`), and the ability to call out to executable code to generate or parse input is really convenient.

RiveScript itself is a loose specification, and thus the conversations can be used in many, many programming languages. A Java port of RiveScript can be found at `https://github.com/aichaos/rivescript-java`, and there's even a Spring Boot starter (`rivescript-spring-boot-starter`) to help create a working RiveScript interpreter for use in Spring Boot applications.

11.6 What's Next?

We hope you've enjoyed learning more about Spring. We've covered the basics of Spring, including why it was written and why it still exists and how it still affects Java developers today. We've also covered using Spring to serve content over the Web and how to interact with multiple data sources; we've also addressed how to identify users and limit what they can do based on their identities and roles. Lastly, we've started gently peeking beyond the Web, persistence, and security to consider the wider Spring ecosystem.

Now it's your turn: develop fascinating applications with Spring! Change the world for the better, and tell the world what you've done and how you've done it. We'll be watching and cheering you on.

Index

© Joseph B. Ottinger and Andrew Lombardi 2019
J. B. Ottinger and A. Lombardi, *Beginning Spring 5*, https://doi.org/10.1007/978-1-4842-4486-9

Made in the USA
Monee, IL
26 May 2021